This is the first book devoted to the Queen's Men, one of the major acting companies of the age of Shakespeare. In describing the troupe's position in the general political situation and the London theatre scene of the 1580s, the authors break new ground, showing how Elizabethan theatre history can be refocused by concentrating on the company which produced the plays rather than on the authors who wrote them.

The book combines a thorough sifting of documentary evidence with textual and critical analysis to provide a full account of the characteristics which gave the company its identity: its acting style, staging methods, touring patterns and repertoire.

Chapters detail the political context in which the Queen's Men were formed; the motives of the Earl of Leicester, Sir Francis Walsingham, and others instrumental in forming the company; the players' national tours; their impact on the commercial theatre of London; the staging of plays and the nature of the texts sent to the printer. A final chapter considers the company's relationships with the plays of Marlowe and Shakespeare, and explores the possibility that Shakespeare began his career writing for the Queen's Men.

The account is illustrated with tour maps as well as photographs and ground plans of several surviving playing spaces. Appendixes include a detailed itinerary of the company on tour between 1583 and 1603, the casting requirements of selected plays and biographical notes on company members.

The Queen's Men and their Plays

The Queen's Men and their Plays

SCOTT McMILLIN

Cornell University

SALLY-BETH MacLEAN

University of Toronto

CAMBRIDGE
UNIVERSITY PRESS

PUBLISHED BY THE PRESS SYNDICATE OF THE UNIVERSITY OF CAMBRIDGE
The Pitt Building, Trumpington Street, Cambridge CB2 1RP, United Kingdom

CAMBRIDGE UNIVERSITY PRESS
The Edinburgh Building, Cambridge CB2 2RU, United Kingdom
40 West 20th Street, New York, NY 10011–4211, USA
10 Stamford Road, Oakleigh, Melbourne 3166, Australia

First published 1998

Reprinted 1999

Printed in the United Kingdom by Biddles Ltd, Guildford, Surrey

Typeset in 11/13pt Adobe Garamond

A catalogue record for this book is available from the British Library

Library of Congress cataloguing in publication data

McMillin, Scott.
The Queen's Men and their plays / Scott McMillin and Sally-Beth
MacLean.
p.   cm.
Includes bibliographical references and index.
ISBN 0–521–59427–8
1. Queen's Men (Theater company) – History.   2. Theatrical
companies – England – History – 16th century.   3. Theater – England –
History – 16th century.   4. English drama – Early modern and
Elizabethan, 1500–1600 – History and criticism.   I. MacLean, Sally-Beth.   II. Title.
PN2599.5.T54M39   1998
792′.0942′ 09031 – dc21   97–18017   CIP

ISBN 0 521 59427 8   hardback

CONTENTS

ILLUSTRATIONS

Plates

Plate 4 is reproduced by courtesy of Norwich City Council and Plate 13 by courtesy of the National Trust; all other photographs are used by kind permission of Paul MacLean.

Ground plans

Maps

The maps are reproduced by kind permission of Records of
Early English Drama.

PREFACE

This book has an obvious motive and an underlying agenda; both should be named at the start. The obvious motive is to draw together the factual information that has come down to us about one of the major Elizabethan acting companies, the Queen's Men, and to set that information within a broader narrative of later-sixteenth-century English drama. The underlying agenda is to suggest that a new approach to Elizabethan drama can be opened by centring on the acting companies instead of the playwrights. That would entail studying the repertories of the companies with the kinds of critical and textual attention that are normally reserved for the canons of the playwrights. Theatre history normally steers clear of criticism and regards textual studies as a useful but separate discipline. We wish to remove the barriers between these fields to see if the overall territory might thereby gain some new prospects.

First, however, come the documents and facts. New information is on the increase for the Elizabethan theatre, especially now that the Records of Early English Drama team of scholars has passed well beyond mid-point in its project of gathering all pre-1642 records bearing on dramatic performance throughout England. A benefit of the REED project is that the routes by which the professional companies travelled can now be mapped for the first time, and one of our purposes is to show how extensive were the touring routes of the Queen's Men, and how important touring itself would have been in the motives which brought the company into existence.

Factual research has advanced on other fronts too: the manuscripts from the Elizabethan theatres have been given thorough examinations in recent years; the office of the Master of the Revels, as well as the biography of the key Elizabethan holder of that office, Edmund Tilney, has come under fresh scrutiny; the unexpected discovery of the Rose foundations has made an outline of one actual Elizabethan theatre briefly apparent; some of the remaining playing places in the provinces have been identified and photographed; and a handful of individual scholars, working through the masses of Elizabethan legal and social documents remaining from this period, have turned up hundreds of facts about actors, writers, entrepreneurs, and theatre-builders. The recent work bears only here and there on the Queen's Men, of course. Everyone working on Elizabethan theatre history, whether on the actors, the provincial records, the playwrights, the theatres, or even the carpenters and plasterers (for the new Globe project on the Bankside has generated some striking discoveries about how earlier playhouses were put together), must share the sense that the field has opened up for fresh exploration.

Nowhere is this sense clearer than for the acting companies. Andrew Gurr's *The Shakespearian Playing Companies* signals the change that has occurred by giving a fresh view of the evidence new and old, and supplying a sweeping narrative for the entire period from the 1560s to 1642.[1] Each company of note now needs to be studied in detail and with an eye for its own special characteristics – the qualities by which it differed from the others, the qualities by which the others would have known this company as something to be reckoned with. Our underlying agenda comes into play on this point. Along with a documentary narrative for the Queen's Men, we are intent upon those special characteristics which gave the company its identity – its acting style, its staging methods, its kinds of versification, its sense of what constituted a worthwhile repertory of plays.

That amounts to saying that acting companies were responsible for the plays they performed and can be evaluated according to that responsibility. Normally playwrights are taken as the responsible agents. The identities of most playwrights seem knowable. That acting companies have identities too is not such a familiar idea, and the troupes sometimes changed in personnel. The Queen's Men often divided into branches in order to tour more widely, so that the 'Queen's Men' appearing in one town were different actors from those appearing elsewhere. Moreover, by 1590 nearly half of the original Queen's Men had died or left the company, and their replacements were not clones but actors with talents and specialities of their own. (The later company appeared more often with acrobats, for example.) Yet the later company continued to perform the kinds of plays and roles of the earlier company: clown roles continued to be a speciality after Tarlton's death, for example, and the English history play, which the company of Tarlton and Knell seem to have brought into the commercial theatre, remained a staple in the repertory of the 1590s. Organizations have reason to develop characteristics of their own *because* they are subject to shifts and losses of personnel, and for a repertory acting company, the stock of older plays, with the style connected to them, must carry through to form the basis of each new season or tour. We think it clear that each company would have had its own style, its own textual procedures, its own sense of purpose, and its own impact on audiences and other acting companies. To some extent these characteristics would have been shared among the other companies, and sometimes actors moved from one troupe to another.

The Queen's Men were first formed of actors from other troupes. But organizations within a profession always develop identities of their own, widely recognized features which stand out from the procedures they share with the other organizations, and we feel that the more urgent consideration is the extent to which each company was unique. Previous generalizations about the Elizabethan companies have tended to assume similarities among them (just as our assumptions about the playhouses did before the Rose foundations were turned up to show unexpected differences), but the test of similarity has not been passed until the possibilities of difference have been given a close look – and when it comes to style, versification, and staging, a close look has been reserved mainly for playwrights rather than acting companies.

The plays of the Queen's Men have never been given a critical and textual reading as a group before, but the more surprising point is that the plays of the other companies have not either, not as bodies of drama brought together under the name of the organization that performed them. Not even the Chamberlain's/King's Men have had their plays studied with the kind of critical and textual attention we bestow on some of their playwrights, although books on the Chamberlain's repertory by Bernard Beckerman, Roslyn Knutson, and Leeds Barroll have made this a more distinct possibility than it is for the other companies.[2] We have always settled for the category of authorship to organize our readings of the drama, while we have reserved the category of acting company to organize our narratives of fact, but a new history of Elizabethan drama *and* theatre might emerge, we wish to suggest, from combining criticism, textual study, and factual narrative under the primary category of acting company.

That undertaking would require many hands, of course, and the present book is intended only as a beginning – a brief for the larger argument, so to speak, and at best an example of some of the guidelines by which this kind of work can be done.

When the Queen's Men were formed in 1583, they were the best acting company in England. That is because the government official responsible for assembling the new company, Sir Francis Walsingham, had the good sense to consult the Master of the Revels, Tilney, about the actors to be chosen. Tilney was in a position to know about actors. As Master of the Revels during the previous five years, he had been responsible for arranging the dramatic performances given at court each Christmas season. He would have known which actors pleased the queen and which were co-operative with authority, two considerations that might have weighed about equally to a man in his position. He seems to have done better on the first score than on the second: he chose Richard Tarlton, who pleased everyone (but no one more than the queen), but he also chose John Bentley and John Singer, whom the authorities in Norwich saw fit to imprison after an affray during the company's first road trip, and

John Towne, who killed another member of the company in a fight in 1587. The Queen's Men were not a tame group, but they could all act – Tilney knew where the talent lay. Anyone would have picked Tarlton by 1583, but Tilney also picked Robert Wilson, John Adams, Singer, Bentley, and John Lanham, among others – actors who were all being recalled with nostalgia twenty-five years later.

No one could have guessed in 1583 that this company would virtually disappear from the London theatre after about a decade. Having many of the best actors of the day, blessed with the patronage of the queen, being larger and better equipped than the other companies, knowing better than the others how to travel far and wide throughout the kingdom, drawing larger rewards wherever they played, with Tilney's schedule of court performances practically to themselves – how could they fail? With the English history play, they hit upon the kind of drama that would revolutionize the theatre of the 1590s. Yet when the revolution came, the Queen's Men were not in the vanguard, not as far as London is concerned. The Chamberlain's Men made the English history play count in the 1590s, and in so far as they learned how to do so from another company, they learned not from the Queen's Men but from the Admiral's Men and Lord Strange's Men. It turns out that Tilney missed two key actors after all, perhaps because they were only about sixteen years old when the Queen's Men were formed: Richard Burbage and Edward Alleyn. These two made a difference in the long run. The Chamberlain's Men were headed by Burbage and the Admiral's Men by Alleyn when these two companies virtually took over the London commercial theatre in 1594. We are not certain the Queen's Men ever performed in London after that. How they managed to lose the advantage in the London commercial theatre is one of the basic stories of English drama.

Yet that is too brisk, calling them losers. They did not lose in the nation at large, but in London. The REED evidence is having its impact, and there is no longer any reason for assuming, as earlier generations tended to do, that Elizabethan drama arose and flourished entirely in London. We now know in detail, through a county-by-county gathering of documentary evidence (two-thirds complete at this point), that English towns and cities were busy with drama and other kinds of showmanship throughout the sixteenth century. The growth of London drama at the end of the century contributed to a shrinking of English theatre – a shrinking into the centre of concentrated population and capital where drama could become a thriving commercial enterprise. The Queen's Men were not very adept in the concentrated theatre and publishing industry of London, but so long as Elizabeth lived, they were the primary company in the country at large. Our account of the company's career in chapter 3 attempts to keep the provincial touring in as sharp a view as the company's London and court performances, and our hope is that in laying out the routes by which the actors travelled and in describing their performance spaces where these can be determined, some of the reality of a flourishing touring theatre will gain a place in Elizabethan theatre studies.

That emphasis will also be found in chapter 2, where we consider this nation-wide touring company in the context of the political and social issues of 1583. It seems to us that the Queen's Men were formed primarily for touring. Walsingham did not just happen upon the assignment to organize a royal company. He was thinking of political advantage, and the political advantage of this particular venture lay in having a group of famous actors banded together under the queen's name and reaching beyond London to the kingdom. The Queen's Men were meant to travel, and in that sense they were always successful, no matter what difficulties they encountered in London.

The first three chapters, then, concern the company's record in the nation-wide theatres of the late sixteenth century. Chapters 4, 5, and 6 are about the plays. Chapter 4 establishes the nine extant plays which can be assigned to the company according to conservative principles of selection. Chapter 5 studies the dramaturgy of the plays, and chapter 6 is devoted to their textual characteristics. The benefits of grouping the plays by acting company must be apparent in these chapters, or they will not be apparent at all.

Chapter 7 places the Queen's Men in the broader context of drama in the 1590s, when their style of performance and writing was rendered obscure. One way Shakespeare dealt with the Queen's Men was by rewriting a sizeable portion of their repertory. Four of their nine extant plays were turned into six Shakespeare plays in an act of appropriation extensive enough to make us think it could have occurred from the inside. Shakespeare knew the plays of this company better than those of any company but his own, and the long-standing speculation that he may have begun his career with the Queen's Men seems to us the most likely possibility. Yet – wherever Shakespeare got his start – the Queen's Men did not take him as seriously as they took Marlowe, the influence of whose plays they sought to curtail in some explicitly anti-Marlowe efforts. Thus, while Shakespeare was dealing with the Queen's Men by rewriting their plays, the Queen's Men were dealing with Marlowe by replying to his. Shakespeare's effort was the more effective – especially in that he learned his method for rewriting the plays of the Queen's Men from no one more obviously than the Marlowe whom the Queen's Men were trying to reject.

That brings us back to the Queen's Men as the losers in the London theatre. There is a cultural divide between ourselves and the years in which the Queen's Men seemed a force to be reckoned with, and we wish to suggest that a good way for historians to cross over that divide is to give first place to the obscure and nearly forgotten agents from the earlier time. If we do theatre history from the point of view of Shakespeare, Marlowe, Alleyn, and Burbage, it becomes an exercise in seeing the continuity between our culture and the past. What could be wrong with that? Nothing, unless the continuity comes to be taken for granted, in the 'Shakespeare our contemporary' vein of thinking. But this does seem to happen in an age which produces Shakespeare as part of its summertime culture, its film culture, and its educational culture – he is so built into our system that we have trouble historicizing him at all. Shakespeare was not our contemporary, and one way to insist on that fact is to study the things which he had to deal with and which our age is free to ignore. Shakespeare had to deal with the Queen's Men. We are free to ignore them – the first summer festival of Queen's Men plays has yet to be held. But if measuring the difference between Shakespeare and ourselves makes for good history, and if the Elizabethans are to be thought of as not another version of ourselves but as strangers from the past, and if things nearly forgotten are the proper objects for historians to keep in view anyhow, then we think the plays of the Queen's Men are worth careful attention.

We should add a word about the division of labour in this collaborative venture. Sally-Beth MacLean has taken the lead in examining the context of touring theatre, particularly as regards Leicester's Men, in which the Queen's Men were formed, and in writing the account of the company's provincial routes and playing places, spelling out the documentary evidence in Appendix A. Scott McMillin's primary assignments have been the plays, their dramaturgy, the casting, and the London theatre scene for which they were written. We hasten to add that each of us has read and offered revisions to everything the other has written, a process in which the invention of e-mail has been an enormous benefit. Portions of our work have appeared earlier in *English Literary Renaissance*, *Shakespeare Quarterly*, *Medieval and Renaissance Drama in England*, *Review of English Studies*, and *Elizabethan Theatre*. To the editors of those journals and books, we are grateful for permission to reprint.

We have also accumulated so many obligations to fellow scholars that it is perhaps best to list their names here, on the understanding that such spare recognition in no way reflects the depth of many of these obligations or the friendship they entail. In addition to Leeds Barroll and Andrew Gurr, whose reader's reports for Cambridge University Press were instrumental in shaping our final revisions, we are indebted to: Simon Adams, Herbert Berry, David Bevington, Anne Brannen, Susan Cerasano, Jane Cowling, Peter Greenfield, Peter Holman, Lynn Hulse, William Ingram, Alexandra Johnston, Arthur Kinney, Roslyn Knutson, Anne Lancashire, Ted McGee, Alan Nelson, Barbara Palmer, Mark Pilkinton, Richard Proudfoot, Alan Somerset, Sandra Siegel, James Stokes, Gary Taylor, Joan Thirsk, David Thurn, Robert Tittler, Brian

Vickers, Philip Virgen, H. R. Woudhuysen, Abigail Ann Young, and all the REED editors whose work is acknowledged more fully in Appendix A.

We owe special thanks to collaborators who have contributed the maps, photographs, and ground plans that enrich our text. William Rowcliffe brought his graphic skills to the adaptation of maps originally designed by Michael Waldin for general REED purposes. Paul MacLean took expert photographs of every nook and cranny of the Elizabethan performance spaces described in chapter 3, from which a selection has been printed here. Conan MacLean assisted in the measurement and exploration of these provincial halls in order to make possible the professionally designed ground plans provided by Carlos Lanfranco, a graduate student in landscape architecture at Cornell University. We are also grateful to Gayle Mault for her help and to the National Trust for permission to publish the photograph of the High Great Chamber at Hardwick Hall.

Friendly assistance and permission to photograph were also given by the following: Tim Aldous, the Halls Manager and the Norwich City Council; the staff of the York Guildhall; Nick Ladlow, the Guildhall Manager, and Simon Gilroy, Museum Assistant in Leicester; R. P. Benthall, Treasurer, and the Custodians of Christ Church, Oxford; R. G. Norton, the House Steward of Hardwick Hall; and the National Trust.

Finally, we gratefully acknowledge generous funding support for our research by Cornell University, the National Endowment for the Humanities, and Victoria College at the University of Toronto. We have also benefited from the ongoing support of Father Edward Jackman, O. P., and the Jackman Foundation for REED cartography.

1

The London theatre of 1583

Giving pause

The year 1583 has been called a crossroads in theatre history, a threshold, and a turning point,[1] but these metaphors of wayfaring and homecoming rest on territory that has not been thoroughly explored. Theatre historians have not thought much about the London theatre of 1583. The founding of the Queen's Men makes the year seem decisive, but the context of evidence which would allow us to fill in the terms of that decisiveness has been glanced at mainly by scholars with other stories to tell, stories that concern Shakespeare and the 1590s. Beyond the crossroads of 1583 playwrights can be discerned whose biographies seem accessible – Marlowe alone would be attraction enough, but there are also Kyd, Greene, and Peele, not to mention anyone more famous. The urgency of reaching identifiable playwrights whose careers seem to have shape and direction carries us past 1583 with little more than an acknowledgement that the founding of the Queen's Men was an important move in the contest between city and crown over the control of the London theatre.

Instead of hurrying on, we would like to pause. We are not accustomed to thinking about an Elizabethan theatre that had never heard of Shakespeare and Marlowe. That in itself makes us suspect that the body of plain theatrical fact which clusters around the founding of the Queen's Men, at that time the most illustrious company of actors ever assembled in England, has not been studied firmly enough. We can tell a crossroads when we see one, but it is of little use unless we have some orientation and can tell in which directions the roads might lead.

At the beginning of March 1583, the best English actors were under the patronage of leading aristocrats – the Earls of Leicester, Sussex, Oxford, Derby, and others, men who must have appreciated the vivid combination of cultural and political attention the theatre entailed. By the end of March 1583, twelve of these actors had been removed from their organizations and formed into a new company, an instant all-star troupe, which would hold the advantage on the calendar of holiday performances at court, would claim royal privileges for securing playing places in the inn yards of London and in the new purpose-built playhouses outside the city walls, and would receive higher rewards than their competitors as they toured the countryside. In the theatre of the time, this was a far-reaching decision. The queen could have enrolled the best actors as her own at any time in her career. She had inherited a royal company when she came to the throne twenty-five years earlier, and that earlier company was fairly active in the provinces until the mid 1570s; yet they did not perform at court after 1569, and they seem to have been allowed to fade away by attrition (the last of the troupe died in 1580). For the first twenty-five years of her reign, the queen evidently preferred to let acting thrive under the patronage of the barons of the realm, the gift of whose performances she would receive at Christmastime. Her theatre patronage was mainly bestowed on the child actors from the chorister schools.

In other words, 1583 marks a shift in the politics of court theatre: where courtiers had offered the queen the gift of dramatic entertainments by companies under their patronage (the opportunity to offer the gift being controlled by the queen, of course), now the queen would take the gift of entertainment into her own name. The advantage of controlling the rivalry of patronage at court was now reduced as far as the holiday performances were concerned, and the loss must have been thought to be offset by some gain to the crown. We may assume that there was a local and factional element to the new arrangement, but much of this is now lost to the passing of time. Behind the scenes a contest over the Lord Chamberlain's office was probably taking shape, and Andrew Gurr has suggested that the new company may have been a special interest of Charles Howard in this regard.[2] The Master of the Revels had special interests too, and later in this chapter we will examine the schedule of court performances with an eye to his family ties, which may have been set back a little with the forming of the new company. Our broader argument will hold that the central government was not protecting the theatre so much as reducing it and gaining control over it. Beneath the 'struggle between City and Court', as Chambers called it, the two sides may have had something in common after all. The political considerations in forming the royal troupe also extended beyond the court, however, and while the remainder of the present chapter will deal with the politics of the court and the London theatre, we will broaden our view to include the national scene in chapter 2.[3]

A pause on 1583 entails further thinking about the children's companies, whose career was undergoing an important change.[4] Two boy companies had been appearing on the holiday calendar for years: the Children of the Chapel and the Children of St Paul's. Their managers having found it possible to open the doors of their dramatic 'rehearsals' to the public for a price, these boys were competing (perhaps sporadically, but with noticeable effect) in the commercial theatre. The Chapel Children gave their commercial performances at Blackfriars. The evidence is less certain about Paul's, but they seem sometimes to have charged admission for the plays they performed at their singing school in the cathedral precinct. In 1583, after the death the year before of the long-term master of Paul's, Sebastian Westcote, these companies were combined under the patronage of the Earl of Oxford. Thus the two children's companies of recent memory became one enlarged company in the year the Queen's Men were formed, and the two decisions may well have been related. Certainly the two companies that resulted, one adult and one children's, became instantly the mainstays of the court holiday schedule. The two decisions would also have had the effect of reducing the extent of the commercial theatre in London, in the case of the boys by combining two companies into one, and in the case of the adults by removing the vital actors from the existing companies and rendering those troupes secondary to the new Queen's Men.

These manoeuvres should be seen in the light of an earlier crown decision. In 1574 Leicester's Men had been granted an extraordinary royal patent to play without hindrance throughout the land. Five actors had been named in the Leicester patent, and three of them were summoned to the new Queen's Men in 1583, leaving little in the way of Leicester's Men behind. Walsingham and Leicester were allies on political and religious issues, and it is hard to think that Leicester would have been taken by surprise when the new company was in part formed of his best players. He certainly maintained an interest in the new company. But the other companies, and those of Leicester's Men who may not have been summoned, must have been disturbed at this turn of events – not only because the important actors were being drawn away from the leading companies, but also because the category of leading company was being instantly redefined.

Why should such a far-reaching decision have been made at all? And why was it made in 1583? Such questions cannot be answered directly, but an examination of the context in which the decisions were taken can lead, we believe, to understanding the possible areas where the answers may lie.

Basic inventory: an actors' theatre

We begin by raising a series of basic questions about the theatre of 1583, questions which playgoers of the day would not have had to ask, because they would have known the answers as part of their normal observation. Who were the recognizable actors of the day in London, the players one would make an effort to see? Which were the leading companies? To what extent were they 'London' companies, and to what extent were they on tour throughout the country? In London, where did they play? Who was writing their plays? And how many of those plays could be purchased by Londoners interested in the theatre – theatregoers, that is, who could read.

The last question is the easiest for us to answer.[5] There were no new plays from the acting companies to be read at all. By 1583 some of the older interludes might still have been on the bookstalls, along with translations from the classical drama. Nathaniel Woodes's *Conflict of Conscience* and the collection of *Seneca's Ten Tragedies* had been published in 1581, and the second edition of *Damon and Pithias*, written fifteen years earlier for one of the children's companies, had appeared in 1582. We have just named the only plays published in London for three years before the founding of the Queen's Men, and none of them came from the large permanent playhouses – the Red Lion, the Theatre, the Curtain, Newington Butts – which had operated near London, at one time or another, to some extent simultaneously, for years. The Red Lion had been built in 1567. The theatre at Newington Butts may have been in business as early as 1575. The Theatre was built in 1576, the Curtain in 1577. Stages at city inns are referred to during these years at the Bull in Bishopsgate Street, the Bell and the Cross Keys in Gracious Street, and the Bel Savage on Ludgate Hill. Children's companies were acting at Blackfriars and probably at St Paul's. Professional theatre was a growing industry in London, and new plays must have been plentiful in such a competitive environment. But the new plays were not being published, probably because the acting companies were keeping their profitable items to themselves. The first play to be published which can be connected with the adult professional companies of the 1580s was *Three Ladies of London*, which came out in 1584.

As for dramatists writing in London by 1583, the list is short. In March 1583, when the Queen's Men were being formed, Shakespeare was still a Stratford teenager, whose wife of a few months was expecting their first child in a few weeks. Marlowe was still at Cambridge, one supposes, and so was Robert Greene. George Peele, after living in London for a while (and perhaps writing plays – we do not know), was back in Oxford. Some older writers were probably living in London, but we can name no plays they had written by 1583: Chapman, Kyd, Chettle, Drayton, Lodge. Who had written plays for the public theatre by then? We can be fairly sure of five names: Stephen Gosson, Anthony Munday, Richard Tarlton, Robert Wilson, and Rowland Broughton. It must be noted that the first two of these, Gosson and Munday, had recently been condemning theatres as sinks of iniquity and plays as enemies to virtue and religion. They might have seemed unlikely to produce many scripts in the future (Munday actually did write more plays – he was hard to predict). All we really know about Rowland Broughton is that he failed to write the eighteen plays which in 1572 he promised to write.[6] Tarlton and Wilson are the two writers on our list who would have seemed certain to write more plays after 1583 (both were named to the Queen's Men), and they were primarily known as actors.

It is when we turn to theatres, companies, and actors that the answers to our questions begin to look more substantial. The London theatregoer of 1583 would have seen Leicester's Men acting at the Theatre to the north of the city, with such actors as Wilson, John Lanham, and William Johnson; and Warwick's Men acting at the playhouse at Newington Butts to the south of the city, headed by the Dutton brothers, John and Laurence, and Jerome Savage. Our playgoer would have been thinking back a few years to Warwick's Men because that company seems to have broken up in 1580, when the Duttons and others went over to a company under the patronage of the Earl of Oxford. So Oxford's Men should be numbered along with Leicester's and Warwick's as troupes known in London. Derby's Men and Sussex's Men had been appearing at court in recent years. Tarlton was with Sussex's Men, gaining his reputation as the first star of the London theatre.[7] There were also three companies well-travelled in the provinces which are likely to have played in London from time to time: Essex's Men, Berkeley's Men (with Arthur King and Thomas Goodale), and Worcester's Men (with a talented youngster, Edward Alleyn).[8]

It would be a mistake – one frequently made – to assume that London was the 'home' of the adult companies, or that they settled into certain playhouses for what we would call a 'long run'. These were touring companies much of the time, and our London playgoer would have been frequently aware of their comings and goings. London was the busiest city for theatre, of that there is no question, and the actors usually made their own homes there. But by 1583 we cannot be certain any adult company was permanently lodged in its own London theatre, not even Leicester's Men. Although the Theatre had been built by the leader of Leicester's Men, James Burbage, and although his company must have played there, the first thing to say about Leicester's Men in the early 1580s is that they spent much of their time travelling the countryside. They appeared in many places, including London, including the court – but they were not a London company. All the companies travelled, but Leicester's toured far and wide – as part of his lordship's political interest, it would seem. The Queen's Men were formed to travel too, and while it is right to think of them as holding an advantage among adult companies on the court schedule, it is even more important to think of them as holding an advantage across the country.[9]

The actors were in circulation – that is the best way to think of them. London was the centre of the circulation, with its rapidly growing population, its new playhouses, and its proximity to the court. Who would not have wanted to play London? But the city government was hostile to the theatre, and the challenge of settling near the city and building a following among Londoners was the challenge of mounting a large repertory of plays and rotating them daily. In feeling the attraction of mastering such a challenge, even the best companies would have noticed how many fewer plays were required on tour. Touring had its hardships too, but it did not require ten or twelve plays ready to be performed in daily rotation. That was the challenge of the London theatre, the challenge of building a repertory large enough to rotate the plays frequently and draw audiences day after day in the face of competition from other companies trying to do the same thing.

It was during the decade of the 1580s that the daily repertory system took hold in the London playhouses. By 1592, when Henslowe's listing of plays begins, a full-fledged repertory was being rotated at the Rose, and programmes so vast do not happen suddenly or in isolation. Yet the nine years separating Henslowe's record from the founding of the Queen's Men is a long time in the life of a competitive industry, and the repertory system evident in Henslowe's *Diary* cannot be taken as a sign of the norm in 1583. It is better read as a sign of the intention. To those companies ambitious for the London market, the need for a sizeable repertory and daily rotation would have been apparent in 1583, and regular weekday performances would have been important in establishing a season of plays by the time the Queen's Men were formed. But the Queen's Men did not settle in one London theatre (they seem to have moved among the playing spaces, as though they were on tour even in London), and we do not know of any other adult company that did settle before Strange's Men at the Rose. One of our themes will be that the 'watershed' years in the London drama were the early 1590s, roughly from 1590 to 1594, and a major development of that period was the establishment of the major companies in particular purpose-built playhouses, offering large-scale repertories. The Queen's Men did not fit into this system. They were peripatetic instead, and their palmy days in the London theatre fall on the distant side of the watershed – the theatre of 1583, but not the theatre of 1594.

What *can* be said of the London theatre of 1583 is that it consistently afforded playgoers a choice. No other city or town regularly offered a choice, not of professional drama. We have named ten companies – two children's, eight adult – which acted in London at one time or another during the five years before the founding of the Queen's Men. That does not mean they all acted simultaneously, and the list includes some little-known or short-lived organizations that may not have acted often. Berkeley's Men may not have made much of an impact in a city where Leicester's and Sussex's Men could hold forth for some weeks before taking their plays to court, or where Tarlton and the young Edward Alleyn could be seen for low prices, or where the children's companies were providing *avant-garde* delights for the wealthier set. But when

Berkeley's Men did play London, they increased the choices available – whereas when they played Bristol or Dover they could hope to be the only show in town for their few days there. The Theatre and the Curtain, the playhouse at Newington Butts, the theatres at St Paul's and Blackfriars had all been built or refurbished in the past seven or eight years, joining the older Red Lion and the inn-yard stages. The theatre was building a centre in London. But that does not mean the adult companies clustered in London suddenly or rapidly. English actors knew how to travel. They had toured for generations. It was their tradition, and they had the routines well in hand. London and its permanent playhouses were the new market, the best market, and the hardest market in many ways, the market of the future for actors ambitious enough to think of rising to fame. But there were many well-known markets across the nation as well.

This busy industry, circulating through the countryside, seeing London as the magnet for expansion, aiming for court performances, serving the interests of its aristocratic patrons, and above all trying to turn a profit, was an actors' theatre. Our inventory insists on this point. The evidence that remains to us concerns players and playhouses more often than writers and books. The information comes in small bits, of course. Nearly everything we want to know about the theatre of the 1580s has vanished over the years, and there is a risk of taking a cluster of facts for a pattern of evidence where it might more properly be called an accident. Should we imagine a writers' theatre after all, lurking behind the fragments of fact? We had never heard of Rowland Broughton until 1981, and we could not have guessed that any playwright would have been thought capable of writing eighteen plays in thirty months, but professional actors signed a contract for him to do that. On the other hand, Broughton failed to meet his contract – that is why his name is preserved in the legal records – and eighteen plays in thirty months sounds impossibly high, as though the contract was an act of hyperbole all round. We are reluctant to take his case as typical. The evidence that we have to go on produces names for actors in 1583, names for companies, and names for playhouses, and it is that kind of detail, the names of things, that one does not find for writers and their plays in the professional theatre of the same time. As far as we can tell, this was an actors' theatre. It had been vigorously on the road for decades, and now the new London playhouses, just beyond the reach of the authorities, along with the other stages within the city, were competing with one another to draw audiences. Londoners had a choice of playhouses, and a choice of famous actors. Moralists and officials were alarmed. Opposition to the stage was on the increase: and it was the actors and the playhouses they attacked, not writers and publishers.

Theatre expansion and the central government

Sometimes it seems that the growth and flowering of English drama occurred in the 1590s, but this is not precise enough. The printing of plays certainly expanded in that decade, producing the texts that have come to be known as 'Elizabethan drama', but the increase of acting companies and playing spaces upon which the printing industry would eventually capitalize had occurred earlier, in the 1570s and 1580s for London and before that nationwide. Our pausing point of 1583 is on the threshold of a change, and the results of that change can be seen in the 1590s, first with the evidence from Strange's Men at the Rose that repertory companies were moving into playhouses with which they would be identified, next with the rapid increase in printed drama during the early 1590s, and then with the establishment in 1594 of two major companies as the centre of the commercial theatre, the Admiral's Men at the Rose and the Chamberlain's Men at the Theatre. The 1590s are a period of concentration in the theatre, not of expansion.[10] From a country busy with showmanship over the previous several decades, London was drawing the theatre into a risky embrace with early capitalism. The capitalization has improved since then, and the embrace continues today.

Our vantage point of 1583 places us at the end of the first expansion-period of the professional drama, and on the threshold of the concentration that would be visible by the earlier 1590s. The founding of the Queen's Men gains clarity in this context. The central government was prepared to see a curtailment of the theatre by 1583, we believe, and the decision to form the Queen's Men was part of that process of curtailment. After 1583 the theatre industry became smaller, probably more stable and profitable, and certainly more manageable in the view of the crown government, whose opposition to the city authorities on matters theatrical may have been less severe than it appeared to be on the surface.

Certainly the illusion of a contest was created between London aldermen and the privy council. In calling it a 'struggle' between city and court, Chambers outlined a conflict between a city government hostile to the playhouses and a privy council protective of the theatre industry, with the city eyeing the playhouses as centres of disorder and idleness, and the privy council guarding them as training grounds for the queen's Christmas entertainments. The evidence for this view consists of repeated statements by the city and the privy council themselves. The city spoke of an immoral and disruptive theatre, which drew people away from religious services, provided a trysting ground for prostitutes and their clients, staged examples of licentious behaviour which spectators would be quick to imitate, and (perhaps the primary concern) served as gathering places for aggrieved and rebellious young people capable of riots.[11]

The privy council spoke of a queen whose 'solace' increased with her attendance at plays, especially at plays performed by actors well rehearsed through regular perfomances in and near the city.

Neither party spoke in directly political terms, and for that reason – politics being obviously the real concern of both – the moral shading of the city and the aesthetic shading of the privy council are to be taken as codes subject to further examination. Yet it must be admitted that the most important generation of theatre historians, the generation of Chambers and Greg, accepted the queen's-solace argument rather at face value. This generation was inclined toward an aesthetic view of the drama themselves. Their shrewdness tended to be directed toward the city position, and particularly toward recognizing the formation of a long-lasting political momentum behind the façade of moralism by which the theatre was resisted. The privy council, however, was taken at its word. 'After all, the people must have their recreation', wrote Chambers of the council's interest in keeping the theatres open, 'and, what was more, the Queen must have hers' (*ES*, 1, 267). Forty years later F. P. Wilson repeated this argument, and concluded that 'by 1584 dramatists and players could realize that they had a friend at court, and proverbially that was worth a penny in the purse'.[12] One wonders if the companies which saw their leading players drawn away by royal command in 1583 shared this view, or would have agreed with Chambers that 'it was really the court play which saved the popular stage' (*ES*, 1, 267).

Elizabeth I's personal interest in drama was keen and well-educated   the privy council was not inventing the queen's-solace argument out of thin air. Beyond the queen's love of drama, however, there was a burgeoning city to be governed, and a nation divided over the basic question of religion. We view it as self-evident that the privy council was motivated by political considerations that came before and outweighed their monarch's aesthetic interest, even though no one on the privy council would have willingly put himself in the path of this monarch's reaction if she thought that an interest so personal to her as the aesthetic was being crossed. And anyhow the queen's personal interests were her way of representing an intensely political attitude. It is in the context of such considerations that some decoding of the struggle between city and court seems necessary.

From our vantage point in 1583, a major event was the accident at Paris Garden in January of that year, when collapsing scaffolds killed eight spectators at a bear-baiting. Religious opposition to spectator sports had been sharply increasing, probably in response to the growth of the playhouse industry, and the issue of Sunday performances came to be something of a lightning rod in the complaints. The Paris Garden accident happened on a Sunday, and even before the pamphleteers were able to announce this as divine retribution for the abuse of the Sabbath, the Lord Mayor wrote to Lord Burghley calling for an end to Sunday performances and seeking Burghley's influence with the Surrey justices, under whose authority the Bankside entertainment places lay. The result, achieved during further correspondence in 1583, was what the city authorities may have regarded as a victory: the council did extend the prohibition against Sunday playing from the city to the suburbs.

In the meantime, Tilney was instructed in March to set about forming the Queen's Men. Left to itself, this outline of events implies that the privy council, having lost a round to the city over the Paris Garden accident and the banning of Sabbath performances, was reasserting its authority and protecting the actors by forming the new company. That appears to be what Chambers meant in calling the new company 'a deliberate and to some extent a successful attempt to overawe the city by the use of the royal name' (ES, 1, 291).[13]

That answer stops short of asking what seem to us obvious questions about the theatrical situation of the time. Would the players, first of all, have seen the Sabbath issue as threatening? To the extent that they were trying to establish themselves in London, the main issue for the players during the 1580s would have been the building up of regular weekday performances in and near the city.[14] The Sabbath is the day for drawing crowds, but the actors who were trying to sustain a London season of several weeks instead of several days were seeking a steady flow of admissions six or seven times a week, and the first six mattered more than the seventh in the business of gaining a reliable and returning audience in this competitive setting. To the players, the Sunday battle might have been worth losing if the weekday war were won at the same time (especially if the occasional Sunday performance could be slipped in behind the authorities' backs). From this perspective those lightning bolts hurled by the religious opposition at the misuse of the Sabbath would have seemed a useful distraction from the main issue. Perhaps the city caught on in November 1583, for upon receiving instructions from the privy council to permit the new Queen's Men to play within London on weekdays but not on Sundays, the Mayor and his fellows promptly tried to reverse the terms by permitting the Sundays and banning the weekdays. The privy council had to write again a few weeks later, to insist that weekday performances be allowed.[15]

From the privy council's perspective, nothing was lost by granting the Sabbath victory to the city. To the extent that the council was looking to the London playhouses for 'rehearsals' for court performances, regular weekday performances were even more effective than regular Sabbath performances. What mattered more, we suggest, was reducing the number of companies and the number of theatres active in London, a point on which the council may have been the silent and unacknowledged allies of the city. Merging the two children's companies after the death of Westcote strikes us as one step in a two-step procedure of 1583 to consolidate the theatre, the other step being the formation of the Queen's Men themselves at about the same time. The merger of the children has been taken – correctly, we think – as a move toward monopolizing the trade in children's theatre,[16] but it cannot have been effected without at least the tacit consent of the Master of the Revels, whose office was supervised by one member of the council and of interest to them all. Would the council not have seen the similarity between the consolidation of the children's companies and the forming of a privileged adult company? If Chambers is right to argue that the combined children's company was known sometimes as Oxford's Boys and sometimes as the Chapel Children, the next two seasons of court performances, totalling thirteen performances in all, were put on by only this company and by the new Queen's Men. All other companies were denied court performances for two years. Whatever other motives may have guided the privy council, they must have been aware that the court schedule was being brought under close control by granting something like monopolies to one children's company and one adult company.

Consider now the founding of the Queen's Men. Our inventory of theatrical activity suggests that London was bustling with theatre before 1583, yet in that year and the year following, the court schedule for adult companies was closed to all but the queen's own players. It is easy to say that the crown was seeking a concentration of the best available talent for royal entertainment, but the more interesting question, which has not often been asked by Elizabethan scholars (although some actors of the period must have asked it quickly enough), is why the government decided to interrupt a busy theatrical scene by removing players from the existing companies and putting them into an all-star troupe. To reply that the queen loved the drama and saw in the new company a way to protect the leading actors from city hostility at the same time as she assured herself of their presence at her Christmas festivities is to place a reasonable idea under a veil of naïvety. There was certainly more to it than that, but the fuller possibilities cannot be seen until the most obvious effect of the founding of the new company is considered. That obvious effect concerns the other companies, the companies from whom the new all-star troupe was formed. How would the Queen's Men have affected them?

The companies we have been discussing from the late 1570s and early 1580s consisted of about a half-dozen leading adult actors, some three or four hired men to play the lesser roles and walk-ons, and some three or four boys.[17] The most important group in each company would have been the half-dozen leading actors. The continuity of the organization lay in their hands. It was from these groups of master actors that the best talent was chosen to join the Queen's Men. At least three of the leading actors from Leicester's Men were called to the new company: Robert Wilson, John Lanham, and William Johnson.

Sussex's Men seem to have lost Tarlton and John Adams. Those are the five whose companies we can be fairly sure of. Possibly John Dutton was from Oxford's Men. But twelve were named, twelve of the most famous performers of the day, drawn from the companies which had built their reputations over the years in a competitive environment. Obviously the Queen's Men were to become, instantly, the largest company London had known, for the twelve leading players would have been joined by boys and hired men too; and at the same time the other companies must have been seriously reduced. In the next chapter, we will consider the possibility that one of those companies, Leicester's Men, virtually ceased to operate as a separate unit in 1583 and 1584. Leicester may well have been party to the formation of the new company, and the majority of his leading players from the 1570s became Queen's Men, but actors were left behind, lesser actors from Leicester's Men perhaps, actors of all qualities from the other companies, and these men must have known their livelihood was being disturbed, not protected.

The most important consideration lies in the quality and experience of the twelve leading actors who were recruited. When a Tarlton leaves, those who remain are reduced by more than one. Obviously the leading companies were damaged. These were not perfectly stable organizations, of course. Personnel had shifted from one company to another before, and one thing all the professional actors of the time must have known was how to adjust to new circumstances. But to lose two or three leading actors at a time would still have been a blow. To the repertories built up in those years, to the companies' financial organization, to the expectations that audiences would have brought to their performances, the players summoned to the Queen's Men had been central. Their departure would have diminished the older companies' immediate prospects, and the government of a queen who loved the drama cannot have been unaware of this.

Royal motives

The thriving theatrical scene we have described in the 1570s and early 1580s, with its variety of companies and acting places, would have been troublesome from the government's point of view. If there is something a little subversive about theatre in the first place, there is something very subversive about a proliferating theatre, which draws crowds into more places than can be easily regulated, to see more plays than can be easily licensed, both in London and across the length and breadth of a realm that was seriously divided over the political issue of religion. The potential for disorder was great. This is, of course, exactly what the city authorities were concerned about within their jurisdiction.

The dimensions of jurisdictions were vastly different for the alderman and the councillor, but the main point was the same. Good order produced good governance even more effectively than good governance produced good order – a connection which increasing numbers of plays and players could only loosen.

The Elizabethan government was especially sensitive about travelling subjects.[18] Men who moved about without licence seemed troublesome – especially men who moved about in bands and drew crowds to inns and taverns. Inns and taverns were worrying too. Disorder was a broad category to the Elizabethan authorities, and travelling players were enough like vagabonds or recusants or innkeepers (some of them *were* innkeepers) to cause suspicion. Of course, the queen was interested in having the best players perform at her Christmas festivities. She loved the drama, it has often been noted. But she loved order too, and it would be possible for a shrewd queen to have both, love of order leading to love of drama, especially drama performed by famous actors banded together so as to be more reliable than their membership in half a dozen distinct troupes would make them appear. It seems likely that the Queen's Men were established not only to bring London's finest players into one unit for the court's pleasure, but also to curtail the growth of the expanding theatre industry.

The long view of Elizabethan theatre history furthers this possibility. If one marks out the most decisive acts taken by the central government toward the London theatre during the reign of Elizabeth I (aside from those stemming from plague epidemics), we believe the list would consist of the renewal of the Acts against Retainers in 1572, the Act for the Punishment of Vagabonds in the same year, the crown patent granted to Leicester's Men in 1574, the patent granted to the Master of the Revels in 1581, the forming of the Queen's Men in 1583, the privy council decree of 1589 establishing a new licensing commission for plays, and the privy council order for the destruction of all playhouses in 1597 (which destroyed no playhouses, but which for a time limited the number of licensed theatres and companies to two). These actions have been fully discussed elsewhere, and there is no need to repeat a story already well told;[19] but the well-told story pits the crown against the city, with the crown attempting through its decisions to protect the theatre industry while gaining control over it, and we would suggest that the events listed above do not 'protect' the theatre industry as clearly as they place limits on its growth. The acts of 1572 made it difficult for companies to operate in the countryside unless they were patronized by barons or persons of higher rank. The crown patent to Leicester's Men granted one company the right to perform throughout the realm, with its plays to be licensed by the Master of the Revels. The Queen's Men gained similar authority a decade later. The Master of the Revels was to license all plays and all playing places according to his patent of 1581 (responsibilities easier to name than to carry out, but still the intention of the crown is clear), and if the tripartite commission of 1589 seemed at first to loosen the Master's control by sharing it with representatives of city and church, it also served to renew and broaden the assertion of censorship itself (in the event, Tilney managed to retain his one-man authority, which was stronger than ever). When the privy council ordered the destruction of all playhouses in 1597, apparently as a pretext for restricting the licensed companies and playhouses to two, the growing theatre industry of a generation before had been brought down to what most administrative minds would regard as manageable size.

This interpretation finds support from another quarter, the list of companies actually invited to perform at court by the Master of the Revels. The Queen's Men dominated the court calendar immediately after their establishment, of course, but a closer look than has perhaps been given to the schedule before 1583 reveals that the tendency to favour one or two companies above the rest had been occurring for about a decade. Table 1 summarizes the evidence.[20] Clearly an attempt was made to single out Leicester's Men in the early 1570s.

Table 1. *Court performances by adult companies*

	Leicester's	Lincoln's Clinton's Warwick's*	Sussex's	Derby's Strange's†	Total adult perf.	Queen's
Winter 1572– Spring 1574 (two seasons)	6	2	1	0	9	
Winter 1574– Spring 1578 (four seasons)	6	11	3	0	24	
Tilney in office by 14 February 1578						
Winter 1578– Spring 1581 (three seasons)	4	3	8	3	18	
Winter 1581– Spring 1583 (two seasons)	1	0	1	3	6	
Winter 1583– Spring 1586	0	0	0	0	14	11

* For the continuity of this company, see Chambers, *ES*, II, 96–9.
† Probably separate companies, although closely allied. See *ibid.*, 118–27.

They dominated the court seasons of 1572–3 and 1573–4, giving six of the nine performances by adult companies during those years. In 1574 they received the crown patent mentioned above. At that point they were nearly a Queen's Men anyhow – the most prestigious company, the company for whom the court schedule was largely reserved, the company whose royal protection was to be displayed throughout the realm. And each of their plays was to be licensed by the Master of the Revels, the price of royal patronage being royal censorship.

What happened to Leicester's Men after 1574, when they would seem to have had the future in their hands, is one of the mysteries of theatre history. Leicester's Men lost their dominance at court during the middle 1570s, as Table 1 shows. During the four seasons between 1574 and 1578 (before Tilney's tenure as Master began), their share of the total adult performances dwindled to one-quarter, and it continued to decline after that. Strangely, the decline at court begins just when the company's leader was putting his money into the future of the London commercial theatre by building a playhouse. It is by no means certain that London commercial success and a permanent playhouse are what the crown intended its favoured company to attain. Royal interest would have been served to the fullest, one imagines, by a company travelling widely throughout the provinces and playing an approved repertory. Leicester's Men continued to travel widely after the building of the Theatre, and, as we noted above, it is not clear that the Theatre was reserved as their London home. Burbage's new playhouse was an early sign of a tendency toward centring the theatre industry in London, however, and the crown was more interested in the counter-tendency, we believe, the tendency toward a theatre that radiated out from a well-defined centre and reached across the country. The centre of such radiation would have to be clearly defined as the court, and not a commercial building in Shoreditch. We are speculating, of course, but the failure of Leicester's Men to hold the court advantage after 1574 has not received even speculative attention before, as far as we know, and one might be permitted to wonder if exactly the right organization had been found to benefit from a combination of crown protection and crown censorship. A company headed by a man of James Burbage's character might not have been soft wax for the royal imprint.

Table 1 reveals that between 1574 and 1578 the most favoured company was the one headed by Jerome Savage and the Dutton brothers, who are thought to have passed from Lincoln's patronage to Warwick's in 1575 (*ES*, ii, 96–9). Thus they were under the patronage of Leicester's brother, Ambrose Dudley, while they took the lead at court. Like Leicester's Men, this company had some links to a playhouse near London, the theatre at Newington Butts, while they were at the zenith of their court career, and like that of Leicester's Men their court career declined soon thereafter.

The change can be pinpointed quite accurately. We now know that Edmund Tilney had assumed his office as Master of the Revels by 14 February 1578.[21] In his first season as Master, Warwick's Men were joined in prominence by a company Tilney had every reason to appreciate, as they were under the patronage of his supervisor and kinsman, the Earl of Sussex, the Lord Chamberlain. In Tilney's second season, Sussex's Men gave three performances for one by Warwick's Men, whose court career thereupon came to an end. Family feeling must have run deep in Tilney. He was also allied by marriage to the house of Stanley, and the next few seasons were graced by several visits from the two companies patronized by that family, the Earl of Derby's Men and Lord Strange's Men. After Tilney assumed office, in other words, the two companies that had successively dominated the court calendar, Leicester's Men and Warwick's Men, receded in favour of Sussex's Men, who along with two other companies from the 'Tilney group', Derby's Men and Strange's Men, gave about two-thirds of the performances by adult companies between the winter of 1578 and the spring of 1583.

This is not to say that the queen's love of drama was not being served, but Tilney was capable of more than one motive at a time. It was part of his genius that he managed to serve the queen's aesthetic interest even as he favoured his immediate superior and boosted the stock of the family troupes. (In the long run he helped make the Chamberlain's Men and the Admiral's Men, both family interests of his, the only two companies in town.)

While changing the direction of favouritism to his own alliances, however, Tilney adhered to what we take to be the general intention of the court toward the London theatre after about 1572 – to restrict the number of companies favoured by court patronage and to grant special prominence to one or two of the restricted group. Two companies gave 75 per cent of the performances by adult troupes between 1572 and 1578; three companies gave 63 per cent of them between 1578 and 1583; the Queen's Men gave 79 per cent between 1583 and 1586. The formation of the Queen's Men was not a change of direction by the crown but an acceleration along a route that had been travelled for a decade. Perhaps 1583 was not a crossroads after all. The crown had long sought to have Queen's 'Men' who would turn playing to a Tudor advantage, and after seeing Leicester's Men, then Warwick's Men, then Sussex's Men adapt themselves, perhaps rather fitfully, to a goal that was never quite declared, it was determined that the goal be declared by taking some of Leicester's Men, some of Warwick's, some of Sussex's – the best of them, for the queen loved the drama – and making them into a company whose name signified its political origin. That the existing companies would be overshadowed was not a new price to be paid, but the price that had been paid all along. Overshadowing is what happens when the source of light becomes selective, and if Worcester's Men, let us say, had been darkened by the patent to Leicester's Men in 1574, the consternation of privy council and crown seems to have been no greater than when Sussex's were darkened by the Queen's Men in 1583. The privileged company should in any case owe its fame to court influence, should the more willingly submit its plays to royal censorship, should have a reliable repertory ready for the Master of the Revels to review before the Christmas season, and should reduce the expenses of the Revels Office in the choosing, rehearsing, and outfitting of the plays.[22] The combination of frugality and censorship, in the interests of holiday pleasure, is hard for a central government to resist.

The companies favoured by Tilney may have fallen short of the crown's interest in travelling theatre, however. Derby's Men toured widely, but Sussex's Men apparently did not. The new Queen's Men would satisfy both interests: they would travel widely and they would help to consolidate the theatre industry by reducing the personnel and influence of the other companies. The damage done to the existing companies by the appointment of their leading members to the new organization would be outweighed by the benefit of increasing the government's influence over the liveliest of the Tudor arts. Tilney read the trend in the later 1570s and continued to maintain a schedule of court performances which celebrated one or two companies at a time, although he shifted the favour away from the Dudley troupes and toward Sussex's Men and the Stanley companies, then shifted it again with the formation of a royal company built to some extent on Leicester's Men.

Our view from the perspective of 1583, then, holds that the formation of the Queen's Men was a more sharply political venture than has been supposed before. Control of a burgeoning theatre was a desirable goal from the viewpoint of authority – so the city authorities insisted, and so the central government thought. The central government's idea of control was not to close the playhouses but to reduce the companies that could act in them, the reduction being accomplished by creating an all-star troupe which could not help but curtail the attractiveness of the other companies at the same time as it spread the queen's name through the country. The crown patent to Leicester's Men a decade before had been a move in the same direction. The scheduling of court performances over that decade seems also to have been motivated by growing selectivity, although there the focus of selectivity moved about, playing over certain leading families of the day. In 1583, the court schedule became monopolized with the consolidation of the children's companies and the formation of the Queen's Men, and at that point the central government seemed ready to take charge of this burgeoning actors' industry and send it along calculated directions.

2

Protestant politics:
Leicester and Walsingham

The Leicester connection

The loss of leading players to the Queen's Men in 1583 must have reduced the prospects for those who remained behind in the existing companies, but Leicester's company may have been in a different position from the others. Leicester's Men seem to have been the main source for the new company: Robert Wilson, John Lanham and William Johnson of the Queen's company had been three of the five actors named as Leicester's Men when they received their landmark royal patent in 1574.[1] The other two from Leicester's company in 1574 were James Burbage and John Perkin. Burbage may have left Leicester's service by 1583, for he was said to be calling himself 'Hunsdon's man' by 1584 (and one surmises that he was occupied with managing the Theatre after 1576). What became of Perkin is unknown, but of the five names of Leicester's Men in the earlier 1570s, when they were a quasi-royal company, more than half appear among the names of the Queen's Men of 1583, the actual royal company. To put that another way, of the six original Queen's Men whose earlier company connections can be detected, half come from Leicester's Men. Obviously there was a measure of continuity between the two organizations.

Six of the new company cannot be traced to their previous troupes. Did two or three of them also come from Leicester's? Were John Bentley, Toby Mills, John Towne, John Singer, Lionel Cooke or John Garland part of Leicester's troupe before 1583? The loss of Leicester's household papers for the period reduces the likelihood that we will ever know, but the chance survival of his personal account book for 1584–6, coupled with the survey of provincial records being carried out by the Records of Early English Drama, allows us a modest patch of ground for speculation.[2]

It is strikingly apparent from a study of the itineraries for Leicester's players over a thirty-year period that there was an exceptional three-year break from 1582 to 1585 in their otherwise constant touring. Between 1580 and their Shrovetide performance at court in March 1583, the company played their favourite circuits in the south-east twice and East Anglia three times, but

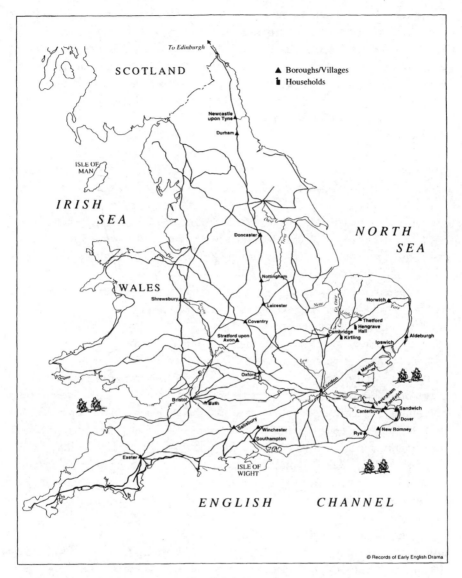

Map 1   Leicester's Men tour stops 1574–82

surviving records show that they also ranged as far as Durham and Newcastle in the north-east; Winchester, Salisbury, and Southampton in the south; and Shrewsbury in the West Midlands (see Map 1).[3] After the summer tour of East Anglia in 1582, however, a troupe under Leicester's patronage does not appear again in the provincial records until June 1585.[4] They were probably in London in later 1582 and they gave a court performance on 10 February 1583. Between then and May 1585, when a reward to them before they set off 'in to the Countrie' was recorded in Leicester's household account book, Leicester's Men do not appear anywhere in the records currently available.[5] An absence of evidence does not prove anything, of course, but Leicester's Men do appear frequently in the records before March 1583, they appear again in the records after May 1585, and the gap between those dates is the more noticeable because it coincides with the formation and early career of the Queen's Men.

The surviving Leicester household account book holds further clues. Intriguingly, and, we would argue, significantly, the only players paid by Leicester between 19 October 1584 when the accounts begin and May 1585 were the Queen's Men, who appeared at Leicester House in London on 28 December 1584 between their three Christmas season performances at court. In fact, the Queen's Men were the only other acting troupe rewarded by Leicester during the two years covered by this household book. They appeared again at Leicester House in mid April 1585 before their summer tour and again in November before their Christmas court shows.[6]

Of related interest is a generous reward to Tarlton, now the Queen's player, in May 1585. On 17 May, Leicester gave Tarlton 40 shillings, and four days later the same amount was given to his own players as they set off on their summer tour. It seems clear that this most assiduous of patrons was showing more than casual concern for the royal company, some of whose members were once his own men. We can add one more familiar nugget of information from a complementary household account for the following year. A Halliwell-Phillipps Scrapbook extract from the now lost source shows that a player named Wilson performed before Leicester in the Netherlands in March 1586 before returning to England. Further evidence (see p. 28 below) supports the likelihood that this was Robert Wilson, joining Leicester only three months after serving as payee at court for the Queen's Men – lured from his new company, it would seem, to augment his old patron's triumphant progress through the Low Countries.[7]

A large company of players accompanied Leicester to the Low Countries, and their names suggest that this was an expanded troupe assembled for grand display. Will Kempe and other actors who eventually came into Lord Strange's Men appear to have been part of the retinue and Wilson's presence suggests that some of the Queen's Men (and former Leicester's Men) were also part of the diplomatic show. The assembled clues point to a special relationship between Leicester and the Queen's Men. Leicester had long shown personal commitment to the theatre in maintaining an acting troupe which we would argue was the most innovative of its time. Indeed, Leicester himself had an enlightened awareness of the power of theatre to affect an audience and to spread cultural and political influence. We can briefly touch upon several actions during his early days as a courtier to illustrate the ways in which Leicester used drama to further his own cause.

A royal favourite from the beginning of Elizabeth's reign, Robert Dudley was ambitious to restore his family's lost fortunes.[8] He was also a committed member of the Protestant reform circle, a cause beyond purely personal gain which he served for the rest of his life. From his early appointment as Master of the Horse, Dudley rose rapidly in influence at court to occupy a controversial but secure place in the inner circle of the queen's advisers.[9] He was quick to see the importance of patronage in developing his position at court – included amongst his earliest endeavours was the formation of an acting troupe which began to tour the kingdom annually in 1559. Dudley ensured through his court connections that his players would have permission to tour beyond the regions of his immediate influence, as a familiar letter to the Earl of Shrewsbury in the north bears witness.[10]

It seems likely that the essential mandate of Dudley's company was to tour as widely as possible, in fair weather and foul. Even during the years of their peak popularity at court in the 1570s they continued to tour, and the establishment of Burbage's Theatre north of London, which they must have used some of the time as a London venue, did not disrupt their regular appearances in the provinces. We have noted the falling-off of their court performances in the later 1570s, but the ebbing of their dominance at court does not signal an eclipse in their fortunes generally. We can now say with some confidence that before the Queen's troupe took over, Leicester's Men were by far the most widely travelled, the most knowledgeable professionals on the road. Carrying their patron's name across the land, the actors made local contacts of undoubted political use. The generosity of their rewards when compared with other troupes illustrates just how aware of Leicester's influence at court were the officials of the towns visited.

Beyond effective public relations, would the players have contributed to any other cause espoused by their patron? We are becoming more conscious of Leicester's use of drama to present his own political or religious viewpoint. Paul White has demonstrated (see p. 31 below) that the stage was used for propaganda purposes by earlier Protestant leaders. Marie Axton has shown how Dudley followed in this tradition, using his new position as Christmas Prince and Master of the Revels at the Inner Temple to sponsor a production of *Gorboduc* and the masque *Desire and Lady Beauty* in 1561. Both the tragedy and the masque when decoded, she suggests, sought to advance Dudley's matrimonial and political aspirations.[11] A remarkable eyewitness report of the first performance of *Gorboduc*, discovered by Norman L. Jones, sheds further light on how the dumbshow in particular urged Dudley's cause as royal consort, a message presumably understood by the audience at the Inner Temple revels on

Twelfth Night 1562 and probably reinforced at its presentation before the queen at Whitehall on 18 January.[12] We need look no further than the dumbshow depicting the murder of Gonzago in *Hamlet* to imagine how potent these mostly unpublished additions to play texts would have been in performance. And if Hamlet could add a speech or two for the actors specially designed to tease a response from his target audience at Elsinore, we can assume that Leicester, the consummate politician, might also have used his position as Master of the Revels at the Inns of Court or as sponsor of productions at court to highlight his own interests. Sadly the plays performed by his own troupe are not specifically identified amongst surviving play texts, beyond the strong possibility that Robert Wilson's *Three Ladies of London*, published in 1584, was a Leicester's play. That the Queen's Men went on to stage the sequel to that play, *Three Lords and Three Ladies of London*, furthers the impression of a connection between the two companies.

Eleanor Rosenberg has studied Leicester's patronage in depth, describing him as 'the greatest Maecenas of his age'.[13] As a patron, his goals were cultural and religious as well as political. Like many Elizabethans, he was keen on English history and Italian humanism, enthusiasms which may also have been reflected in the plays performed by his actors. But his overriding concern during the 1570s and 1580s was for the security of the English realm and the Protestant faith at home and abroad. This concern he shared with Sir Francis Walsingham. During the decades when Mary Stuart was a focus for Catholic sympathies in England and on the continent, Leicester and Walsingham were the dominant members of what has been characterized as 'an aggressively Protestant party' in the privy council.[14] Together with Warwick, Bedford, and Knollys, they formed a 'family compact' at court, related by blood or marriage as well as bonded through religious sympathies. In their policy of active hostility toward Spain, they formed an opposition to Burghley, who had an aversion as strong as the queen's to war abroad. Tactically, Leicester and Walsingham shared more than policy and influence. While Walsingham was the undisputed spymaster of the Elizabethan era, there is ample reason to think that Leicester too employed secret methods to gain advantage. Alan Haynes names both men, with Burghley, as the three most important initiators of spying as a government resource. As Haynes observes, 'The political slant of Leicester's career, his contacts at home and abroad, though ill recorded, suggest with remaining data that he would have wanted a wide-ranging clutch of informers and intelligencers.'[15] It is possible that Leicester's players may have served on occasion in the transmission of information; one of the best-known examples of an Elizabethan actor acting as messenger is 'Will my Lord of Leicester's jesting player', who was given letters to carry from Sir Philip Sidney in the Low Countries to Walsingham.[16] (Will may only have been given such an assignment once: he delivered the letter to Walsingham's wife by mistake.)

In acting from time to time as informers, Leicester's Men would once again have been perpetuating a late-medieval tradition. Spying was not initiated under Elizabeth – her grandfather is on record for establishing a domestic spy ring, and some of his predecessors seem to have made *ad hoc* payments for intelligence reports as well. Ian Arthurson's research on late-medieval espionage practices has identified the touring royal or noble minstrel as one of the likeliest spies: 'The norm for spying was the itinerant: the servant, the merchant, the priest or the musician, the individual who, "in a society in which mobility was indubitably an important characteristic", would hardly be noticed. Every town account notes the gifts which the town gave to the minstrels of the aristocracy . . . The status of such men, not merely their peregrinations, made them spies.'[17] The minstrels as household servants had intimate access to those in power, but much of their time was spent on the road. Leicester's Men would have shared similar access to their patron, who would have drawn upon established Tudor practice in gathering intelligence reports to serve and protect his political interests.

Certainly Leicester and Walsingham both helped to define what Conyers Read has described as 'one of the characteristic attitudes of Tudor government . . . its increasing interest in public relations, that is to say, in the relations between the Crown and its neighbours and the Crown and its subjects, through public channels of communication'.[18] Read identifies the drama and the popular ballad as two obvious channels of approach to the people, although 'there is little evidence that they were used by the government'.[19] We would suggest, however, that Leicester recognized early just how effective drama could be as a means of influencing public opinion and of maintaining cultural and political links between the patron at court and local society, even in remoter parts of the kingdom. In this regard at least, he had greater experience than Walsingham and would have been ideally placed to advise the secretary of state on how to harness the theatre for their common cause.

Good public relations between crown and people were clearly of urgent importance in the 1580s, and it is into this context that we would place the formation and touring habits of the Queen's Men. If Walsingham was involved in their creation, Leicester seems likely to have collaborated wholeheartedly, as the most influential member of his circle and patron of several of the key players drafted for the new company. It is not impossible that all the core professionals of his troupe were yielded to the larger enterprise and that Leicester himself took an ongoing personal interest for the first two or three years in their repertoire and performance itinerary. He would seem to have had the greater experience and appetite for the politics of theatre in any case.

Leicester's players brought not only top-rated acting talent to the queen's service. They were masters of the touring tradition – the most knowledgeable about the best routes across England, the most lucrative towns to visit, the most sympathetic households. Their preferred circuits lay through East Anglia, the south-east and the Midlands leading to the north-east, but they had extended their travels to the south-west or into the north-east on average two years out of three. While personal profit and responsive audiences must always have been central issues for enterprising actors, service to the patron was also an essential part of their bargain for his protection. Leicester's Men would have been aware of the value of their touring for him. Not only was his name kept before the public through their performances, but local connections would be made and useful political information picked up while on the road, in the inns or at private residences. If he took the same interest in their repertoire as he had shown as an impresario at court, then they would also have acted as his agents in presenting to a wider audience plays that reflected his perspective on national and religious issues.

In sketching the profile of this most dynamic of early Elizabethan troupes, we catch more than a glimpse of the model we are proposing for the Queen's Men – a company designed to increase the prestige of their patron throughout the land, to harness the theatre in the service of a moderate Protestant ideology, and to add a vivid group of travellers who might serve the council's needs for secret information about recusants or foreign visitors in more than one way. Whether some or all of Leicester's Men joined the new company in 1583, the influence of their former patron must have been felt. We do not think that he was dismayed to lose his star players. He was too close to the urgent concerns of the inner ring of the queen's advisers at the time. Leicester and Walsingham had the same political agenda in 1583 and their personal and religious sympathies ran deep. What evidence we have accumulated suggests that Leicester maintained a mentoring link with the new troupe, previewing some of their performances and encouraging their tour. He understood the advantages in forming a travelling company for purposes of cultural influence reaching into the countryside from the court. How the Queen's Men absorbed this purpose is evident from the earliest years of their existence, and how they further shaped the existing model for touring the kingdom with a royal patent will be the subject of chapter 3 below.

Walsingham

The government official who instructed the Master of the Revels to appoint the Queen's Men in 1583 was not the Lord Chamberlain, under whose authority the Revels office operated. It was Sir Francis Walsingham. Why should the man who was in effect secretary of state have undertaken this assignment? E. K. Chambers assumed that the Lord Chamberlain, the Earl of Sussex, failed to act because he was ill. Walsingham was simply filling in, according to this interpretation, which better explains why Sussex did not act than why Walsingham did. It is true that Sussex had been ill the previous year, and he died a few months after the Queen's Men were formed. The authority of the Chamberlain's office may have been in some disarray. On the other hand, this was one of the most important and powerful offices in the government, and when the Chamberlain was incapacitated, his role was normally filled by experienced officers within the Household. Henry Carey, Lord Hunsdon, had served as Sussex's deputy since November 1582. The Vice-Chamberlain was Sir Christopher Hatton. The Household was not lacking in responsible and experienced officers who could enact Sussex's authority. Why should Walsingham, a political opponent of Sussex's on most matters, have filled his role when it came to the appointment of the Queen's Men? A few months later, when the city authorities attempted to limit the new company's playing times in London, it was Walsingham who wrote on behalf of the Queen's Men and explained that they should be permitted to give regular weekday performances. His concern for the Queen's Men seems to have been more than incidental.

In 1583 Walsingham's alliance with Leicester was about to be tightened by the marriage of his daughter to Leicester's nephew, Sir Philip Sidney. The degree of continuity between Leicester's Men and the new Queen's Men should be considered in the context of interests shared between these two leading puritan politicians of the day.[20]

Not for a moment does one suppose that Walsingham cared personally for the theatre – there is no sign that he ever set foot in a playhouse or sponsored performances at his own houses, as Leicester did. Yet he was aware of the cultural influence drama could have. The view that the literary culture passed by an untouched Walsingham simply will not do. Conyers Read could assume Walsingham was 'clearly no patron of the drama' and 'quite indifferent to the fact that a group of obscure young men in the Mermaid Tavern and elsewhere were about to produce the greatest monuments of the English language', but new information has appeared and it helps put the old in a different light. It is now clear that Marlowe was no 'obscure young man' to Walsingham, and some writers who are obscure to us, like Thomas Watson and Anthony Munday, were well known to him.[21] The leading Queen's player, Richard Tarlton, wrote from his deathbed to Walsingham, seeking protection for his survivors against possible fraud. Walsingham's son-in-law, Sir Philip Sidney, was godfather to Tarlton's son, and later, in 1592, the Countess of Pembroke, Sidney's sister, patronized common players who can be identified with the Queen's Men (see below, pp. 29–30). Walsingham was probably not being a 'jack-of-all-trades' when he set the formation of the Queen's Men in motion. He was attending to business – not because he cared for theatre or did errands for the queen, but because he cared for the demands and opportunities of his office.

Local in-fighting among members and would-be members of the privy council must have been a consideration. A behind-the-scenes contest over the naming of the next Chamberlain was probably under way by March 1583, and the long-standing dispute between the Leicester and Sussex factions would not have been put aside at such a time. From our distance, we must guess at such matters, but in observing a degree of continuity between Leicester's Men and the new Queen's company, we should note that the most important member of the new company, Richard Tarlton, was apparently drawn not from Leicester's Men but from Sussex's.[22] The advantage of removing the most famous actor of the day from Sussex's patronage and teaming him with the best of Leicester's Men may not have escaped notice in the Leicester–Walsingham circle.[23]

Walsingham's larger political concerns centred on the religious arguments of the day, issues imbued with dangers from the old faith and problems from the new. On the surface of things, the threat from Catholicism was the leading danger. A little under the surface, but perhaps as close to the point of Walsingham's and Leicester's considerations in 1583, lay the danger within the more active elements of the Protestant movement itself, where a radical faction was using attacks against the theatre to gain ascendancy. The puritan attacks on the theatre grew strident from the mid 1570s into the 1580s. They were the leading edge of a Protestant radicalism that could not be ignored, and because the attack centred on the theatre, the theatre would have mattered to Walsingham – not because it delighted the imagination of the beholder, but because it drew lightning from the articulate extremists among the puritans and threatened a storm from which moderation might have to seek cover.

Against Catholicism, the government's most general aim was to unify the country. A touring company bearing special licence from the queen obviously carried royal influence through the realm, and both Leicester's Men with their extraordinary royal patent of 1574 and the Queen's Men of 1583 were meant to serve this general cultural function. The 1580s were the decade when the effort to spread a court-inspired culture took on mythical proportions under the queen's name, not the name of 'Elizabethan' (that was a nineteenth-century invention) but of 'Eliza' or 'Gloriana', the semi-divine monarch before whose beauty and authority ancient boundaries became pervious. The real queen did traverse some of the land on her summer progresses, but her influence was spread by a public-relations campaign which grew effective in the 1580s, gained an enormous boost from the defeat of the Armada, and culminated with the publication of Spenser's glorification of Elizabeth in the first three books of *The Faerie Queene*. It is not hard to see the Queen's Men as belonging to this general cultural effort, but in thinking about Walsingham we are thinking about an official who dealt in specific issues and used specific administrative methods.

Sixteenth-century England was a vast space to unify, with areas of Catholic resistance remaining far from court influence, especially in the north. To make inroads upon these centres of the ancient faith, the privy council built two administrative networks, one public and one covert, during the time of Walsingham's greatest influence. The public network was the lord lieutenancy system, which was completed during the 1580s and brought each county under the control of an authority whose primary allegiance was to the queen. The covert network was Walsingham's intelligence system, his leading method of tracking and controlling the Catholic underground. He began receiving large Treasury outlays for this purpose in 1582 (larger than has been noted before), and from then at least until the execution of Mary Queen of Scots in 1587, the spy system ranked among Walsingham's principal undertakings.[24]

The formation of the Queen's Men in 1583 should be regarded particularly in connection with the intelligence system – not because the Queen's Men were spies, but because Walsingham used licensed travellers of various kinds to give the impression of an extensive court influence within which the actual size and constitution of the spy system could not be detected. He was creating the impression of a larger intelligence system than he in fact possessed, and licensed travellers from court, who crossed the land on their own business, were serving as something of a smoke-screen to obscure the locations of a few flames.

Moreover, Walsingham could sometimes learn a thing or two from the licensed travellers and other alert persons – writers, for example – who could be employed for specific tasks. Professional spies like Robert Barnard, Walter Williams, Malivery Catlyn, and Thomas Rogers (who used the name 'Nicholas Berden') were the foundation of the network, but men of other professions – publicly recognized professions, especially recognized professions in which travel was a normal component – could pick up and deliver things too. The connection between travel and foreign service was fully recognized by Edmund Tilney, who compiled a massive reference guide about England and the major continental nations.[25] Only recently has this book gained much notice and been recognized as a foreign-service undertaking (it is called by its recent editor, W. R. Streitberger, 'a heroic example of an attempt to give shape to intelligence material'). Tilney was trying to advance his career by writing a foreign-policy reference guide which took the form of a book for travellers. He knew that the licensed traveller was useful to the government.

Thus a travelling company of Queen's Men would not only carry the name and influence of the monarch through the country but would also give the impression of a watchful monarch, one whose 'men' ranged over the land. They would perform useful fictions before crowds throughout the country, but they would also be something of a fiction themselves, coming into town dressed in their vivid livery coats, drums and trumpets heralding them: the Queen's Men on the move. Here is another way the Queen's Men helped to spread a new court culture – not only by acting stories the court wanted the country to hear, but also by letting some in the country wonder what stories the actors were telling the court. The actors may not have been telling the court anything, but it is the possibility of information-gathering that mattered to recusants and their sympathizers, whose attention Walsingham would gladly have drawn to the wrong travellers so that the real spies could set about their tasks more easily. The Queen's Men would seem to have had the privilege of access to court. Their actual privileges at court were restricted to performing plays on command, as far as we know, and the privy councillor who would regularly trust a Tarlton or a Bentley with matters of political sensitivity would in all likelihood find his career coming to an early end; but the impression was what mattered, and the impression given by the Queen's Men on tour was that of a central government whose influence was active and penetrating.

There are in fact correspondences between the names of the Queen's Men and the names of messengers listed in the court records. A Laurence Dutton and a John Symons appear regularly in the Declared Accounts of the Treasurer as messengers of the queen's chamber in the 1580s and 1590s; a Lawrence Dutton, perhaps the same man, was earlier named as a queen's messenger in an Essex household account book in 1576.[26] Actors named Laurence Dutton and John Symons were with the Queen's Men in the provinces in the late 1580s and early 1590s. Robert Wilson, a member of the original 1583 company, is said in one record to have been dwelling at court in 1585 and in another to have carried letters into the Low Countries in January 1586.[27] John Dutton, John Garland, and (later) William Smith were Queen's Men, and these names also appear in the messengers' records.[28] These are common names, of course, and it would be unwise to build an argument on their occurrences in different sorts of records. There was another John Garland who served as an informant in Ireland, for example, and he rather than the actor John Garland probably accounts for all the 'Garland' references in the messenger records.[29] Yet actors did on occasion carry letters. Will (quite possibly Will Kempe), 'my Lord of Leicester's jesting player' who misdelivered the letter from Utrecht according to Sir Philip Sidney, may not have been a good messenger, but he was carrying letters and he was a player. A record of 1603 shows four unnamed players giving intelligence information.[30] It is likely that some of the Queen's Men did bear messages on occasion, and some of the names in the messengers' records may indeed belong to the actors. There is no way to be certain. The point is not that the Queen's Men were spies, but that travelling players wearing the queen's livery would have been useful to Walsingham – perhaps for occasionally bearing messages to the right persons, more obviously for showing that the central government was attending to the nation through its licensed travellers.

Walsingham certainly made use of writers. Anthony Munday was spying when he was a guest at the English College in Rome, and Marlowe nearly missed out on his Cambridge degree by spending some of his final student months on her majesty's service at Rheims. One of Marlowe's acquaintances was the engineer and writer on fortifications, Paul Ive. Another was the poet Thomas Watson. The men of letters who gathered around Sir Philip Sidney at Walsingham's country estate at Barn Elms, or at his cousin Thomas Walsingham's house at Chislehurst, saw their own careers as consistent with the Protestant reform movement that the Walsinghams were instrumental in forwarding. Did the circle at times include common stage players? Tarlton's connection with Sidney and Walsingham suggests that the most famous of the Queen's Men was known there. John Bentley, another of the original Queen's players, was said to have been moulded out of the pens of Watson, Achlow, and Kyd, all writers involved in the Sidney circle. Only Kyd is known to have written for the common stage among this group, and he is not known to have written for the Queen's Men. But 'known' is a rare quality when it comes to the authors of plays in the 1580s, even the titles of which have disappeared, with few exceptions. It is quite possible that the *Felix and Philiomena* or the *Phillyda and Corin* (both now lost) which the Queen's Men played at court in 1585 came from writers like Watson, Achlow, or Kyd, the three who are said to have moulded John Bentley with their pens.[31]

We are on firmer ground with the Countess of Pembroke, Mary Herbert, who certainly was acquainted with players. The discovery of the will of Simon Jewell, an actor who died in 1592 and is otherwise unknown to posterity, shows that a contribution toward burial expenses was expected from 'my ladie Pembrooke'.[32] Jewell's company is not named, and some have taken the mention of Lady Pembroke to mean that he belonged to an acting company under the patronage of the Earl of Pembroke. The other names mentioned in the will, however, indicate that Jewell's company in 1592 was the Queen's Men. The will refers to a 'Mr. Johnson' in such a way as to indicate that he had been a sharer in the company, it names 'Roberte Nicholls', 'Mr. Smithe', and 'Mr. Cooke' as though they also belonged to the company, and it mentions 'Robert Scott' as Jewell's landlord. These are common names, but they form a cluster with William Johnson and Lionel Cooke, original members of the Queen's Men, Robert Nichols and William Smith, who seem from evidence in

Henslowe's *Diary* to have joined the Queen's Men in the 1590s, and the Robert Scott who is named in the will of another of the original Queen's Men, John Bentley. In being acquainted with stage players, the Countess of Pembroke was probably no more following after her husband's interests than Walsingham was filling in for Sussex when the Queen's Men were formed. Both were probably looking after their own affairs, and both were deeply interested in the religious/political issues of the day. The literary circle sponsored by the Countess of Pembroke at Wilton paralleled the group Walsingham and Sidney supported at Barn Elms, and the point to grasp about both endeavours is that their bias toward what we might call 'high culture' did not exclude what we might call (and they certainly did) the 'common' stage. Sir Philip Sidney has not a good word for the common stage in his *Apology for Poetry*, which he worked on during his Barn Elms sojourn, and the drama written for and by Mary Sidney at Wilton was not to be clapper-clawed by the vulgar. But it would be a mistake to think these writers were above propaganda. The idea of a high culture that refused to descend to propaganda and popular literature cannot be maintained for the Walsingham–Sidney set. Mary Sidney may not have appreciated the conventions of the common stage any more than her brother did, and Walsingham may not have known what those conventions were, but that does not mean they rejected the cultural usefulness the common stage had to offer; and in that context their acquaintance with actors like Tarlton and Simon Jewell should be understood as signs of the larger efforts which forward-looking Protestants near or in the central government were undertaking.[33]

In 1583, those larger efforts may well have seemed more sharply focused on forward-looking Protestantism itself than on the unifying, anti-Catholic purpose we have so far considered. By 1583, the cultural rift that had been opening within radical Protestantism for about a decade would have seemed dangerous. Earlier generations of reform had used art, drama, and music as methods of propaganda, but now, since the mid 1570s, in what Patrick Collinson has called the secondary phase of the Reformation, the radical edge of the movement had rejected these cultural media. Particularly it rejected the drama. Articulate and vehement spokesmen were attacking the London theatre industry from the ground up – the buildings as sinks of iniquity, the actors as extravagant immoralists, and the audiences as youth on the verge of corruption or adults daily engaged in its practice. The building of permanent playhouses like the Red Lion in Stepney and the Theatre and Curtain in Shoreditch alarmed writers and preachers like Philip Stubbes, John Northbrooke, John Stockwood, and Thomas White because the new theatres institutionalized this concentrated and crowd-pleasing form of corruption. And they provided the zealous with a new opportunity for leading the Protestant movement. Authorities who sought to use the growing literary and theatrical culture for national political purposes had to see the new vehemence as a problem. Its dimensions must have increased between 1579 and 1583, when two writers of plays themselves, Stephen Gosson and Anthony Munday, the sort of talent Walsingham would have hoped to use (and in Munday's case probably did), joined the puritan attack.

The puritans on the privy council of the 1570s and 1580s – Walsingham, Leicester, and Knollys in particular – would have seen signs of danger in the attacks on the stage from within the reform movement. These men had a government to manage, and a nation to steer through a potentially disastrous political and religious conflict. From their perspective, the danger was not so much that zealous reformers would harm a form of entertainment in which the queen took special pleasure, but that the radical reformers would drive the reform movement apart from a developing English culture and create a division which the government would find unbridgeable. Patrick Collinson has used Eliot's phrase, 'the dissociation of sensibility', to describe the cultural separation that resulted; it was 'without precedent in English cultural history'.[34] Puritanism eventually sought to strip its approved culture of all fictions and images that were not literally attached to scripture and the new faith. Karl-Josef Holtgen has called attention to the extremity of this drive by naming it 'iconophobia'. The commercial theatre, drawing afternoon crowds to witness spectacles presented by men pretending to identities other than their own (and boys pretending to be women), was the false icon run mad.

The theatre had been a useful instrument to Protestant leaders in the past. As Paul Whitfield White has demonstrated, earlier secretaries of state – especially Cromwell and William Cecil – had controlled the stage for propagandistic purposes.[35] White also shows that some of the bands of travelling interluders of the earlier Tudor period served the Protestant interests of their patrons: six members of Edward VI's privy council known to have supported the Protestant cause were patrons of acting companies, for example.[36] To use the theatre in behalf of the reform movement would have been nothing new when Walsingham first entered government service.

But the puritan attack on the growing London stage in the 1570s and 1580s created a complex situation. With puritanism divorcing itself from the drama that Protestantism had earlier sponsored, the stage was losing contact with religious doctrine and developing its own system of language, characterization, and the generic intricacies we now think of as Shakespearean. Collinson notes that the drama, left to its own devices in this way, 'became, in the perception of the hyper-religious public, "filthier", more abandoned than ever', and that this degeneration is now known to us as the flowering of the Elizabethan drama.[37]

A politician like Walsingham did not deem the flowering of the drama a primary concern. Walsingham cared about holding the reformed religion together with a strong centralized government, exactly the connection that was threatened by puritan extremism. The queen was not about to accede to the radicals. Every well-reasoned attack on the episcopacy left unstated the question it fully implied: where did the supreme governor of the church, the queen herself, belong in an establishment fully reformed along puritan lines? The queen's refusal to negotiate with the reform movement of the 1570s and 1580s was firmly based on knowing that 'nowhere' was the answer to this question, and the task of Walsingham and her other councillors who supported reform was to find avenues that would accommodate both the religious ideology in which they believed and the monarch they served with no less devotion. Finding himself addressed in the preface to Gosson's attack on the stage in 1582 (*Plays Confuted*), where he appears to be called upon to combine the function of Scipio and Hercules in cleansing the realm of theatre, Walsingham may have felt his position was not sufficiently understood. Whatever he thought of the theatre in his personal life is not to the point. Extreme puritanism was a real threat to the religious politics of the government, a larger problem than the growing theatre industry, and one which the growing theatre industry could even help to allay.

That the monarch was prepared to suppress the radical movement posed delicate issues for a man in Walsingham's position. Among the manoeuvres by which he sought to maintain the influence of advanced Protestantism should be numbered the formation of an acting company bearing the queen's name and performing plays of such English and Protestant moderation as could displease only those reformers opposed to playing itself.

Truth and plainness staged

When the extant plays of the Queen's Men are read in the light of the political interests we have just reviewed, several elements fall into place. Their first published play, Robert Wilson's *Three Lords and Three Ladies of London*, acts out the defeat of the Spanish Armada. Most of the characters carry over from the predecessor play, *Three Ladies of London* (probably from Leicester's Men), but the three lords of London themselves are new, and their names are not casually chosen: Pleasure, Pomp, and Policy. What is Pleasure doing in a play about the Spanish Armada? He is being told to publish plays and other entertainments that the puritan zealots would have banned from the realm – publish them now, publish them quickly, for the Spaniards are coming. 'See that plays be published', Pleasure is urged (by Policy) as the Spanish approach,

> May-games and masks, with mirth and minstrelsy,
> Pageants and school-feasts, bears and puppet plays.

Pomp should join the battle against Spain too. He is to put on shows and solemn feasts, triumphs and bonfires. This amounts to calling the puritan extremists who opposed such festivities unpatriotic – the plays and other entertainments they would expunge are contributing to the nation's defence. *Three Lords and Three Ladies* is obviously an anti-Catholic play, but puritanism is being shown its place too, and its place is in the centre of a strong and unified London. Conscience is married to Pleasure at the end of the play, Love to Policy, and Zeal has helped the ladies with new clothes.

The most important kind of play performed by the Queen's Men was the English history play, which they were the first professional company to undertake extensively. We will examine their history plays more fully later on, but for the moment we should notice that the particular stamp they placed upon historical drama was called 'truth' – truth as opposed to shadows and images such as 'poetry'. In calling their plays *The True Tragedy of Richard III*, or the *True Chronicle History of King Leir,* they were advertising the point enacted at the beginning of their piece on Richard III, when Truth comes onto the stage and takes the leadership of playing away from Poetry. Poetry provides but 'shadows' upon a stage, but Truth will 'add bodies to the shadows' in an English tragedy that 'will revive the hearts of drooping minds'. That last phrase makes one yearn for the return of Poetry, but we should meet the Queen's Men on their own terms and try to see what they meant. Their 'Truth' is of a piece with their 'Pleasure' in *Three Lords and Three Ladies.* The business of plays is to gain an edge over those who trade in alluring images for their own sake – i.e. 'Poetry'. It is to display the plain, unvarnished substance of history in a form appealing to all the people. *Selimus* is one of their history plays on a non-English subject, but it makes the same point as *The True Tragedy of Richard III* and *The True Chronicle History of King Leir*. The prologue to *Selimus* disavows 'forged tragedy' in favour of what has been acknowledged as 'true', and then proceeds to offer thirty scenes of chronicle about dynastic warfare in post-Tamburlaine Turkey, all of it done in answer to Marlowe's glorification of ruthless individualism. (Several of the Queen's Men plays are replies to Marlowe – see chapter 7, pp. 155–60 below.) There is no question but that these plays are a campaign to give legitimacy to a Protestant drive for substantial truth and plain speech. Their *King Leir* is virtually an exercise in plain speaking, as we will see. But the campaign is not just for truth and plainness – it is for truth and plainness set forth on the stages which the radical reformers had been attacking since the 1570s, and the Queen's Men were formed to conduct the campaign. From the perspective of men like Walsingham and Leicester, the Queen's Men of 1583 would have seemed an avenue for bringing the theatre back into the service of a Protestant ideology which could also be identified as the 'truth' of Tudor history.

How does this reading of the Queen's Men differ from previous accounts? An earlier generation of scholars (those who thought Walsingham was filling in for Sussex when the Queen's Men were named) believed that the cultural and educational movements we have learned to call humanism eventually set the theatre free from religious ideology. The Queen's Men were thought to be part of humanism. This argument held that the suppression of the Catholic stage in the banning of the miracle cycles under Protestant governments cleared the way for the drama to develop along aesthetic and commercial lines. The use of drama for a *Protestant* ideology played but a small role in this narrative.

The commercial playhouses of London were a centre of the humanist effort as far as drama was concerned. Over these London playhouses, there was a 'struggle between City and Court' (Chambers's phrase), with the court often protecting the playhouses because they served as rehearsal places for the shows which would be performed before the queen. This made the court an ally of the free enterprise system that was being found to flourish in the playhouses. With the support of the privy council, 'the stage won its way, against the linked opposition of an alienated pulpit and an alienated municipality, to an ultimate entrenchment of economic independence'.[38]

In the previous chapter, we have wondered what sort of protection for the theatre industry can be found in the decision to draw the best actors away from their older companies in order to form the new all-star troupe. We imagined that the crown's interest lay in gaining control over the burgeoning London theatre rather than in protecting the companies by decimating the best of them. As we now consider the particular motives of Leicester and Walsingham in the 1580s, we find specific political intentions for the Queen's Men becoming evident, and these motives are not so much humanist as royalist and Protestant – Protestant particularly in regard to the division being opened by the most strident reformers. The company's engagement in the Marprelate broil of 1589– 91 will not seem an anomaly from this point of view, and the extent of their career in the provinces should be recognized as a measure of their success in spreading a court-sponsored culture through the realm.

The older view held that the queen decided to form the Queen's Men because, loving the drama, she wanted an all-star company for performances at court. This may well be so. Nothing we have said rules it out. We do feel that the queen's desire is not the most important part of the motives for organizing the company and that the queen herself would have been more concerned for the political/religious factors we have reviewed than for the delectability of the court play. But perhaps she would not have minded having Tarlton banded together with the actors from Leicester's Men, and it is more than likely Leicester would not have minded either.

B.S.! Leicester's taste is reflected in the Kenilworth entertainments of 1575!

What can be said of humanism at this point? The titles from the court schedule during the decade before 1583 belong to the classical and romantic veins associated with humanism: *Predor and Lucia*, *Mamillia*, *Philomen and Philecia*, *Panecia*, *The Collier*, *A Greek Maid*, *Delight*, *Talomo*. These titles sound as though they were meant to make a broad cultural assertion about England's position in a European world. To prove that England had a literature and a drama that could stand among those of the continental nations – that was a challenge being met by the companies that were called to play such pastoral and classical pieces at court, and it was a full-fledged motive in what we call humanism. Yet the pastoral romance had subtexts that a sophisticated Elizabethan would have understood in terms of the politics of the regime, which centred on a monarch willing to be described as a matchless shepherdess herself. John Michael Archer has shown the connections between pastoralism and the growth of intelligence systems in the 1580s, and his account makes it clear that Walsingham's country estate at Barn Elms figured at once as pastoral retreat and as centre of political espionage.[39] When the new Queen's Men brought *Phillyda and Corin* along with *Felix and Philiomena* to court in 1584 (both lost, but the titles are clearly pastoral), they were participating in a movement which can be thought of as humanist so long as humanism retains its edge of association with the specific political interests of men like Walsingham and Leicester.

Humanism is capable of many agendas. We have argued in the previous chapter that Tilney was building his career through favouring one or two companies on the court schedule, but this personal motive fits into broader political considerations which would have been apparent to an aspiring Elizabethan official. If the privy council sought to limit the growth of the London playhouses by drawing the best players of the day into a single company, they also sought to extend the queen's influence throughout the nation, and the puritans among them would have known that drama could have a telling effect in religious controversy. Does that deny the older argument about humanism? Of course not. The creation of a national literature, permanent and influential in the later Renaissance, is a political goal in the first place, and to connect a particular event like the founding of the Queen's Men with particular interests like Tilney's family ties or the operation of Walsingham's espionage system or the opportunity to steal Tarlton away from Sussex's Men is not to topple an edifice in literary history called humanism but to describe some of the political and social parts the edifices of literary history are composed of.

The Protestant text running through the plays of the Queen's Men insists on the value of fiction, image-making, and playing so long as two concepts are being served. Those concepts are 'truth' and 'plainness'. It need not be imagined that Leicester or Walsingham always dictated those terms. Writers in a

35

Who?

controversial age can handle the terms of the argument for themselves, and the writers of the plays of the Queen's Men would have known how to solidify an opposition to attacks on the theatre without advice from a privy councillor. Walsingham probably did not preview the plays of the Queen's Men or dictate the inventions on 'truth' and 'plainness' by which they are organized, although Leicester may have done so on occasion – the dates of the company's visits to Leicester House occur shortly before court performances in 1584–5 and shortly before their provincial tour in 1585. It requires no great stretch of imagination to think that Walsingham or others from the Barn Elms literary circle regarded English history as the best field for the new company to dramatize, or that this thought had earlier occurred to Leicester when his company was the quasi-royal troupe. We do not know much about the Leicester repertory. We do know that the Queen's Men, with former Leicester's Men at their centre, established the English history play in the popular theatre before other companies took it up, and their approach to English history combines broad anti-Catholicism with a specifically Protestant style, 'truth' and 'plainness' intertwined. It need be no mystery why Walsingham was involved in the formation of the company.

Why should these writers be so hard to identify?

3

The career of the Queen's Men

The inherited tradition

From the year of their formation in 1583, the Queen's Men were the most active touring troupe on record. Standard narratives would encourage us to discount their provincial activities as of secondary importance to London and court performances during their heyday in the 1580s and as a sign of their decline in the 1590s.[1] Yet a wealth of recently uncovered evidence suggests otherwise and demands that we reassess their career in the provinces as we explore the political and cultural motives for their formation.[2]

Before revising the tale of the Queen's on tour, we may want to ask a couple of basic questions. What was the inherited tradition for travelling professional companies? Did the most successful act at court or in the London area by preference, touring only during time of plague or crackdown by city authorities?

It has become apparent in recent years that touring in the provinces was a well-established custom long before the Queen's Men went on the road. Although relevant records become at best fitful as we move back through the centuries, surviving accounts of late-medieval and Tudor towns and households allow us to chart at least some of the movements of hundreds of entertainers throughout England.[3] Some of these travellers were very localized, amateur acts, but many claimed members of the royal family, nobility and gentry as their patrons. This second group, approximating what we might consider early 'professionals', received some rewards as servants of their patrons' households for performances at Christmas and Shrovetide especially, but they were also free to earn money by performing elsewhere when they were not needed at home. Such troupes would typically visit cities and market towns in regions where their patrons had influence, as well as other private residences belonging to friendly associates. When we locate the places visited on a map and combine the performance evidence with what is known about major roads linking London with the provinces, it is easy to conclude that most troupes followed the principal routes in pursuit of paying audiences, though they did sometimes venture off the well-beaten tracks when a hospitable household or monastery (before 1540) held out the prospect of higher rewards augmented by room and board.[4] The 'home base' for such a touring troupe would have been their patron's principal residence; certainly some performed at court and in the London area before the establishment of the theatres, but the focus for their efforts would seem to have been the provinces.[5]

By the 1570s, then, the tradition of touring would have been adopted by all companies with any enterprise. Audiences could be guaranteed throughout the kingdom, with official rewards varying according to the prominence of the patron, the economic resources of the town or household, and possibly the scope of the performance itself. In this era of maturing urban communities, towns were alert to the advantages of nurturing good relations with powerful patrons who might support their quest for expanded civic privileges.[6] Provincial performances could foster stronger ties between the nobility and local communities, yoking pleasure, profit and political advantage in ways which we would assume were recognized by all involved.

In the first chapter we looked at the leading London troupes of the decade preceding the formation of the Queen's Men. Companies patronized by the Earls of Leicester, Warwick, Derby and Sussex are likely to have performed in playhouses and inns in the London area as well as at court during the 1570s, with the possibility that some of the other more active troupes such as Essex's, Berkeley's and Worcester's may have included London playhouses in their itineraries though they did not appear at court. But were such prominent companies essentially based in the new 'theatres' in London or did they maintain a provincial tour as their performing predecessors had done? For Leicester's and Derby's Men the answer decidedly favours the provinces. We have already developed a profile of Leicester's troupe, concluding that they were masters of the touring tradition (see pp. 18–21 above). Derby's can furnish us with another example, a company singled out for court appearances at Shrovetide 1580 and during the Christmas season, 1581 and 1582, while touring the southwest and Midlands regularly as they had before.[7] In fact, we know more about their provincial activities than we do of any London-area performances apart from Whitehall.[8] In the main, Leicester's Men, Derby's Men and the company newly organized as Oxford's Men in 1580 were very active touring companies in the years shortly before the formation of the Queen's Men.

How much can we learn from documentary evidence which has survived centuries of erratic treatment to become the recent focus for scholars interested in Elizabethan acting troupes? While admitting that financial accounts provide only the most pragmatic and partial details of theatrical experience, we can nevertheless benefit from a careful review of the dramatic records available to us from towns and private households across Great Britain. If we lay aside earlier accounts of the Queen's Men, bypassing old assumptions about plague-driven tours and scrambled dating systems, we can newly analyse a remarkable accumulation of information about their provincial itineraries.

While surviving evidence is far from comprehensive, it is sufficiently detailed for us to reassess the number and relative popularity of circuits favoured by the royal troupe. Collaborative research in recent years has yielded many new records of provincial performances. We have learned to pinpoint dates more accurately as we have searched both new and familiar sources, although we must cautiously note that the date of recording a mayor's payment to players should not be taken as the exact date of performance or even as the precise day of the payment itself in every instance. Nonetheless, verification of transcriptions from Elizabethan manuscripts and the increase in evidence make it possible in many instances to deduce the direction that the annual tours took. Where a payment is entered under a specific day or week within a set of annual accounts which are clearly organized and detailed, rather than summarized, in chronological order, then we may reasonably assume that both the performance and the payment concerned occurred not too long before. The itineraries of the Queen's Men reconstructed in Appendix A (pp. 170–88 below) will illustrate how such dates can complement each other and strengthen the evidence for seasonal tours in specific regions.[9]

Established tour circuits existed throughout the kingdom, as illustrated in Map 2. We may broadly categorize these as East Anglia; the south-east through Canterbury to the Cinque Ports and their coastal affiliates; the south-west via the coast through Southampton and Dorset or along one of several inland roads to Bristol; the Midlands centring on Coventry at the hub of a network of roads running in all directions; the West Midlands along the hilly terrain of the Welsh borders; the north-east via the Great North Road or another important road through Leicester; and the mountainous north-west most commonly reached across Coventry or from the north-east through the breach in the Yorkshire hills in Airedale. Lacking relevant journals or travel expenses, we cannot know for certain how many days were needed by entertainers to tour each of these circuits. Circumstances varied greatly: mid spring through mid autumn would have offered the best travel conditions, but the quality of roads must have varied as much as the terrain through the kingdom. Some companies would have travelled on horseback, as evidence suggests the Queen's Men did, and consequently their pace would have been faster, but we do not have a record of all stops made on route nor, in most instances, of the length of time spent in each place.

An influential scholar of the English road system has suggested that the late-medieval 'high ways' (to use Grafton's term) brought every part of the country within a fortnight's ride of London.[10] Others have postulated the average speed of travel on foot or horseback and noted the increase in travel despite road

Map 2   Post-1550 performance locations in England visited by
travelling players with patrons

conditions which we may too easily assume were prohibitive: Norbert Ohler, for example, reckons that 15–25 miles a day was feasible for the medieval traveller, while the 'average traveller' on horseback going slowly with followers and baggage (merchants, for example) could cover somewhere between 20 and 30 miles daily.[11] An early-seventeenth-century English journal provides one instance of an early-modern traveller on horseback achieving that average: Nicholas Assheton left London on 5 March 1618 and travelled at a comfortable pace along the road north through Ware, Royston, Huntingdon, Lincoln and Doncaster to York, Skipton and then home to Downham in Lancashire by 13 March. Although on the road for nine days, he made a couple of stops for rest and pleasure, so that there were only six days of actual travel. While his mileage figures may not be accurate by our modern reckoning, he estimated the distance of his trip as being 178 miles, for an average distance of 30 miles a day.[12] This is the context into which we may place the touring achievements of the Queen's Men in the late sixteenth century.

The Queen's Men: the first two years

How soon did the newly formed company begin to explore the performance opportunities along these well-travelled circuits? The first two years of their existence are indicative of the balance struck between their appearances in the London area and their travels in the provinces.

The company was formed by Tilney at Walsingham's instigation in March 1583. Their earliest recorded appearances are in East Anglia, where a cluster of entries from Kirtling, Norwich, Aldeburgh, and Ipswich show that the company was travelling by early June. The first specific date is a 3–4 June entry for 20 shillings reward in the household account book of Lord North, whose home at Kirtling, not far from Cambridge, had also welcomed the troupe of his friend Leicester in the 1570s.[13] Their next stop along the north-eastern road through East Anglia offers us an extraordinary glimpse of the flamboyant circumstances that sometimes characterized theatre in the period and drew the wrath of local authorities. In mid June 1583, the royal players visited Norwich and were paid the generous reward of 40 shillings for their performance before the mayor.[14] It is frequently only this type of official payment in town account books which allows us to track the progress of a professional troupe on the road in England during the period before newspapers and journals became common. However, a County Quarter Sessions Minute Book and a set of depositions taken on 15 and 17 June 1583 for eventual presentation before the King's Bench have a further story to tell.

We are probably safe in assuming that visiting troupes in this period would have performed more than once and in several locations within a city of the size and population of Norwich. To interpret the mayor's officially set reward as the only profit taken at such a performance stop is to be naïvely conservative.[15] There is evidence to suggest that even the official reward may have been augmented at that performance by additional donations taken from those invited to attend.[16] Records seldom survive from other venues such as inns or churches to add to our understanding of how much profit could be made by actors determined to make their travels lucrative, but we know it had been the rule in Gloucester from 1580 to allow any royal troupe three performances in the city, while other companies were allowed two or less.[17] For the 1583 Norwich visit, we have an additional summary account from Norwich cathedral as witness that the dean and chapter may have viewed a performance by the Queen's Men, but whether it was in company with the mayor or on a separate occasion cannot be traced.[18] Clearly the Queen's Men went on to play at the Red Lion Inn in Norwich, where an affray broke out that led to dire consequences.

The importance of getting a good gate lies at the heart of the story. Presumably after their performance for the mayor, the queen's new company played on the afternoon of 15 June in the yard of the Red Lion Inn. A recalcitrant customer at the entrance refused payment and roused the attention of first Tarlton and then Singer and Bentley from the stage. Their stage exit, rapiers in hand, to pursue the customer and the ensuing struggle resulted, alarmingly one would expect, in the death of an innocent bystander. Here the tour ground temporarily to a halt. Two days later twelve witnesses were called before the Quarter Sessions court and on the evidence Singer and Bentley were committed to gaol until they had found sufficient security for their good behaviour. They were not alone in their crime, as a local man named Henry Browne had joined in the affray and struck one of the first blows against the victim. When Browne was called to witness, he recollected Singer's confident words of assurance over the corpse: 'be of good Chere for yf all this matter bee layed on the thowe shalt haue what ffrendshipe we can procure thee'.[19] He may have thought this aside cold comfort when he found himself in gaol alone in July.

The principal culprits behaved well enough in the early stages of the case. On 19 June both Singer and Bentley provided guarantees for the required bail money of £40 apiece, with a further £40 each from two local residents, for appearance at the next sessions. Oddly, perhaps, new bonds were set for the players at half the former amount, while the hapless Browne's was left at the same level of £80. Between 19 June and 1 July, their next court date, we do not know for certain where Singer, Bentley and the rest of their troupe were, although they cannot have strayed far from Norwich. On 1 July, Browne went to gaol until the next Quarter Sessions court, but Bentley and Singer gave new bonds at the lower rate, with a significant change of guarantors. The four local men who had acted on their behalf dropped out, leaving the actors, who were London residents, to act as each other's guarantors, with the helpful addition of Tarlton. At this point we must assume that the players were free to resume their tour until their next required appearance in the Norwich court in September. But when 23 September came, Bentley and Singer were not to be found in Norwich, although Browne appeared and was discharged for felony and homicide by benefit of clergy, good fortune at last coming his way.[20] The Norwich authorities apparently did not pursue the players for the amounts of the forfeited bonds. That the bonds were reduced to half the original amounts and that Tarlton replaced the local guarantors suggest that they may have been unwilling to press a case against the queen's players. Did they suffer further consequences for a crime which should have been taken seriously? Though the Queen's Men continued to visit Norwich once a year on average (their next entry in the official city records is in mid 1586, but the cathedral records refer to them in 1584 and 1585), there is no further trace of the actors' names in the Quarter Sessions records for the period, despite their legal requirement to appear to answer the original charges, as well as those for non-appearance. We have not been able to find further evidence of prosecution of the charges in London courts either, although the depositions taken at the time of the affray in June 1583 were brought before the King's Bench in Trinity term 1585, two years later. It seems that the outcome of the case may not be retrievable but we may well ask whether influence was indeed brought to bear on their behalf.[21]

Another stop on the same East Anglian tour was the coastal town of Aldeburgh, just off a principal route from London to Norwich.[22] This was a well-established and lucrative circuit through flat terrain and prosperous towns with a rich tradition of sponsoring amateur and professional drama stretching back into the Middle Ages. At Aldeburgh the troupe received 20 shillings from the mayor, and it is likely that their payment of 40 shillings from the Ipswich civic purse in the 1582–3 accounting year occurred at around the same time.[23] Their East Anglian circuit in the first year of their existence had therefore grossed at least 120 shillings or £6 in official rewards, not including other unrecorded stops on the route and income from performances not hosted by the mayor of each town.

Proximity to London was not at the top of the Queen's Men's agenda for most of their first year, however. Queen's Men can next be found in the west country, with a Bristol record dated 24 July and a Bath record of *c*. June or July. Very possibly the company that had been in Norwich crossed the country to the south-west via Abingdon in the Thames Valley and Gloucester near the mouth of the Severn. But later in the summer there are signs that the company had divided into two branches (see below), and the division may have occurred earlier, perhaps even from the beginning of the tour. What is certain is that the south-west was being visited by Queen's Men before the end of July. Whether these were the players who had been in Norwich or a second branch of their troupe is not certain. Then follows a cluster of entries datable in late August and early September at the south-eastern coastal towns of Dover, Lydd and Rye, as well as inland at Faversham and the cathedral town of Canterbury.

(Their route from Bristol to Lydd may have run through Salisbury Plain to Southampton and the south-east coast, although a visit is not recorded at Southampton during this year; unfortunately mayors' bills were no longer entered after 1582 in the town ledger extant, so we have no record of the identities of visiting troupes after that date in Salisbury.) A single company could have made this entire sweep through the country, but the probability that two branches were involved arises unmistakably at the end of the summer. For there are Queen's Men in Nottingham by 2 September, surely the same company also recorded in Leicester in the late summer, and these cannot have been the same Queen's Men who were playing the south-east towns at about the same time.

It has always been known that the Queen's Men divided in their later career, after 1587, but we are now looking at the virtual certainty that they divided during their first summer's tour. The usual interpretation of this practice has been to take it as evidence of a failing company, but we must read the evidence differently. If the Queen's Men were formed to reach far and wide into the kingdom, the best way was for the company to divide and send branches in different directions. The political intentions behind the formation of the company reviewed in the previous chapter fit with the early signs of a divided company in the provinces and lead us to conclude that division was not a sign of despair, but a sign of purpose. The largest company ever formed in the professional theatre had the resources to divide and it may have occurred to some minds that income would approximately double as well.

That income would have been high in any event. The known rewards from the Thames Valley–West Country circuit of 1583 are worth pausing over. Abingdon, for example, was a relatively small town which seems to have been a less popular stop on the professional tour routes. Rewards even to prominent troupes such as Worcester's or Derby's Men in this period were more typically in the 5 or 6 shilling range, but the Queen's Men were given 20 shillings, with a further 16 shillings' worth of wine at the mayor's command.[24] Gloucester was a more popular stop for players and had given out as much as 20 shillings to troupes with prominent patrons in the previous decade but the Queen's company was the first to receive 30 shillings.[25] Moreover, as we mentioned above, Gloucester allowed the Queen's Men three performances in all, rather than the customary one or two for other troupes, so the town was a lucrative stop.

A similar economic imperative underlies the payment at Bristol. Here the reward to the royal players was double or triple the amount usually given to visiting troupes. In the same year that the Queen's Men received £2, Oxford's players were given 20 shillings, while Hunsdon's and Morley's combined company was paid 13 shillings 4 pence.[26] This first year's recognition of the importance of the Queen's Men establishes the striking preferential treatment observable for years to come. Bath also fell into line with its higher payment of 20 shillings 7½ pence to the royal players while others received between 5 and 10 shillings.[27]

The south-east coast circuit was as profitable as the others for the Queen's Men. They collected official payments of 20 shillings at Faversham, Lydd and Rye, while Canterbury and Dover each rewarded them with the handsome sum of 40 shillings.[28] The higher value accorded the royal players is typically illustrated by the comparative figures in performance accounts at Dover: in the same year, Stafford's Men received 3 shillings 4 pence and, in the next, Berkeley's got 5 shillings while the more prominent troupe patronized by the Earl of Oxford gained 20 shillings. Only the Queen's Men were deemed worthy of twice that amount.[29]

Payments in the Midlands were similarly high. At Nottingham we know the Queen's Men received 20 shillings and at least 38 shillings 4 pence at Leicester.[30] Leicester is another excellent example of dramatically contrasting rewards: the players of the local patron, Sir George Hastings, received only 10 shillings while the Earl of Derby's were given 15 shillings above what was gathered. The 38 shillings 4 pence for the Queen's Men paid in addition to what was 'gathered at the door' was therefore exceptional.

Which road they took across the Midlands is not apparent from surviving records, but there is a clue that their return to London was via the west. Hilly terrain along the Welsh border seems to have made the western marches a less popular circuit for the major companies during this period, although borough accounts from the area other than Shrewsbury's are at best spotty and erratic. An undated bailiffs' payment of 40 shillings 6 pence to the Queen's Men at Shrewsbury during the year running from Michaelmas 1582 to Michaelmas 1583 is more likely to have been in connection with their Midlands tour than with the earlier summer circuit in the south-west.[31] This would place some members of the royal troupe in the West Midlands in September 1583 while others in the company toured in Kent. By subdividing in this way, the Queen's Men managed to tour half the kingdom during their first summer, a custom they were to continue into the next decade.

All of the Queen's Men seem to have reached London by November 1583, with the evident intention of preparing for their first Christmas season at court. The Midlands branch of the troupe seems to have returned to London by way of Marlborough, as a payment of 7 shillings to the troupe at that town occurred sometime during its accounting year running 15 November 1583 to 15 November 1584.[32] If the Marlborough appearance can be dated in 1583, they would have reached London sometime after 15 November. One or both branches may have acted at the suburban playhouses upon their return, but this is an assumption. What seems clear from the evidence is that both branches were in the city and were looking for central playing spaces by 26 November, when the privy council asked the Lord Mayor to license them. The permission was given for the Queen's Men to play at the Bull in Bishopsgate Street and the Bell in Gracious Street on holidays, Wednesdays, and Saturdays – but not on the Sabbath – between late November and Shrovetide. As Gurr notes, some of the open days each week may have been used for playing in the suburban theatres again.[33] Soon the city was reinterpreting the terms of the licence, permitting the holidays and preventing the other days, and Walsingham intervened in December to restore the original terms. We take the two-inn arrangement to indicate that the company was keeping open its option of playing in division, although we also think that they would have united for their three court performances – two in December and a third on Shrove Tuesday in March.

The first tour by the Queen's Men had lasted for some four or five months, with no sign of London performances during that time, and with many signs that the company whether subdivided or as a whole was making more money than touring companies had ever done before. The enhanced fees they received at every stop had almost certainly been profitable. The winter strategy was to play near London and move in toward the centre as the weather worsened, with major performances at court to be ready by Christmastide. The most important point may be that they had no fixed home and no evident interest in attaining one. Even in London they used more than one playing space and apparently maintained their division to some extent. Oscar Brownstein's remark that even in London they were on tour seems perceptive on this point: they were following 'the pattern of the provincial tour within the limited geographical scope of London, its liberties, and suburbs'.[34] Moving in from the outlying playhouses, occupying two inns only a few streets apart, and then moving to court for command performances – all this would have been normal for the company that had spent the bulk of its career to date on the road. In spending most of their first year on tour apart from their patron they were, in fact, following a familiar precedent, and following it vigorously.[35]

Their three performances at court earned a reward of £20 in all. They appear to have stayed in London into the spring: the third performance at court was in March, and the court payments were made on 9 May. They were still in London when riots broke out in June and they were summoned by the City Recorder, William Fleetwood, who had secured a letter from the privy council to close all the playhouses.[36] One would like to know more about the company's relations with James Burbage at this point. The Queen's Men, all co-operation according to Fleetwood, recommended to the authorities that they seek out Burbage and place him under bond while the order against the playhouses was carried out. At least three of the Queen's Men had been

Burbage's fellows in Leicester's Men, and the new company might well have acted at the Theatre from time to time. Perhaps they were counting on Burbage and his overbearing ways to have some effect in their behalf (or perhaps they were willing to see Burbage discomfited and his playhouse threatened). Burbage did try his overbearing ways. He 'stowtted me owt very hastie', according to Fleetwood, and claimed privilege in the Vice-Chamberlain's office as 'Lord Hunsdon's man'.[37] But this act of defiance lost its effect against the signatures of both the Chamberlain and the Vice-Chamberlain on the letter authorizing the destruction of the playhouses. Exactly what was going on is anyone's guess.[38] In the event, the playhouses were not destroyed, but the week had been filled with disturbances associated with the playhouses, and soon the Queen's Men were on the road again, undertaking their second summer tour.

By early July they were again playing the East Anglian circuit and this year there are two more towns which document that tour. Not far from Cambridge lay the attractive market town of Saffron Walden, close to one of the main roads running from London to Norwich. This was to become one of their most frequent stops, presumably reflecting a lucrative route, not adequately represented by the small size of Walden's first official reward of 6 shillings and 2 pence to the players in 1584.[39] At Cambridge itself they had a mixed welcome: the town treasurers note a civic reward of 20 shillings to the company on 9 July, but the university, notoriously hostile to players other than its own, paid them handsomely to go away. Safe in his chamber, the keeper of the university audit book was free to express himself vehemently: '. . . gyven vnto the *Queens* players forbiddinge theim to playe in the towne/ & so to ridd theim cleane away L s'.[40] The university of Cambridge was virtually unique in turning away the royal troupe and we know that they did play elsewhere in the town during this visit.

Beyond Cambridge lay the road east to the familiar stops at Kirtling and Norwich. From here the evidence suggests that one branch of the troupe went north through the Lincolnshire wolds to York, where the Queen's Men are on record in early August 1584.[41] This was a significant early venture into Yorkshire in the north-east, where recusancy remained a challenge to Protestant authorities of church and state for decades to come. It was also profitable. Not only did they receive £3 6 shillings and 8 pence from the mayor (easily triple the usual payment at York), but they also netted 40 shillings from the minster.[42] Early autumn was spent in the Midlands, covering a different route south to London through Leicester, with a stop at the first private household traced for the itinerary of the Queen's Men. At Wollaton Hall, the residence of Sir Francis Willoughby, a powerful local landowner and patron of the arts, a minor payment to a boy travelling with the players gives us evidence that the royal troupe must have played at a family occasion around 10 October.[43]

Meanwhile, once again conflicting dates appear to confirm that another branch of the company spent much of the summer and early autumn in the south. They were paid 20 shillings in a specifically dated account in mid September at Rye, along the Sussex coast. The tour of the south-east coast probably encompassed Southampton, Lydd, Hythe, Folkestone and Dover during the same period.[44] The company must have reunited in London, where in November they were once again seeking to move from the playhouses outside the city to more convenient quarters, presumably within the walls.[45] 'The season of the yere beynge past to playe att anye of the houses without the Citye of London', and the time of the queen's recreations drawing near, they wished to 'excercise within the Cittye' and to gain 'some order to the Justices of Middlesex' to ease the way back to the suburban theatres. As before, having theatres available to them in various neighbourhoods appears to have been one of their goals.

The city objected strenuously, claiming the Queen's Men had abused their licence the previous year. They had divided themselves and played in all the acting places. They violated the spirit of the prohibition against playing in time of divine service by admitting spectators during evening prayer and beginning the play directly thereafter. They were anathema to godliness. 'How uncomely it is for youth to runne streight from prayer to playes, from Gods seruice to the Deuells.'[46] It is the most energetic of the corporation's complaints against the theatres, and the ingenuity of the argument runs high. Playing when plague deaths are low is dangerous, for example, because the growing number of *survivors* is a menace in itself – they go to plays carrying the disease in their sores, on their clothes. But the corporation must have known the case was hopeless. Their reply ends with stipulations that if the Queen's Men must play in public, they be permitted only when deaths in London number under fifty a week for three weeks running. There must be no playing on the Sabbath and no one may be received into the auditory during times of evening prayer. Plays are to end in time for the audience to be home before dark. Only the Queen's Men are permitted to play, they must not divide themselves, and their lordships on the council are requested to provide a list of the players' names.

Their lordships' reply is not extant, but we have no reason to doubt that the company's petition was successful, and they were ready to entertain the powerful during the Christmas season. Four of their plays were given at court, and they received a total of £40. The titles sound humanist and learned. A 'pastorall of phillyda and Choryn' was given on 26 December, according to the Revels Accounts, and the 'history of felix and philiomena' on 3 January (this would seem to be a 'Felix and Philismena' plot from Montemayor). Between these performances, they appeared before Dudley at Leicester House on 28 December. An 'invention' called 'Five Plays in One' was given at court on 3 January, and another, 'Three Plays in One', would have been played on Shrove Sunday but her Majesty 'came not abroad that night'. Finally, on 23 February they performed an 'antick' play and a comedy. Nothing of the company's repertory from these early years of 1583–5 appears to have survived. (F. G. Fleay's guess that the 'Three Plays in One' and 'Five Plays in One' combined to form Tarlton's play of the 'Seven Deadly Sins' was allowed to pass by Chambers and Greg, but it is not secure.)[47]

The first two years of existence thus established a consistent performance pattern. In the good weather of the summer months and through the early autumn, the Queen's Men were on tour, sometimes perhaps together but more often subdivided in order to cover most regions of the kingdom, earning higher rewards than had ever been paid for travelling players. There is no evidence that they travelled with their royal patron when she was on summer progress; rather, they pursued an independent course, travelling to every region except the further reaches of the south-west and the Scottish borders and north-west.[48] Sometime in October or November, they came to London and brought their tour in toward the centre of patronage. Beginning in the outlying playhouses, they sought permission to move to the city inns sometime in November, and from the city inns they were ready to play at the most prestigious sites – at places like Leicester House, before the earl who had once patronized some of them, or at court, before the queen who now patronized them all.

London career and the Marprelate controversy

This pattern, of touring widely in the good weather and playing various locations in London in the winter, formed the basis of the company's career during their first decade. The extent of their touring from 1583 to 1593 can be seen in Map 3. After ten years they were the best known and the best rewarded acting company the country had ever seen, but in London their situation was giving way. By 1592 they were no longer the favoured company on the court calendar. In May 1594, Philip Henslowe recorded a loan to his nephew Francis of £15 'to laye downe for his share to the Quenes players when they brocke & went into the contrey to playe'.[49] Their final court performance – ever – came on 6 January 1594, and they played a short season at the Rose, in conjunction with Sussex's Men, in April 1594. A major reorganization of the acting companies was occurring in 1594, and the result was that two other companies were established as the most powerful in the city: one under the patronage of Henry Carey, the Lord Chamberlain, and the other under the patronage of Carey's son-in-law Charles Howard, the Lord Admiral. Andrew Gurr regards the reorganization as an extension of the policy which set up the Queen's Men

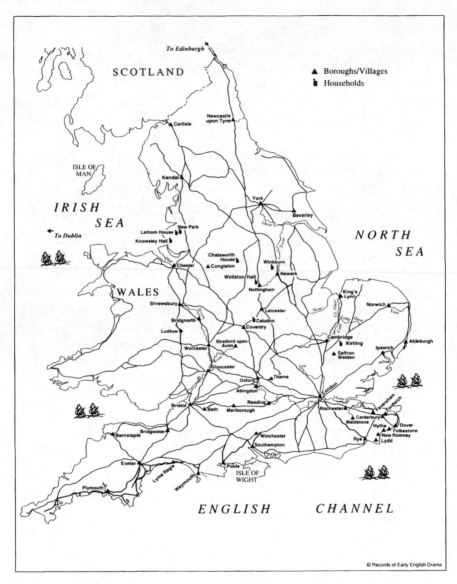

Map 3   Queen's Men tour stops 1583–93

as the favoured troupe in 1583, only now the Queen's Men were out of the picture and their virtual London monopoly had become a duopoly for the Chamberlain's Men and the Admiral's Men.[50] Henceforth the purpose-built playhouses would be central to the successful companies. The Theatre to the north was now known to be the venue for the Chamberlain's Men; for the Admiral's Men it was the Rose to the south. The peripatetic movement of the

Queen's Men was giving way to fixtures near the city, and after 1594 there is no doubt that London was the dominant centre of the commercial theatre.

It is possible that the Queen's Men tried to establish themselves at the Swan when it was built as the second Bankside playhouse in about 1595. William Ingram has found that Francis Henslowe, who borrowed money for a share in the Queen's Men in 1594, took up quarters in the summer or fall of 1595 in the tenements which Francis Langley constructed near the Swan. Francis Henslowe's loan was witnessed by William Smith and Robert Nichols, who can otherwise be linked to the Queen's Men.[51] Langley must have had some company in mind when he ventured to build the Swan, and the Queen's Men were still the best-known organization after the Chamberlain's and the Admiral's. A connection between the Queen's Men and the Swan is plausible, but there is no proof. At any rate, even if the company did play at the Swan, their mandate and their experience lay in being a road company, and to the road they certainly returned. During the rest of the 1590s, they continued to tour more often than the other major companies, but we have no further record of their playing in London.

That makes it all too easy to treat the Queen's Men lightly and to assume that serious history can be limited to the ascendant companies. Some theatre historians even assume the Queen's Men 'broke up' in 1594,[52] although they are on record for over a hundred performances in the provinces after that date. The London decline of this company is part of what makes the early 1590s a watershed in English drama, but the decline has often been misdescribed. In our belief that serious history should attend as well to the process by which obsolescence occurs as to the innovations which emerge from that process, we would like to convey an accurate impression of the decline of the Queen's Men. But other kinds of narratives must be unravelled along the way – particularly the one set forth in Greg's influential *Two Elizabethan Stage Abridgements*.[53]

Greg turned the change in the company's London fortunes into a tale of disaster and rascality. He claimed that the Queen's Men, 'in very low water' from 1591 on, and in an 'embarrassed state', sold one of their plays twice, having vamped up a 'corrupt' version in the meantime. The play was Greene's *Orlando Furioso* and there is no evidence that the Queen's Men sold it even once. But Greg was using the myth of the desperate actors to prove that the published *Orlando* of 1594 was another 'memorial reconstruction' to add to the 'bad' quartos then accumulating around the name of Shakespeare. He invented a story that the Queen's Men not only sold *Orlando* to the Admiral's Men, but also then reconstructed an inaccurate version from their bad memories and staged the sorry result to uncomprehending audiences in the country.

What is the basis for all this? The evidence in the case says that the *playwright*, Robert Greene, sold *Orlando* twice, first to the Queen's and then to the

The two London companies were an addition, not a conflation or rivalry.

Admiral's. So Greg's narrative blames the Queen's Men for what Greene did, according to the evidence. It turns the victims of fraud into its perpetrators, in order to invent a new 'memorial reconstruction' and advance the 'bad quarto' theory in Shakespearean textual studies. The Queen's Men thus became the playthings of the Shakespeare narrative. They are starving and unscrupulous, 'forced to part one by one with the hired men who had accompanied them into the country', unable to remember their lines, looking for opportunities to cheat their way to survival.

This must be resisted. The Queen's Men were not impoverished or crooked. The provincial records now being gathered in the REED volumes show that they continued to tour widely, successfully and (one must assume, from the relatively high rewards they continued to receive) profitably. Greg (p. 356) said that they suffered from 'the competition' when all the companies were touring in 1592–3. On the contrary, they continued to out-earn their competition in the provinces, as they always had. Their practice of dividing into separate companies can more easily be read as a shrewd – and early established – method of increasing earnings than as the token of despair Greg saw in it. As for their crookedness, this is a matter of pointless surmise all around.

Let us try to set the elements in balance. That the company failed in London in the 1590s seems undeniable. But Henslowe did not say that they 'went broke' when Francis Henslowe bought his share. He said they 'broke', by which he could have referred to a number of things, including the division of the company into touring branches. We think that they had lost out in the London commercial theatre and that Henslowe would have been among the first to know of their disadvantage. We also think that they had a good career going in the country and that Henslowe, not known for investing in sinking ships, was putting his money into a promising venture when he backed his nephew. When they were acting at the Rose in 1594, they were playing *King Leir* and *Friar Bacon and Friar Bungay*, both influential plays, and there is no reason to suppose they were playing them badly or in 'corrupt' versions. The company had declined in the London theatre, but it must be understood that London is only part of the story.

Tarlton's death in September 1588 was certainly their most serious loss, but there is a tendency to suppose that the company more or less collapsed as a result. In fact, death had affected the Queen's Men almost from the beginning: John Bentley and Tobias Mills were both buried in 1585 and the actor who probably replaced Bentley in tragic and heroic parts, William Knell, was killed at Thame in a fight with his fellow actor John Towne on 13 June 1587.[54] Tarlton's death was the worst blow but it came at the end of a series of losses which would have sunk a small company or a company which depended on only one

Could it be that only the names changed?

star. The Queen's Men did not founder in 1588. They continued to receive the highest rewards throughout the country, travel more widely than the other companies, and maintain an important role in the London and court theatres into the earlier 1590s.

If the notion of a collapse upon the death of Tarlton can be laid aside, the company's diminishing role in London can be seen in balance with their continuing success in the provinces. The Queen's Men without Tarlton appeared at court more often than did the companies headed by Edward Alleyn – Strange's Men and the Admiral's Men – down to 1591–2, but the Alleyn companies were narrowing the gap. Then in 1591–2 there was a drastic shift, with the Alleyn company (Strange's Men) playing six times at court to only once for the Queen's. By that time, commentators on London culture could see the Queen's Men as figures of the past. In 1592 Thomas Nashe named the four English actors whose fame he would immortalize throughout the continent (in *Pierce Penilesse*). Three of them had been Queen's Men – Tarlton, Bentley, and Knell – but all three had died within the first six years of the company's career. The fourth was Edward Alleyn, young and very influential, the new star of the London theatre – a different kind of actor in a different kind of play.

Another setback to their London career must have been the Marprelate controversy of 1588–90, in which their role is obscure but clear enough to show us that they ran into trouble. The usual view is that their difficulty was political, and this is certainly so. It can also be seen, however, that the Martin row was a stylistic battle, and in this regard the part played by the Queen's Men is ironic. For the style at issue was their own, and Martin was giving it back to them in hardened and gross terms, as though the former mode of theatrical pleasure was now sufficiently shopworn as to be exaggerated into a virtual parody of itself.

The first Marprelate tract appeared in October 1588, just weeks after Tarlton's death. Here was one of the very things the Queen's Men were formed to allay – vehement Protestant attack. Now, after a relatively quiet period since 1583, fresh outbursts from the reformers erupted. But this time the reformers were different in name, intention, and method – and their method, in a fine irony which may not have been appreciated on the privy council, was an outsized version of the kind of comic routine for which the Queen's Men were known. Martin Marprelate spoke uproariously, and the source of the uproar was the spontaneous jest, the impious lampoon, the improvised satire – it was Tarlton and one phase of the theatre of the Queen's Men turned into vitriolic and irrepressible prose. The earlier reformers had despised the theatre. Martin outdid them by using it. As his opponents knew, the most popular actors of the day were being taken as a model.

> These tinkers termes, and barbers jestes,
> first Tarleton on the stage,
> Then Martin in his bookes of lies,
> hath put in every page,

was how one of Martin's opponents put it, and another urged 'let old Lanham lash him with his rhymes'.[55]

The Queen's Men were in a difficult position. Old Lanham and his fellows were indeed pressed into service by the government in its anti-Martin campaign. But Martin had already mastered their style and extended it into the excesses of bad taste. The Queen's Men were not experts in bullying an opponent. What little we know of Tarlton's jigs, and what more we know of Wilson's plays, combine into an impression that corruption in high places was a favourite target and that the church was not exempt from laughter induced from the common man's point of view. Tarlton was said (by Martin) to have discovered Simony in Don John of London's cellar, and Simony is one of the four rogues in Wilson's plays on the Lords and Ladies of London. But Wilson's Simony is generalized, a walking offence in any church, while Martin's method was to zero in on the Church of England, name her bishops, and call them fools, sometimes with a persuasive text from the bishop himself at hand. The actors had to find an extra burst of satire to answer him, and they came up with something more like scurrility instead. As was reported in the *Return of Pasquill of England* in October:

> Vetus Comoedia beganne to pricke him at London in the right vaine, when shee brought foorth Divinitie wyth a scratcht face, holding her hart as if she were sicke, because Martin wold have forced her, but myssing of his purpose, he left the print of his nayles uppon her cheekes, and poysoned her with a vomit which he administred unto her, to make her cast uppe her dignities and promotions.[56]

Companies other than the Queen's Men may have been involved in this effort – the boy actors seem also to have been answering Martin, and the government warned the Admiral's Men and Strange's Men to desist from the fray – but there should be no doubt that the stage efforts at driving Martin into silence were headed by the Queen's Men and that they were serving the political interests of their patroness more directly than they had before. It is the Queen's Men who are cited for staging Martin in *Martin's Month's Mind*, and the style which we will describe as the 'literalism of the theatre' in our chapter on the company's dramaturgy (see pp. 121–54 below) seems pressed and harried beyond effectiveness in the descriptions given in the tracts: an actor emerges from a sack as an ape, who 'delights with moppes and mowes, with jesting and scoffing, with flouting and kicking' (*A Whip for an Ape*); on the stages of the

Theatre and the Curtain, Martin is 'drie beaten, and therby his bones broken, then whipt that made him winse, then wormd and launced, that he tooke verie grievouslie, to be made a Maygame upon the stage' (*Martin's Month's Mind*).[57]

Tilney's role in this sorry business is obscure. He certainly declared himself offended at some point, and Richard Dutton may be right to think he and the privy council were bothered because these satiric performances were staged without his authority.[58] It may also be that Tilney's authority launched the satiric effort from the beginning, then found itself offended when the gross results became apparent. This may be one reason why the Queen's Men began to share the court calendar with other companies in the seasons of 1588–9 and 1589–90, and why they lost the court advantage drastically in 1591–2.

Chambers held that the Queen's Men were sent into the provinces as a kind of punishment, the government having been forced to disavow its own instruments in the Marprelate fracas. This seems a plausible reading of the London events, but it misses the point of touring for the Queen's Men, for whom the provinces were not a kind of purgatory but the largest part of their territory. That they travelled further than ever before in 1589 shows that they could serve the crown's general cultural/political purpose during the same year as they struggled against Martin at home. This was the year they travelled to Ireland and Scotland – the latter trip being intended to grace a royal wedding which finally had to be postponed. Their travels were ranging further than ever. It is true that in these years they were sometimes travelling with rope-dancers, acrobats, and children's companies, but anyone who has seen good rope-dancers, acrobats, and children's companies will draw back from thinking this a disaster. Dividing into separate troupes, which they certainly did during these years, has been taken to mean that they were ragged and hopeless wayfarers, but we have shown that division was practised in their palmy days and was a sensible way of increasing income and spreading the influence of the queen. The career of the Queen's Men for theatre historians does not end with the death of Tarlton, in other words, but continues in areas where historians are only now gaining a perspective. We must think of the provinces and the business of professional touring: which routes the company favoured, what sorts of spaces they performed in, how much they earned – questions which have not often been addressed in our London-centred annals of the Elizabethan theatre.

Two decades in the provinces

The easiest circuits for a Renaissance troupe using London or the court as its base were those leading through the comfortably situated and prosperous towns of East Anglia or the south-east coast. Logically enough, these two have proved to be the most popular and lucrative of the routes travelled by the Queen's Men during their first decade as they had been earlier for Leicester's company. Their tour of the south-east earned them the most, almost £81 in official rewards alone, over seven summer seasons, two of which extended into the fall (1586, 1587) and another which kicked off in the spring (1589).[59] In the years when the royal troupe was elsewhere in the summer, they visited the south-east in either spring (1588, 1592) and/or fall (1592, 1593). They were encouraged to make appearances during the more difficult winter months of December and January as well in 1588–91, years when they were also performing at court during Christmas and Shrovetide.

The south-east could offer a readily mounted short tour encompassing ten significant towns only a short distance apart. Yet we may get the measure of their mandate when we recognize that, together or subdivided, the Queen's Men took the longer tour to the south-west almost as often. Map 3 (see p. 50 above) shows the company's visits during the first half of their career, eleven years down to 1594. Nine of their first eleven seasons included the region of Devon and Somerset; in at least seven of these years, we know that they took a less frequented route through the south via Southampton and that about half the time they stopped at smaller towns such as Lyme Regis, Poole or Weymouth in Dorset, where travelling entertainers did not venture as often.[60] While summer was preferred for the south-western circuit in 1583–8, 1590 and 1592, there were separate spring and fall tours in 1589, an extended annual tour beginning in the spring in 1591, and a spring tour in 1593.

The large cities of Bristol and Exeter would have been major attractions for a troupe looking to increase its profits. Perhaps in order to maintain their appeal at such a distance from the capital, some of the prominent south-western towns set their civic rewards at a higher level than many in the east.[61] Yet it was more costly to travel the greater distance and there must have been more than pure profit luring the Queen's Men to the towns of the Dorset coast where rewards were relatively small.[62] In this context it is interesting to note too that the route south-west to Bristol through the Thames Valley is less frequently on record for the Queen's Men generally. Admittedly, the Thames Valley seems to have been one of the least favoured by play troupes, judging by civic accounts which survive for several of its key towns.[63] The central towns were small and the level of payments even for a troupe like Leicester's was comparatively low. However, the size of reward for Queen's was in a class of its own. The royal troupe routinely received at least £1 for their official performances and often more, so economic motives may not have influenced the direction of their tour to the same extent. It is possible that the roads across marshy terrain may also have been a deterring factor, yet it is equally possible, in the case of Queen's, to speculate that it was more important for them to visit towns in the south which were less familiar with royal progresses and visits to residences, such as were common in the Thames Valley. During the politically troubled decade of the 1580s, the queen did not go on progress at all, but when she resumed her summer travels in 1591 and 1592, she did not stray further than Sudeley Castle in Gloucestershire.[64] All the more important, then, for her performers to concentrate on extending the royal outreach to Dorset and Devon in the south-west and the north beyond Coventry where their patron did not go.[65]

The preferred route north lay on the east side of the Pennines through country more level than the undulating hills of the West Midlands. The tours to the north were certainly longer, but the fact that they occurred in eight out of eleven years after the formation of the Queen's Men surely demonstrates the importance of this form of royal outreach to an area notoriously resistant to intervention from the south, especially in matters of religion. The concern of Walsingham and Leicester about pro-Catholic plots before the execution of Mary Stuart in 1587 and the attack of the Armada in 1588 was matched in the early 1590s by official anxiety about recusancy in Yorkshire and the north-west. This was the era when Burghley had his map of suspected papist households in Lancashire drawn up.[66] As we have already suggested, the players may not only have been emissaries in the royal name to these far-flung regions; they may also have been useful as observers on the road and in the private household.

Despite only partial accumulation of evidence for the northern tours, we can still see their strategic importance.[67] In the north-west, where there were fewer large towns and more challenging terrain to cross, there are minimal civic accounts extant. The most influential family in the recusant county of Lancashire was the Stanleys. In the late 1580s and 1590s, they became the focus of pro-Catholic plots, because William Stanley, a cousin of the Earl of Derby, had defected to the Spaniards in 1587. As Barry Coward has noted in his study of the family, William Stanley's intrigues built up the hope of English Catholic exiles that the earl and his son, Lord Strange, would lend their support to the cause of securing a Catholic succession to the throne of England.[68] Clearly the uncertain religious sympathies of the Stanleys, as well as their territorial power, would have made them an object of particular attention for the central government. Their three residences at Knowsley, Lathom and New Park would therefore have been important stops on the northern route for any politically motivated tour.

Although we have only a meagre four years of household accounts to draw upon for the Stanleys in this period, the evidence therein corroborates their significance for the Queen's Men. Another troupe with a Protestant patron, the revitalized Leicester's Men, visited Lathom in 1587, but in 1588 the Queen's Men make the first of several trips to the Stanley homes, playing New Park in the fall of that year. One branch probably led by the Duttons went to Lathom for two nights in July 1589, presumably around the time of their trip to Ireland. In early September 1589 they were back amongst the Stanleys again, this time at Knowsley, for two nights in company with Essex's Men.[69] It was while they were at Knowsley that they received the invitation sent via the governor of Carlisle to perform at the royal wedding of James VI and Anne of Denmark.[70] Adverse winds held Anne at Oslo but we know that the players went in good faith to Edinburgh thanks to an October letter to Lord Burghley sent by the English ambassador in Scotland, commending the Earl of Bothwell for 'great kindness to our Nation, using her Maiesties players and Canoniers with all Courtesie'.[71] This 1589 tour by the Queen's Men was by far its most adventurous, as they travelled into both Scotland and Ireland in the same year. The following June, 1590, the company subdivided again, with a branch led by the Duttons once more in the north-west visiting the Earl of Derby at Knowsley. It would indeed seem that the royal troupe made the Stanley homes a regular stop in planning their itineraries despite the greater distances involved.

Household records, however partial, have proved to be the most informative sources for the north-western circuit in the late sixteenth century. They may yet prove to be so for the north-eastern itinerary as well, although major cities like York and Newcastle upon Tyne, as well as the towns of Beverley and Durham, can also help to fill out the picture of touring in that region. Even more than the cities of the south-west, the northern centres of York and Newcastle paid highly for their entertainment, giving the Queen's Men the best rewards in the provinces.[72] The frequent appearance of Leicester and Nottingham on their itinerary indicates that the preferred route north for the Queen's Men was the road leading through those towns in the Midlands and along the eastern side of the Derbyshire Peak district. From here they were within relatively easy striking distance of some important households – Belvoir, Wollaton, Winkburn, Hardwick and Chatsworth, all of which have accounts surviving to attest to their drawing appeal for travelling entertainers.[73] The extended family of the Cliffords, the Earls of Cumberland, with their residences at Skipton Castle and Londesborough not far from York, represented one of the most influential branches of the nobility. The Cavendishes at Chatsworth, the Middletons at Wollaton and the Manners at Belvoir and Winkburn were families of significant regional influence and extensive landholdings – like the Cliffords and the Stanleys, less engaged with affairs at court than with managing their own estates in the country. As such, they too may have invited the watchful eye of the more politically minded members of the privy council. We note that the Queen's Men visited Wollaton Hall in 1584, Winkburn in 1591, and Chatsworth House in 1593 as they were to continue to visit other private homes during the second decade of their career.

The popularity of the eastern road north for the Queen's Men appears understandable, given the easier terrain, a network of well-travelled roads, the proximity of important towns promising generous rewards, and an inviting cluster of private households where bed and board might be obtained. Yet their recurring appearances at the Stanley homes in Lancashire during the few years for which we have evidence, together with three visits recorded by the dean and chapter of Chester cathedral, make it apparent that they expected to tour the north-west also.[74] Did they go north on the east side of the Pennines and travel the road south through the Welsh Marches on the west? Here we are frustrated by inadequate resources upon which to base an answer. In this area there were fewer important families in permanent residence and virtually no archive treasuries to compare with Belvoir or Chatsworth. The principal towns along the route through the western hills were Shrewsbury, Ludlow, Leominster, and Hereford, with an alternative route branching off through Bridgnorth to Worcester. Apart from Shrewsbury, evidence from all these towns is patchy at best. During their first decade, we know that the Queen's Men travelled one of the roads through Shrewsbury in 1583 and 1590; only in 1590 do we know that a circuit was made through Bridgnorth and Ludlow. The Leominster–Hereford stretch of the road is otherwise undocumented, perhaps because only two years of summary accounts in this period survive, and those only for Hereford.[75] Occasionally attempts to retrace the tour are foiled and the western circuit is the most obvious gap in the record.

Like the tours in the south, those to the north occurred outside the summer season. Extended travel which began from the south through the Midlands in the summer would easily lead into a fall circuit in the north. The Queen's Men went through the Midlands in ten of their first eleven years and in four of these they were in the north-west during the autumn months. However, so far they have been found on record in the north-east only in the summer; neither winter nor spring seems to have been chosen for northern performances.[76]

Undoubtedly more demanding, these northern tours were clearly an important part of the troupe's mandate. They seem to have been less profitable than those in the southern provinces, although there were more comfortable household stops on the itinerary through the Midlands and north. While the evidence from the north-east is still incomplete and the records from the north-west and West Midlands too limited to be representative, we can presently calculate that the rewards from a number of important towns and households in the Midlands total less than those from the south-west accumulated over the first decade, while those from the north-east amount to roughly half what was earned on the Bristol circuit.[77] We would argue therefore that the maintenance of public relations, for obvious political gain, may have been the key motive for the northern tours, as financial profit could be more readily had in the south.

As the Queen's Men crossed the country along the routes outlined above, they faced practical considerations which have not figured strongly in Elizabethan theatre history. Little thought has been given to the economics of touring theatre, for instance, in part because London has always been the centre of scholarly attention, and in part because the economics of anything in Tudor England are difficult to reconstruct. The Queen's Men must have thought about the economics of touring as a daily concern, however, and the record they left behind in the provinces raises some businesslike implications which we wish to outline. Our intentions are more in the spirit of opening questions for further thought than of supplying definitive answers.

Touring companies must have looked for locations where they could perform for several days running. This is a matter of common sense – profits outweigh expenses for travelling entertainers the more often performance days outnumber travelling days. In Norwich during their first summer tour, for example, even incomplete records make it clear that the Queen's Men gave at least two performances. They played for the mayor and council sometime before 15 June when the fracas broke out during their performance at the Red Lion Inn, and they may have played on a separate occasion at some point for the dean and chapter of Norwich cathedral. A good location would probably have produced four or five performance opportunities. When the Gloucester authorities of 1580 set limits on the number of days different companies could play in their city, they limited any company sponsored by the queen to three performances within a space of three days. The number of 'great-house' visits on record for the Queen's Men reminds us that touring routes would have been chosen for the combinations of playing opportunities they provided. From one performance before the mayor to another in the great hall of a nearby manor, from there to an inn for perhaps two or three performances, or to the market-square or the church for another – such combinations of opportunities must have been sought by companies on the road.[78]

A preliminary estimate of touring costs has recently been made by William Ingram.[79] Considering details which have not made their way into theatre history before – would it have been cheaper for the players to hire post horses than buy them? how much might lodging and board have cost for the players? (and for the horses?) – Ingram estimates that travelling expenses would have run about two shillings per man per travelling day. This is an admittedly speculative figure, but it opens the way to further thinking about the business of the tour. The original Queen's Men had twelve leading actors, plus hired men and boys. On Ingram's estimate, touring costs would have run to the range of 32 to 40 shillings per day if a company of sixteen to twenty Queen's Men travelled as a unit. The relatively high official payments to the Queen's Men normally run 20 to 40 shillings, sometimes rising to 60 shillings, sometimes dropping below 20. These amounts may not have been the total income from the mayor's performances (as we know, further collections were sometimes made), but by themselves they would have averaged out to cover *per diem* costs of 32 to 40 shillings for the entire company. This is a way to break even, but it is only a way to make a living if the mayor's performance is the prelude to further performances and further collections.

Obviously, a way to increase profits would have been for the company to divide into branches.[80] Two groups of Queen's Men, each numbering about six main actors and a few hired men and boys, could aim to double the overall income of the company without entailing a similar increase in road expenses. If travelling expenses run only 16 to 20 shillings, a 40 shilling reward from the mayor's performance looks quite profitable for the first day in a town.

Ingram bases part of his survey of touring costs on the will of the actor Simon Jewell, which was brought to light by Mary Edmond in 1974. Jewell was previously unknown to us, but he now appears to have been a member of the Queen's Men in 1592, the year of his death, for his will refers to several Queen's Men as his 'fellows' and associates.[81] The will is important evidence about the business of touring in any event, but it may well speak directly about the company we are studying. There were clearly six sharers in Jewell's touring company. If these were Queen's Men, the original company of twelve was divided exactly in half for touring in 1592.

The will was proved on 23 August 1592. Among the debts or bequests linked with Jewell's fellow actors are some suggestive items – his share owing from 'horses waggen and apparrell newe boughte', more due for 'plates suger and banquetinge stuf', and gifts of 'a black veluet purse imbrodered with golde and siluer', and 'all my playenge thinges in a box and my veluet shewes'.[82] These actor's possessions may be modest in detail but their value was considerable. The stock of 'apparrell' owned by the company was worth £80 and had been increased, apparently for the tour, by another £37. In addition to Ingram's estimates of travelling costs, in other words, a capital expenditure lay behind the tour, and this would have increased the need to build up multiple performances in each location and/or to divide into branches.

If Jewell's 'playenge thinges' could be willed to another actor, Robert Nichols, in a box, we can assume that these were primarily costumes, with some small hand props, and that they represented the essential gear of the touring player. If each actor in the company brought his own box or trunk of costumes on the road, these would take up much of the space in the wagon specified as part of the troupe's expenses. Modern performances have proved that Shakespearean theatre requires no more than the actors themselves, colourful costumes, and some portable props such as crowns, swords and banqueting cups to engage an audience – there is no reason to think that more was needed by the Queen's Men on tour.

While Jewell's will gives us a glimpse of one branch of the Queen's Men in the early 1590s, the provincial records hold other clues about the way the company toured during what we would regard as their heyday. We have already reviewed the signs that there were separate branches in operation as early as 1583 (see p. 44 above). It seems that these subdivided troupes came to be known by their leaders' names in the later 1580s. One touring branch becomes identified with John Lanham and the other with John Dutton and his brother Laurence. Specified first at Nottingham in 1589, the Duttons seem to have been especially well known in the towns along the tour routes.[83] A 'Mr Dutton' is singled out at the Stanley household of Knowsley in 1590 and at Southampton in 1591, while both are paid at Lyme Regis in 1593.[84] More notoriously, the Dutton name as principal member is highlighted by Cambridge University officials seeking to discredit the Queen's Men in 1592 when they sought to play in the area during the lucrative period of Sturbridge Fair.[85] Lanham is not named in the provincial records, but he is recognized as the leader of one branch, with the Duttons leading the other, in the court payments of 1590–1. The Duttons were paid for four of the Queen's Men court performances that winter, while Lanham was paid, according to a separate warrant, for a fifth. The Lanham performance fell on 1 January, and some unusually early records of Queen's Men in the south-east between 2 January and 14 February suggest that this branch went on tour immediately after their one court date, while the Dutton branch was giving three of their court performances during January and February.[86]

Each branch entered into occasional collaborations with other acting companies. At Poole in Dorset, joint payments were made in June 1591 to the Queen's Men with the musical Children of the Chapel.[87] Very little is known about the Chapel Children during these years. They did not perform at court between 1585 and 1600 and provincial touring may have been limited to East Anglia in 1587, where they appear in the civic accounts for both Norwich and Ipswich, and this tour, perhaps sometimes in company with the Queen's Men.[88] Other payments at Fordwich, Lydd and Leicester during the summer of 1591 specify the Children of the Chapel, while complementary payments to the Queen's Men during the same period occur in accounts for neighbouring towns on the southern and Midlands circuits.[89]

In the spring of the same year, Lanham collaborated with a different troupe. While the Duttons mounted the required court performance at Greenwich at Shrovetide with some of the Queen's Men, Lanham must have been on the road through the south-west and Midlands with others, including Sussex's newly reformed troupe.[90] This partnership was to be renewed in London in 1594 when Henslowe's *Diary* notes their collaboration at the Rose during the week of 1 to 8 April.[91]

It is in this spirit of touring showmanship that one should read the other evidence that attends the Queen's Men when they divided for provincial travelling. They joined up with acrobats, rope-dancers, and musicians to put on displays of all theatrical kinds. There are numerous specific references to tumblers travelling with the Queen's Men from the summer tour of 1588 through the summer of 1590. The mere fact that they are mentioned suggests their particular appeal, intriguing even to the usually stolid civic accountants. The Nottingham records in the fall of 1588 identify their leader during that first season as the tumbler John Symons, who had previously made his reputation under Strange's and then Oxford's patronage at court.[92] The July 1590 stop at Shrewsbury inspired an eyewitness account of the excitement of an acrobatic act added to the regular programme during that spring and summer tour: '. . . he shewyd woonderfull feates and knackes in fallinge his head and handes downewardes and hangid at the roape by his feete and assendid vp agayne and after that hangid by his handes and all his feete and bodye downewardes and turnid hys body backward & forward betwyxt his handes & the rope as nymbell as yf it had been an eele in sutche woonderfull maner that the licke was neuer seene of the inhabitantes there before that tyme'.[93] More circumspect accounting references to the 'Turk on the rope' or the 'hongarian' at other locations show that he travelled with the Queen's Men on a continuous tour through the country during 1590.

Music is customarily assumed to have been part of stage performances during the Elizabethan period. Although the actors themselves may have played instruments as needed, there are a few special payments to musicians performing with the Queen's Men at Nottingham in August 1587 and at Canterbury in 1592. At Nottingham they are specifically designated as royal musicians but whether they were also on tour or hired locally at Canterbury is unclear. At Worcester, sometime during the 1591–2 season, trumpeters, otherwise unremarked, are rewarded with the actors.[94]

The first decade draws to a close with one of the most serious outbreaks of plague on record for London, affecting not only the schedule of the Queen's Men, but also the activities of all the professionals accustomed to performing in the London area. Plays were restrained by a privy council order on 28 January 1593 for almost a year and there is no evidence that the royal troupe performed in the area until their week at the Rose with Sussex's Men in the spring of 1594.[95] Nor did they appear at court during the Christmas or Shrovetide seasons; a letter from the Cambridge vice-chancellor and heads to Lord Burghley in early December 1592 makes the reason why and the proposed alternative apparent: '. . . by reason that her Maiesties owne servant*es*, in this time of infection, may not disport her Highnes w*i*th theire wonted and ordinary pastimes: his Ho*nor* hath moued our Vniu*er*sity (as he writeth that he hath also done the other of Oxford) to prepare A Comedie in Englishe, to be acted before her Highnes, by some of our Student*es* in this time of Christmas . . .'[96] In fact, neither university rose to the challenge, leaving Strange's and Pembroke's Men to fill the bill at court. Most of this year featured the Queen's Men touring energetically, one branch going to the south-west while another moved north-east through the Midlands.

If the spring of 1594 marks the end of the career of the Queen's Men in London as we know it, there was less immediate change in their performance schedule in the provinces, so far as we can detect. Their travels from 1594 to 1603 (shown on Map 4) are marked by some regional adjustments but, in the main, Queen's Men continued to tour the country to loyal audiences along all the circuits described above.

East Anglia and the south-east continue to be favoured for seven of the ten years in the second decade, in spring, summer or fall; these remained lucrative routes, but still less so than the south-west, which was also visited in seven of the ten years.[97] The southern coast circuit appears to have been linked with the tour of the south-west at least four times during this decade, with an independent visit to Winchester in 1600.[98] An increase along the north-east route came in the good weather of summer: Queen's Men travelled as far as York six times, with the generous level of reward at that city continuing.[99] By contrast, evidence for the north-western circuit drops off during these years, along with the profits. Only once is the royal troupe known to have appeared in that region, although we are reminded that the Stanley accounts which might have extended our knowledge do not survive for this period. The Midlands remains the preferred route to the north; only in three of the ten years do stops in the north-west or West Midlands indicate that the Welsh border road was taken.[100] Some of the private households visited during the first decade disappear from the annual itinerary – the Stanley homes in Lancashire, Chatsworth in Derbyshire, Winkburn and Wollaton Hall in Nottinghamshire and Kirtling in Cambridgeshire – but we suspect this has more to do with the imperfect survival of corresponding household accounts. Caludon Castle, home of the Berkeleys near Coventry, remained on the itinerary (1594, 1601) and although we have as yet found no further notice of Winkburn as a performance location in the 1590s, the scraps of household records available in print from the otherwise inaccessible family archives show that another important Manners home, at Belvoir in Leicestershire, was a tour stop in 1602. And as more household accounts begin to pick up, we learn of additional private homes on the tour of the Queen's Men: Hardwick Hall (1596, 1600), the Derbyshire residence of

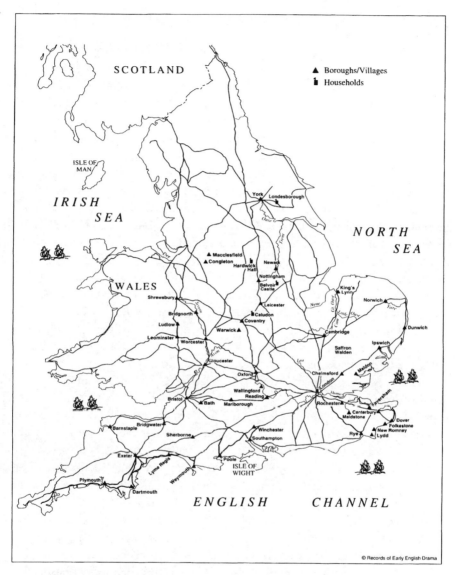

Map 4   Queen's Men tour stops 1594–1603

Elizabeth Hardwick, former wife of Sir William Cavendish, and the Cliffords at Londesborough in the north-east (1595).[101]

Signs of a divided company continue to be a possibility until 1597 (see note 80, p. 211 below, for divisions in the first decade) but for the rest of the second decade a single united company could have reached all the stops presently before us. Partnerships may have characterized the middle years of the company's existence, but after 1594 there are no indications of performances expanded by special acts or associations.

At this time it is possible to identify a total of 183 itinerary stops between 1583 and 1593; from 1594 to 1603, there are 140 stops on record, with a dropping off on the provincial circuits starting in 1598. In part the drop in tour stops in the second decade may be attributed to the loss of records at such key locations as Nottingham, Southampton and Gloucester, but in the last years it may also reflect a smaller troupe with reduced touring capacity. Were the Queen's Men reduced in number by this time or were they meeting with local resistance? In the late sixteenth century it is rare to find instances of players' dismissal by hostile town authorities – the determined rejection of the Queen's Men by the Cambridge University authorities in 1584 was a significant presage of what was to come in the opening decades of the next century, but it was no more than a presage. Apart from Cambridge, during their first decade the royal troupe is noted as paid but 'played not' in only two other instances: at Bristol in the summer of 1586 and at Norwich in May 1592, when plague in London may have caused concern to local officials, though the company maintained a vigorous and successful tour schedule elsewhere.[102] These isolated occurrences should not be interpreted as an indication of local disregard for the Queen's Men, however. They continued to visit Bristol, rewards as high as ever, and Bristol officials are never on record as debarring them in any hostile way from performance. Although a stern ordinance passed by the Bristol Common Council in February 1596 forbade the use of the Guildhall by players, nonetheless rewards to players, including the Queen's Men, continue to specify performances in the Guildhall until 1598.[103] Norwich was an even more regular and consistently lucrative stop for the Queen's Men throughout their career.

Only Cambridge University authorities are known to have actively discouraged the troupe – debarring them four times, in the summers of 1584, 1591 and 1592 and at the time of Sturbridge Fair in September 1592.[104] Under such circumstances, why include Cambridge on the tour, we may ask? A broad survey of local records shows that others were more welcoming. Even as the players were pocketing a substantial payment from the university not to play, they were lining up performances elsewhere in town: in 1584 and 1592, as well as in 1585, they appeared before the mayor and in 1592 Trinity College made a payment to one of the Queen's Men just as it had rewarded one branch of the troupe once before in 1587.[105] Anxious letters from the university's vice-chancellor to Lord Burghley and other members of the privy council reveal that the troupe also played in a private house at Chesterton, after posting notices near the college gates in flagrant disregard of official prohibitions. Both peril of plague and the luring of students from their books are cited as reasons for the university's disapproval of touring players.[106] The Queen's Men may have been effectively discouraged by their 1592 experience: they are recorded as making only one stop at Cambridge in their second decade of touring – in 1597 – when, somewhat ironically, they were welcomed by town and gown alike.[107]

What we have learned from a review of the documentary evidence, then, is that the provincial tour was the cornerstone of the troupe's existence. While others may have taken their place at court or in the London area theatres after 1594, the Queen's Men continued to pursue the performances in the provinces which had dominated their schedule from the year of their formation. Going primarily to locations north and south where their royal patron never ventured, they spread her name and garnered the highest rewards of any professional company. How typical of professional companies was their touring in the 1590s? The London-based Admiral's and Chamberlain's Men travelled comparatively little, reserving their energies for their now-established theatres and special performances at court. More active touring companies such as Pembroke's or Worcester's Men cannot compete in the distances covered or the number of locations visited. This remains true even in the last years of their provincial career, when the Queen's Men may have become a smaller troupe, still touring more widely than other companies, but no longer reaching the same number of audiences and no longer distinguished by the star acts that they once could boast. Despite the contrast between the tour in 1602, say, and the ambitious far-flung travels of 1589, it is still apparent from what we know of their annual itineraries that the Queen's Men, from the beginning of their career in 1583 to their final year, 1602–3, were quite simply, the best known and most widely travelled professional company in the kingdom.

Playing places in the provinces

There is much to be learned about the performance spaces which touring actors used in the provinces, although no evidence remains about the exact positions of stages and audiences. We may mourn the loss of the Curtain or the interrupted excavation at the site of the Rose, but we can rejoice that some of the provincial performance halls used by the Queen's Men survive, meriting attention after years of being overlooked. A total of twenty-two performance locations used by the troupe can be identified with confidence, and of these at least five remain, in original, restored or renovated form.

The touring tradition required flexibility on the part of entertainers who had to adapt their acts to both indoor and outdoor locations. If we can trust the admittedly partial evidence, we can deduce that their preference was for indoor halls where the gate could be more readily controlled and a performance mounted come wind or foul weather. Alan Somerset's recent survey of performance spaces known to have been used between 1564 and 1642 suggests that this was indeed a common preference for professional actors both in London and the provinces: 'During the seventy-five years during which converted or purpose-built theatres were used in London, it is significant that in only nineteen of these years (1567–76 and 1590–1600) were outdoor unroofed theatres the only ones available to audiences.'[108] Somerset's interim census of provincial playing spaces turned up forty-two locations, thirty-three definitely indoors, with a further seven (unidentified inns) perhaps also to be added to that category. A mere two were indisputably outdoors. Perhaps typically, then, the only unmistakably open-air productions on the Queen's Men's itinerary were the infamous inn-yard performance at the Red Lion in Norwich in 1583, another in the cathedral churchyard at Gloucester in 1590,[109] and a third at the Cornmarket in Shrewsbury (1590), where a large performance space may have been needed because of the rope-walking act so enthusiastically described by a member of the crowd and quoted above. It is possible that another stop featuring tumblers the same year at the Bristol Free School was in the courtyard rather than indoors.[110]

Much more favoured were the town or guildhalls and the private halls of the nobility or gentry which are distinguishable in the dramatic records. While we may be justified in assuming that the Queen's Men presented their official performance to the mayor and guests in the main town or guildhall of each town visited, we can only verify the following from specific references in our period sources: Canterbury's Court Hall, Norwich's 'New' Hall, York's Common Hall, and the guildhalls at Abingdon, Bristol, and Leicester.[111] Of these, the Leicester Guildhall remains remarkably intact, a small half-timbered late-medieval building originally belonging to the Corpus Christi Guild but purchased to replace an older town hall in 1563 (see Plate 1).[112] It endured as a centre for civic activities until Leicester's expansion after the industrial revolution created the need for a larger hall in the later nineteenth century. Varied tenants and subsequent neglect of the medieval hall almost led to its demolition but in 1922 the City Council agreed to restore the building, removing unsightly annexes and other additions which masked its original character.

The oldest section of the Leicester Guildhall is the great hall on the ground level of the courtyard's north range. Although the gallery and staircase at its eastern end were added during nineteenth- and twentieth-century renovations, the hall retains its original measurements, stone floor, timber-framed walls and pitched cruck frame ceiling from the era when the Queen's Men would have performed before audiences conservatively estimated at three hundred (see Plates 2 and 3).[113] There are five bays, the three at the east end being the oldest (later fourteenth century), with three windows having three lights each on the north wall and two similar windows on the south. The two fifteenth-century bays at

Plate 1   Leicester Guildhall

Plate 2   Leicester Guildhall interior: upper end

Plate 3 Leicester Guildhall interior: lower end

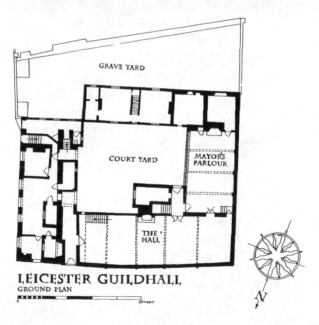

the western end have more light coming in on the north side thanks to two seven-light windows of a very different style. The hall's dimensions are 62 feet long by 20 feet wide, with the ceiling rising to 27 feet at its peak, providing a relatively small but congenial performance space with excellent sight lines that

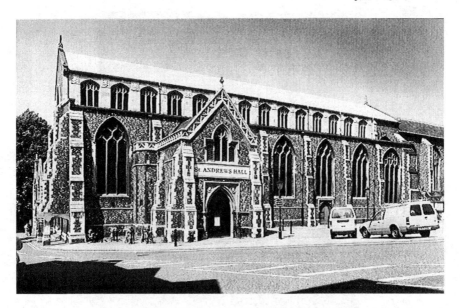

Plate 4   Norwich Common Hall

is still used for Christmas pantomimes. Both the fireplace in the south wall and the wooden dais at the western end post-date the sixteenth century, but it is likely that they represent the approximate location of earlier features of the room.[114] The original doorways are long gone, but there remains an entrance in the east end, and an early door from the courtyard is known to have existed to the east of the present double panelled door in the south wall near the dais. Two entry points for actors were therefore possible, but whether the only adjacent room, the Mayor's Parlour, would have been used as a tiring-house is subject only for speculation.

On a grander scale, befitting one of the largest urban centres in the country, Norwich's New or Common Hall had been acquired by the city in 1540 very soon after the dissolution of the monasteries.[115] The nave of the former Blackfriars' church was blocked off from the chancel and converted into an assembly hall used for a variety of purposes, including official entertainment, and remains in similar use to this day, part of the most complete medieval friary building complex in England (see Plates 4, 5 and 6). The interior is largely a fifteenth-century structure, designed as a great open preaching hall with excellent sight lines and acoustics. The nave is an impressive 126 feet in length and almost 35 feet across its centre, with a further 15½ feet of width provided in each of its north and south aisles. The arches of the seven bays spring from high and slender pillars, allowing light from the seven large windows in both aisles to illuminate the central space.[116] Fourteen three-light

Plate 5   Norwich Common Hall interior: upper end

Plate 6   Norwich Common Hall interior: lower end

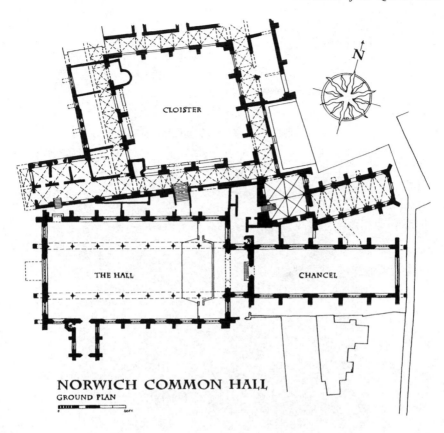

NORWICH COMMON HALL
GROUND PLAN

clerestory windows below the hammerbeam ceiling brighten the interior further. The roof of the nave rises to approximately 65 feet, with the side aisles reaching a generous 45 feet in height. One original doorway (presumably giving access to the sanctuary) survives in the second bay of the north aisle and another at the north-west corner of the nave which would have led into the former cloister. The main south door was moved by the Victorian restorers from the westernmost bay to its neighbour and a porch added.[117]

The Blackfriars' nave would have made an imposing and spacious civic hall after 1540: its walls were whitewashed, rails were made for hangings, benches built within each of the seven bays, and the crossing arch at the east end blocked up to create the new space.[118] Although it is not possible to give an accurate estimate of the maximum audience size for performances in this space, it is worth noting that a crowd of 2,066 people were accommodated here on one occasion in the nineteenth century at the city's popular music festival.[119] Since that time the addition of raked seating at the west end and the organ recess and

Plate 7   York Common Hall

modern stage at the east end have considerably altered the layout of the hall but bear witness to its continuing vitality as a civic performance location.

York's fifteenth-century Common Hall falls between those of Norwich and Leicester in scale. The hall was bombed during an air raid in 1942 but its present incarnation is not a replica, as commonly reported, but a faithful restoration reopened in 1960.[120] Although the roof was destroyed and the windows blown out, photographs taken after the bombing show that most of the sturdy limestone walls withstood the impact.[121] The hall therefore retains its original dimensions and aisled plan, with six bays lighted by three- or four-light windows (see Plates 7 and 8). The dimensions of the Common Hall are 93 feet long by 43 feet wide, the reconstructed roof rising to 31 feet 1 inch at its apex.

The ten slim octagonal oak pillars supporting the new timber roof are replacements of similar proportions to the originals, rising high to create an open

Plate 8   York Common Hall interior: lower end

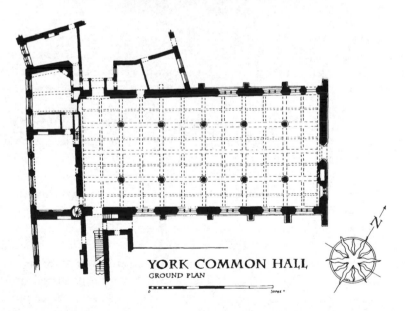

and flexible space with excellent sight lines for performance. Like many medieval halls, there was once a screens passage with an upper gallery above across the east end, a dais enclosed by a wooden screen at the west end and an open fireplace in the middle. A combination of surviving and vestigial architectural

Plate 9   Sherborne church house, Dorset

evidence shows that there were several points of entry to the Renaissance hall: the central entrance at the east end; another door at the east end of the north aisle which gave access to the screens passage, with a corresponding door on the south side; a narrow door at the west end of the south aisle and another door in the south-west corner leading to the medieval Committee Room.[122]

However various their dimensions, the Leicester, Norwich, and York guild-halls are probably representative of the most typical performance spaces available to Renaissance troupes like the Queen's Men in substantial towns and cities along their tour routes. Some cities had more options than others. At Bristol, for example, we know that the Free School was used during the visit with the rope-walker, but neither the sixteenth-century school buildings nor the more commonly used Guildhall survive.[123]

At the other end of the scale, in towns or villages where civic buildings were lacking, troupes are known to have made use of church houses. Such a space was available at Sherborne, where the royal troupe made a stop on their route through the south-west in 1597 and 1598.[124] The golden hamstone building where they performed is situated on Half Moon Street to the east of the former Sherborne Abbey church, which was taken over by the town parish shortly after the dissolution (see Plate 9).[125] Even in the Elizabethan era, the ground floor was divided into shops, rented out by the churchwardens who also rented the upper room on occasion to visiting players. After 1700, the building ceased to function as a church house and was converted into three separate tenements.[126] Today there are four tenants, whose signs and shop fronts distract from but do not obliterate the original character of the exterior.[127]

Although altered structurally over the years, the Sherborne church house retains enough of its sixteenth-century features to help us recapture the original long room on the second storey where the Queen's Men mounted their productions. Without the later addition of a ceiling to create a third storey, the roof of the upper room would have risen to a peak of approximately 18 feet 2 inches. The room's original width of 19 feet remains and its interior length has been estimated as 116 feet, not an easy measurement to recover, divided as it is by walls into several sections reflecting the various needs of the three tenants.[128] Twelve of the fourteen four-light windows (41 inches high × 12 inches wide) are intact along the south wall and a larger four-light window at the west end (68 inches × 76 inches) – the north and east sides of the hall are now encompassed by later buildings. The large fireplace in the east wall is now partly plastered over and the elaborate stone staircase which gave access to the upper room at the west end is long gone.[129] Sherborne churchwardens' inventories from the late sixteenth century indicate that there were benches by the walls, as well as forms and trestles, to provide seating for at least some spectators – as with most other performance locations in the provinces, it is not possible to determine whether or where in the room a stage was set up.[130]

The Sherborne church house was therefore a substantial hall which could readily accommodate performers and audience. Its dimensions, although less easy to recover accurately, were comparable to those of the Guildhall at Leicester, but its appeal was apparently not as great for travelling players, perhaps because of its somewhat rural setting on one of the less frequented tour routes in the south-west and the terms set for the rental of the space by its entrepreneurial churchwardens.[131]

In the category of private halls, the performance spaces could have been made available by either colleges or families. Between 1602 and *c.* 1608 Trinity College, Cambridge, rebuilt the hall where college performances had customarily been mounted since about 1546. A payment of 30 shillings by the Trinity authorities in 1587 may indicate that the Queen's Men played there, although we have no direct evidence that the hall was the space used.[132] But if it was, they probably worked within what Alan H. Nelson has described as a fairly uniform plan: 'All [college halls] were substantial rectangular rooms with distinctive upper and lower ends. In general, doors to the outside were often separated from the body of the hall by a light wooden wall called "the screens", normally in three panels defining two openings. When the screens passage was covered, as was usually the case, the natural result was a gallery above, overlooking the hall . . . At the upper end of the hall was generally a single door through which

Plate 10   Christ Church Hall, Oxford (view from the quadrangle)

persons of higher standing entered the hall, and a wooden platform – the dais – raised perhaps a foot above the hall floor. This upper end dais was usually reserved for the dining table of college dignitaries and guests.'[133]

In the same category, as an unverifiable but tantalizing possibility, is a payment by Christ Church, Oxford, during 1589–90 which may have been for a performance in that college's hall, the largest pre-nineteenth-century structure of its kind in either university (Plate 10).[134] Christ Church had hosted the queen herself in 1566, when the Great Hall was converted into an elaborate theatre for 'spectacula apparatissima' (sumptuous spectacles) described in detail by an eyewitness, John Bereblock.[135]

The early-sixteenth-century Great Hall, which remains remarkably intact, does indeed provide space fit for a royal court (see Plate 11). Its dimensions are approximately 115 feet × 40 feet with a lofty hammerbeam roof and eight bays lit by large windows on the upper level above walls panelled in the nineteenth century.[136] The principal bay window is the second from the west on the south side of the hall with two three-light windows, three transoms and a fan vault over the alcove; with the high two-transom light bay window in the north wall at the west end facing the quadrangle and the central seven-light window high in the west wall of the hall, the dais would have been better illuminated than the lower end of the hall.[137] Differing from the conventional plan described by Nelson, Christ Church features a large anteroom in place of the screens passage

Plate 11   Christ Church Hall interior: lower end

and gallery, from which a single doorway leads into the hall. There are currently two other entrances, one at the lower end in the south wall giving access to the kitchens and another at the upper end through the panelled wall on the left side of the dais, but neither may be original.[138]

The Great Hall, with its generous proportions and important setting in one of Oxford's wealthiest colleges, would have furnished an attractive performance space comparable to others used at court or to the popular venue at Norwich Common Hall. If it was used by the Queen's Men, however, we cannot assume that they enjoyed the same conditions as college-based performers. Although there are detailed staging and costuming records for both Oxford and Cambridge college productions, there are no direct indications of where, or even if, temporary stages were placed in the college halls for touring players.

A generous assortment of private households belonging to the nobility and gentry also played host to her majesty's players. Although the performance spaces are not specified at these locations, we know that it was a tradition to entertain guests with food, wine and performers, usually in the family's 'great' hall or its equivalent. We may reasonably deduce that such was the case at the Cavendish home at Chatsworth and the Hardwick family's hall, both in Derbyshire; the Clifford home at Londesborough in the East Riding; the Stanley homes at Knowsley, Lathom and New Park in Lancashire; the Manners residences at Belvoir Castle in Leicestershire and Winkburn in Nottinghamshire;

Plate 12   Hardwick Hall, Derbyshire

the Berkeley seat at Caludon Castle in Warwickshire; and Sir Francis Willoughby's older home at Wollaton in Nottinghamshire. Of these ten private
provincial halls, only one remains complete as a witness to the size and grandeur of such playing places.[139]

By the time the troupe arrived in the early autumn of 1600, Bess of Hardwick,
widowed Countess of Shrewsbury, and her granddaughter Arabella had moved
into the splendid new hall designed for them by Robert Smythson. Adjacent to
the now ruinous old hall, Hardwick Hall had been completed in 1597, a monu-
ment to the aspirations of its redoubtable owner.[140] Bess was wealthy and ambitious for a royal marriage for Arabella, who already had a claim to the throne
through her father, Charles Stuart.

Rising high on a hill in the Peak district of south-eastern Derbyshire, the six
great towers of the new hall proclaim its ownership in the stone initials 'E S'
(for Elizabeth Shrewsbury) crowning their tops (see Plate 12). The High Great
Chamber on the first floor has been described as 'the ceremonial pivot of the
house'.[141] Its principal use was as the room where formal meals were served,
but it was also where guests were entertained with music, dancing, plays and
masques. It seems probable that the High Great Chamber served as the performance space for the Queen's Men in 1600 and it remains to this day 'the
most undilutedly Elizabethan room in Hardwick, as well as the most magnificent' (see Plate 13).[142] The west wall of the room is almost entirely given over to

Plate 13 Hardwick Hall High Great Chamber

eight huge mullioned windows that allow glorious views over the surrounding countryside. The frieze, chimneypiece and Brussels tapestries of the original unified design scheme have survived the centuries, their colours faded but their design intact. The coloured plaster frieze features forest scenes, with Diana's court prominently featured, undoubtedly a deferential allusion to the virgin queen. Politically motivated too would have been the royal coat of arms above the alabaster and blackstone fireplace in the centre of the east wall, but characteristically Bess's initials 'E S' are intertwined in the queen's motto 'Dieu et mon droit'. As well as the tapestries depicting the adventures of Ulysses covering three of the four walls, it is known that there were thirteen pictures in the room (probably in the alcove) and a looking glass also decorated with the royal coat of arms. An inventory drawn up in 1601 itemizes the other furnishings: a long table of white wood covered with two carpets, a needlework chair with gold and silk fringe together with a footstool for Bess, six forms and sixteen upholstered and cushioned stools for her guests, an inlaid table in the window, a gilt cupboard and a pair of brass firedogs.[143]

The High Great Chamber is approximately 66 feet long, with an entrance at its south end leading to the main staircase, another adjacent at the south-east corner giving access to the gallery next door, and a third at the north end by the east wall leading into the withdrawing chamber.[144] The basic width of the chamber is $32\frac{1}{4}$ feet, but there is a deep alcove in the long outside wall created by a bay window distinguishing the tower facing the fireplace. The alcove measures approximately 21 feet across and 19 feet deep, a generous space which could have provided additional seating for guests as well as affording good sight lines for any performance staged in the chamber. This was a space well designed for a longed-for visit by the queen, who never came but who may instead have heard eyewitness reports of it from her itinerant troupe.

We may conclude that performance conditions for the Queen's Men, as for other play troupes on tour, were more congenial than has often been assumed. Many, if not most, of their performances would have been indoors, in halls that may have varied in size but would have been comfortably appointed. This was an era of secular building closely related to evolving civic pride, and efforts taken to dignify and maintain the environment of town halls undoubtedly were characteristic of private halls also.[145] We learn from more than one source that concern for furnishings led some civic authorities to remove prize possessions before performances and that costly repairs were sometimes needed afterwards, as the payment for mending the Guildhall windows at Abingdon after a performance by the Queen's Men bears witness.[146] Such notices also suggest that audiences were large and enthusiastic to the point of rowdiness, despite the official nature of the mayor's sponsored show. There must have been some, but perhaps not enough, seating in the public halls, though we can reasonably assume that performances in private households would have been more auspiciously controlled and accommodated.

These provincial 'theatre' spaces were not designed for a uniform purpose, however, and flexibility in adapting plays to differing audiences and varying locations would have been a basic requirement for all touring players. Given the range of locations involved on a tour, they could not have counted on more than minimal furnishings such as scaffolding, hall benches, forms and trestles at their tour stops, although other props such as housekeeping equipment may have been available to them on site.[147] Our survey of the staging requirements of the Queen's Men plays in chapter 6 (pp. 138–43 below) shows that most of them would have travelled easily, so long as a portable 'canopy' or 'pavilion' was among their properties. Without detailed accounts or eyewitness reports, we cannot be specific about how the provincial halls on record were set up for performances by the Queen's Men, although the possibilities become apparent when the surviving spaces are viewed with an eye to their periodic use as theatres.[148] Whether purpose-built stages were mounted toward their high or low ends, or plays were staged in the centre with spectators seated or standing, it is clear from the relatively small hall at Leicester to the imposing open space at Norwich's converted Blackfriars nave that most had generous audience capacity, adaptable layouts, and good sight lines. We would suggest that even a troupe such as the Queen's Men, familiar with the grandeur of royal halls at court, would have found most of these provincial indoor spaces versatile and accommodating for their accustomed needs. However, it is true that the players also had to be remarkably quick-witted and resourceful in mounting their performances. We have limited our analysis here to the provincial spaces known to have been used, but had other direct references survived in the records, an even greater variety of alternative outdoor and indoor performance spaces during their twenty years of touring would bear witness to the adaptability of the Queen's Men.

4

The Queen's Men in print

Actors out of their element

The plays of the Queen's Men were among the first to reach print from the adult professional companies, but this did not begin to happen until 1590. Very few plays from the adult professional companies were published during the 1580s. We have noted in chapter 1 (see p. 4 above) that when the company was organized in 1583, no plays from the commercial companies had been published for three years. This was an actors' theatre, and publication did not have an important place in it. Plays printed and read would have reduced the demand for plays staged and seen – so the reasoning seems to have gone. It is not necessarily correct reasoning, for publication has boosted live performance in some cultures, but in the culture of the 1580s, the companies thought their advantage lay in keeping their plays to themselves. The only commercial plays published between 1583 and 1590 were *Three Ladies of London* in 1584, probably from Leicester's Men, and *Rare Triumphs of Love and Fortune* in 1589, perhaps from Derby's Men.[1]

The situation changed in 1590, when Marlowe's two-part *Tamburlaine* and Robert Wilson's *Three Lords and Three Ladies of London* were both published – the former from the Admiral's Men, the latter from the Queen's. This was a defining moment. The same publisher, Richard Jones, brought out both plays, and one of his ventures clearly outpaced the other. *Tamburlaine* was a tremendous success on the stage, but it made a similar impact in print. We will discuss this cultural phenomenon in chapter 7 (see pp. 155–8 below), where the reaction of the Queen's Men to Marlowe's success can be treated at greater length. Suffice it to say here that the Queen's Men seem to have known from the start that *Tamburlaine* had the advantage. When their *Troublesome Reign of King John* was published in 1591 (not by Jones), it was printed in a two-part format, in imitation of *Tamburlaine*.

Plays from the adult companies were printed in every year after 1590: at least one in 1591, probably three in 1592, probably three more in 1593; then a deluge of nine or ten in 1594 (probably owing to a major reorganization of several troupes into the Chamberlain's Men and the Admiral's Men in that year).

It will be apparent in the chapters that follow that print-culture and the Queen's Men were not a good match. The defining moment of 1590 left the royal company behind. Their plays continued to be published during the 1590s, but they were competing with texts from the Admiral's Men and the Chamberlain's Men – texts from Marlowe and from Shakespeare would be another way to put it – and they were not competing well. Theirs was not primarily a literary drama. Tarlton liked to make fun of learning, and although he was very much a writer himself, part of his stage-pose was that of the illiterate jokester whose freedom from the written word allowed him all the more dexterity with speech. Comic routines almost always suffer in print, and the original Queen's Men were rife with comics. No Queen's Men play was published while Tarlton was alive, and for those comics who survived into the nineties – Wilson, Singer, Lanham – we must assume that much of their knock-about improvisation was never recorded or lost its point in translation to the medium of print. The company's serious plays are fully composed texts, but here too, as we will demonstrate in the chapters to follow, performance is required for the seriousness to come across, and they all have interludes for the clowns as well. One must imagine the routines by which the clown Bullithrumble made his mark on *Selimus*, for example, for the text is of very little help.

Serious or comic, the writing of the Queen's Men is for players and audiences. The fourteeners of *Clyomon and Clamydes* can be a wonderful challenge to actors who have an ear for the comic pace of a long line that comes out on a rhyme, but the fourteener quality shifts in the act of reading – to moral sententiousness among the readers of the sixteenth century (the fourteener was favoured as 'weighty' verse for several generations) and to nursery-rhyme silliness among readers today. Set the blank verse of the Queen's Men against the blank verse of Marlowe and Shakespeare, and the difference will be spotted in the unrelenting end-stopping of the former. We will have more to say of this feature of their verse in later chapters, but as our present business is to account for the published plays of the Queen's Men, at least those that have come down to us, we wish to make it clear from the start that publication took their plays out of their normal element. To some extent that can be said of all plays written for performance, but there are differences of degree, and the degree to which the plays of the Queen's Men are meant for the physical space of the theatre, as distinguished from the inner space of reading, is very great.

Yet the published plays of the Queen's Men are our most specific source of information about them and are to be trusted in detail. Quite the opposite impression has been created in the annals of textual scholarship, where such plays as *The Famous Victories of Henry V* and *The True Tragedy of Richard III* have been passed off as corrupt texts of the sort that have come to be known as 'bad' quartos in Shakespeare studies, and *The Troublesome Reign of King John* has sometimes been described as nothing more than a redaction of Shakespeare's play on the same subject, a 'bad' quarto of another kind. We find, on the contrary, that while the printed plays do contain some errors and garbled passages, they are coherent in dramaturgy and informative down to the details of casting and doubling. The dramatic style and playhouse practices they reveal deserve to be described for their own sake and not just as a foil to the examples of Marlowe and Shakespeare. Since the printed versions of their plays will be the basis for the chapters that follow, we are concerned to lay a proper foundation at this point by dwelling on the facts of publication and setting forth the logic for determining the company's extant repertory.

Published plays from the Queen's Men

Upwards of twenty Elizabethan plays have been attributed to the Queen's Men at one time or another, but in about half of these cases the connection is more a matter of speculation than of evidence. The speculations do have their place, but we think it is not here. A conservative approach is best for the kind of study we are engaged upon, for if plays are to be read closely as evidence of an acting company's artistic identity, they must be chosen on evidence which connects with that acting company and no other.

Speculation would open up some interesting possibilities – we are aware of missing some good bets. G. M. Pinciss, arguing that a special relationship can be detected between the company and the printer Thomas Creede, has placed such Creede plays as *James IV* and *Locrine* with the Queen's Men despite the absence of title-page attribution.[1A] It perhaps defines what we mean by 'conservative' to say that even such a reasonable hypothesis as this does not fit our method, which takes title-page attribution as the first line of evidence, or looks for other explicit indications that the company performed the play before it reached the publisher. Creede did publish texts from the Queen's Men, but nothing about *James IV* and *Locrine* indicates that these were Queen's plays.

Orlando Furioso, to choose another good speculation which we do not follow, was performed by the Queen's Men at some point in their career, but (as noted at p. 51 above) it was also performed by the Admiral's Men. The published text names neither company, and as it could as well reflect the Admiral's Men as the Queen's, we feel obliged to exclude it at this point. Eventually, *Orlando Furioso* should be studied with a view to the Queen's Men and/or the Admiral's Men – we are only saying that it should not be studied in the first instance for these two companies. Further work on the acting companies will be done, and we hope that restrictive approaches followed early will allow broader avenues to be opened later.

In that spirit, then, we will base our analysis upon the seven texts which were published with the Queen's Men named on the title-page and upon two others – *Three Lords and Three Ladies of London* and *King Leir* – for which there is reliable external evidence of a Queen's Men provenance: nine published plays in all. We take the title-page attributions as the clearest guide because in the absence of evidence to the contrary, one can assume that the publisher stated the facts of the case. One must be on one's guard against the possibility of false advertising on title-pages, of course, but there is also the risk of inventing the myth of the unscrupulous publisher to bolster other theories, particularly theories about 'bad' quartos and 'memorial reconstructions'. Some publishers of Queen's Men plays have been castigated from time to time – Thomas Creede and John Danter, for instance – but competence is gradually coming to be recognized as a quality of their work. Patricia Binnie's estimate of Danter's printing of *The Old Wives Tale* exemplifies the new attitude:

> The quarto of 1595, printed by John Danter, was evidently set up by competent workmen. In the previous year, Danter had printed QI of *Titus Andronicus*. The printing is notably regular, with only minor variations in method . . . The compositors appear to have followed a clear manuscript copy conscientiously and exactly.[2]

There is no reason to suspect someone like Danter of incorrectly stating the name of an acting company on a title-page. Some fabrications have been detected on Elizabethan title-pages, of course, but these involve authorship rather than acting company. We prefer to assume that the publishers knew more than we know about where their plays came from.

This chapter will accumulate the facts for the nine plays which can conservatively be attributed to the Queen's Men. That little catalogue will be followed by a discussion of leading points of evidence, then we will set forth a list of the speculative possibilities which we are ignoring – the good bets plus some lesser prospects. In the chapters that follow, we will read our nine chosen texts closely for implications about the kinds of drama the Queen's Men performed, the dramatic techniques by which they staged their plays, the size of the company at different periods in their career, the process by which their texts were transmitted in the playhouse, and the place of the company in Elizabethan drama. Obviously this is a lot to derive from nine plays, but we believe the risks are worth running. Only about 20 to 25 per cent of the entire Elizabethan drama has come down to us, and this partial evidence is skewed toward the more popular authors, who were well published. All Elizabethan theatre history must make its way by means of careful extrapolation.

Here are the nine Queen's Men plays, listed alphabetically and with a summary of publication information in each case:

>*Clyomon and Clamydes*. Published, without Stationers' Register entry, by Thomas Creede in 1599, with the Queen's Men named on the title-page.
>
>*The Famous Victories of Henry V*. Stationers' Register 14 May 1594, Thomas Creede. Published by Creede in 1598, with Queen's Men named on title-page.
>
>*Friar Bacon and Friar Bungay*. Stationers' Register 14 May 1594, Adam Islip (but Islip's name is crossed out and Edward White's substituted). Published in 1594 for Edward White, with Queen's Men named on title-page.
>
>*King Leir*. Stationers' Register 14 May 1594, Adam Islip (Islip's name is crossed out and Edward White's substituted). No edition is known to have followed, and another Stationers' Register entry was made on 8 May 1605, this one by Simon Stafford who assigned the title to John Wright provided that he, Stafford, should have the printing. This may have followed from the earlier Stationers' Register entry, for Wright had been apprentice to Edward White.[3] Published in 1605 by Stafford and Wright, with no company named. Henslowe lists performances of a *King Leir* in 1594, when the Queen's Men and Sussex's Men were acting together at the Rose. Since Henslowe's earlier list of plays by Sussex's Men does not include this title, the play is assumed to have been provided by the Queen's Men.[4] The 1594 entry was made on 14 May, the same day that other plays of the Queen's Men (*Famous Victories*, *Friar Bacon*) were entered. This is perhaps the least certain of our attributions to the Queen's Men. It rests on the evidence from Henslowe that the Queen's Men did play a *Leir* and on assuming that the second Stationers' Register entry links to the first by virtue of the Wright/White connection.
>
>*The Old Wives Tale*. Stationers' Register 16 April 1595, Ralph Hancock. Published in 1595 by John Danter, to be sold by Hancock and John Hardie. Queen's Men named on title-page.
>
>*Selimus*. Published, without Stationers' Register entry, by Creede in 1594, with Queen's Men named on title-page. This was said to be the first part, but no sequel is known.
>
>*The Troublesome Reign of King John*. Published by Sampson Clarke, without Stationers' Register entry, in 1591, with Queen's Men named on title-page. The division of the text into two parts seems to be a publisher's device; the piece should be regarded as a single play.[5] The plot closely resembles Shakespeare's *King John*, with which it seems to have been treated as identical from a publishing viewpoint. The exact relationship between the two plays remains unsettled. Some have considered this as

belonging to the class of texts known as Shakespearean 'bad' quartos. For further discussion, see pp. 161–6 below.

Three Lords and Three Ladies of London. Stationers' Register 1590 for Richard Jones. Published by Jones in 1590. No company is named, but Robert Wilson's authorship ('R. W.' on title-page) is no longer questioned, and the play's lament for Tarlton indicates that it was performed by the Queen's Men. The date must be after the Armada as well as the death of Tarlton. Chambers's estimate of *c.* 1589 seems right.[6]

True Tragedy of Richard III. Stationers' Register 19 June 1594, Thomas Creede. Published by Creede in 1594, with Queen's Men named on title-page.

Something may be said about the leading points of difficulty and interest, especially in regard to accepting the title-page attributions. The title-page claim that *Clyomon and Clamydes* was played by the Queen's Men, for example, may seem doubtful on the grounds that the style of the play, relentless in its fourteeners, points back to the 1570s, well before the Queen's Men were formed.[7] But an early date of composition does not invalidate the title-page statement. Old-fashioned plays do often make their way in a new-fashioned age. Our experience of theatre in other periods should warn us not to assume that a trim evolutionary pattern sums things up. The fourteener was not laid to rest with the arrival of Marlowe, Kyd and Shakespeare, any more than the Viennese operetta style of the late nineteenth century was laid to rest with the revolution in the American musical created by Irving Berlin, the Gershwins, and others in the 1920s. Berlin and the Gershwins made Romberg and Friml look old-fashioned, but operettas in the Romberg and Friml vein continued to be written (by Romberg and Friml among others) after the 1920s, and they were successful. The Queen's Men used fourteeners from time to time for special effect in plays like *The True Tragedy of Richard III* and *The Troublesome Reign of King John.* It was a mark of their style that they could handle this challenge well. There is no reason not to think that *Clyomon and Clamydes* was being performed by the Queen's Men and that they released it for publication, just as the title-page says. (This leaves open the possibility that it *was* an old play which the Queen's Men took over and refurbished.[8])

The date of *The Famous Victories of Henry V* is important, for it may be the earliest of extant English history plays among the professional companies. A story in *Tarlton's Jests* tells of Tarlton and Knell performing at the Bull in Bishopsgate. The actor who normally played the Lord Chief Justice was absent, so Tarlton stepped into the role, took a blow on the cheek from Knell, who was playing the Prince of Wales (see scene iv), then returned to his normal role as the clown (Derick in scene v) and made a joke about still feeling the effect of the blow.[9] If the anecdote is to be believed, it means that the Queen's Men acted the play before mid 1587, when Knell died. As Bullough notes (p. 167),

the mentioning of both Tarlton and Knell of the Queen's Men gives the anecdote authenticity. Moreover, the story specifies a performance at the Bull in
Bishopsgate, where the Queen's are otherwise known to have played; it hinges
on the need to double the role of the Lord Chief Justice, who does appear when
the casting becomes most difficult; and it claims that the clown's role occurs in
the following scene, another point supported by the text. The anecdote seems
to be generally reliable.[10] Its claim that Tarlton doubled the clown and the
Lord Chief Justice is impossible as the text now stands, for the two characters
appear together in scene iv, but the Lord Chief Justice's role is the kind that
was normally doubled in Elizabethan plays – brief but distinctive, more than a
walk-on, and entering the play relatively late. The role of Oldcastle is strangely
missing from scene iv. It seems clear that the normal doubling was for the
Oldcastle actor to double the Lord Chief Justice. The anecdote indicates that
Tarlton's doubling the role was extraordinary, and seems to be on target in
identifying a role that would have been doubled. The clown's role can be
cut from the scene without difficulty.[11] All things considered, the anecdote is
unusually circumstantial, and we take it as valid evidence for dating *Famous
Victories* before mid 1587.

Greene's *Friar Bacon and Friar Bungay*, attributed on the title-page to the
Queen's Men, has sometimes been claimed for Lord Strange's Men, for whom
Henslowe lists a 'Friar Bacon' in 1592. So long as only one 'Friar Bacon' play
was known – and this was the case when Chambers and Greg set forth their
foundational works in Elizabethan theatre history – it appeared that the piece
passed back and forth between Strange's Men and the Queen's Men. This
notion should have been laid to rest in 1936 with the publication of a second
'Friar Bacon' play, a manuscript play called *John of Bordeaux*, with Friar Bacon
as hero.[12] The manuscript play records the name of John Holland, an actor
known to have been with Strange's Men. Thus it appears that Henslowe used
'Friar Bacon' in reference to two separate plays: *John of Bordeaux* for Strange's
Men and *Friar Bacon and Friar Bungay* (as the title-page says) for the Queen's
Men.[13]

The provenance of *The Old Wives Tale* has become one of the mysteries of
the Elizabethan stage. The standard earlier view followed the title-page attribution to the Queen's Men and held that the unusually short text (1170 lines in
the Malone Society Reprint) was an abridgement prepared for the company's
provincial touring. The clearest statement of this view was made by Harold
Jenkins in 1939.[14] Later commentators have thought that the title-page must
be misleading: such a sophisticated play cannot so well be attributed to the
Queen's Men and can best be imagined as performed by a boy company. A
sampling of opinion: the play is an hour-long afterpiece, intended to follow a
romantic comedy now lost and written for an audience of literary sophisticates

(S. Musgrove, 'Peele's *Old Wives Tale*: an afterpiece?', *Journal of the Austral-asian Universities Language and Literature Association* 23 (1965), 89–95); the play is not an afterpiece, but is rather a full-fledged entertainment perhaps performed by a company of boys (Frank S. Hook, introduction to his edition in *The Dramatic Works of George Peele* III (New Haven, 1970), pp. 303–76); the play can hardly have belonged to the Queen's Men, but may have been a provincial abridgement from one of the children's companies which had taken to the road (G. M. Pinciss, 'Thomas Creede and the repertory of the Queen's Men, 1583–1592', *Modern Philology* 67 (1970), 321–30). Whether it was long or short, a play or an afterpiece, played by boys or adults, the common theme in these views is that *The Old Wives Tale* belonged to the aristocratic, courtly, sophisticated milieu of Elizabethan drama, and not to the Queen's Men. This perhaps ignores the fact that the Queen's Men were the most courtly of companies, if the number of performances actually given at court can be taken as a sign of 'courtliness'. That this would be a wonderful play performed by boys is an expression of taste with which we agree, but it is not a statement of fact.

The only fact we have is the title-page attribution, which names 'the Queenes Maiesties players', exactly the form used for the Queen's Men on the title-pages of *The Troublesome Reign of King John*, *The Famous Victories of Henry V*, *The True Tragedy of Richard III*, and *Selimus*. Nothing in the text prevents *The Old Wives Tale* from being performed by a company of the structure and size of the Queen's Men at about the time of publication (for further discussion, see pp. 109–12 below). Pinciss suggests that, inasmuch as the Queen's Men built their reputation on romances, this play, with its parody of romance conventions, cannot easily be placed in the company's repertory, but it is not beyond a group of actors to parody conventions which they have been accustomed to perform straightforwardly. Indeed, parodic treatment of serious action within the same play is the heart of the clown's scenes in Queen's pieces like *The Famous Victories of Henry V* and *Friar Bacon*. The title-page is to be believed.

We now supply information for other plays which have been attributed to the Queen's Men. None of these texts names the company on the title-page, and our subsequent chapters do not take them up. We also include the titles of plays now lost which the company is on record as presenting.

A Looking Glass for London and England. Stationers' Register 5 March 1594, Thomas Creede. Published by Creede in 1594. Played by Strange's Men at the Rose, 8 March 1592. That the clown is called 'Adam' hardly points to John Adams of the Queen's Men, as has been supposed.

Alphonsus of Aragon. Published, without Stationers' Register entry, in 1599 by Creede. Pinciss includes this as a probable Queen's play because of Creede's involvement and Greene's authorship.

The Cobbler's Prophecy. Stationers' Register 8 June 1594 by Cuthbert Burby. Published by Danter for Burby in 1594, with Robert Wilson named as author. Wilson's authorship is tempting to read as evidence for the Queen's Men, but it is impossible to tell when the play was written, and we do not know how long Wilson continued a member of the Queen's Men (he was writing for Henslowe's companies at the Rose later in the 1590s). So the company responsible for this text is unknown.

Felix and Philiomena (lost). Given by the Queen's Men at court, 3 January 1585.

Five Plays in One (lost). Given by the Queen's Men at court, 6 January 1585. Not to be confused with the extant plot of *2 Seven Deadly Sins* (see below).

James IV. Stationers' Register 14 May 1594, Thomas Creede. Published in 1598, by Creede, 'as it hath bene sundrie times publikely plaide'. The Stationers' Register date is that of other Queen's Men texts, including *Famous Victories of Henry V*, also entered to Creede. G. M. Pinciss's speculation that plays published by Creede are from the Queen's Men even when they are without title-page attribution is attractive for this play, and the combination of history play and romantic drama would certainly fit the company's style. But Creede's title-pages do name the Queen's Men in three other instances, a custom he did not follow here. The parallel case of *King Leir* (also entered on 14 May 1594, although not to Creede, and published in 1605) tips in favour of the Queen's Men with Henslowe's indication that the company performed a play of that title at his theatre, but there is no similar corroborating evidence for *James IV*. The use of 'Adam' in a prefix for the character Oberon has been taken as indicating John Adams of the Queen's Men, but this is fanciful.

Locrine. Stationers' Register 20 July 1594, Thomas Creede. Published in 1595 by Creede, with no attribution to a company and as 'newly set foorth, ouerseene and corrected, By W. S.' Included as a Queen's play by Pinciss because of the Creede connection. That it shares some borrowings from Spenser's *Complaints* (1591) with *Selimus*, an undoubted Queen's play, adds an extra suggestion of a Queen's connection, as does the cautionary attitude toward *Tamburlaine* (for this factor in known plays of the Queen's Men, see pp. 156–60 below).[15] For the possibility that a 'W. S.' may have written for the Queen's Men, see under Shakespeare in chapter 7 (pp. 160–6 below).

Orlando Furioso. Stationers' Register 7 December 1593, John Danter. Transfer to Cuthbert Burby, Stationers' Register 28 May 1594, so long as Danter has the printing. Published 1594, 'as it was plaid before the Queenes Maiestie'. John Danter for Cuthbert Burby. According to a passage in the *Defence of Conycatching* (Stationers' Register 21 April 1592) Greene sold the play to the Queen's Men for twenty nobles, and when they were acting in the country sold it again to the Admiral's Men. The story may be true, but the published text could well have come from the Admiral's Men, or Strange's Men (when Alleyn was acting with them). Strange's acted *Orlando* at the Rose on 22 February 1592. Alleyn's part for the role of Orlando is preserved at Dulwich College. *The Old Wives Tale*, attributed on the title-page to the Queen's Men, shares the spelling of 'Sacrapant' and two brief passages with *Orlando*.[16]

Pedlar's Prophecy. Stationers' Register 13 May 1594, Thomas Creede. Published by Creede in 1595. The Creede connection, along with the usual conjecture that Robert Wilson wrote the play, caused Pinciss to assign it to the Queen's Men, but this is nowhere stated in the evidence.

Phillyda and Corin (lost). Given by the Queen's Men at court, 26 December 1584.

Seven Deadly Sins. Tarlton wrote a play of the Seven Deadly Sins, according to Gabriel Harvey. As Gurr points out (*Playing Companies*, pp. 210–11), Harvey probably saw it on the visit of the Queen's Men to Oxford in 1585 or 1586. The extant 'plot' of 2 *Seven Deadly Sins* preserved at Dulwich is often taken to be related to Tarlton's play, but there is no convincing evidence for this connection. The 'plot' does not mention Tarlton or any other Queen's Men, and lists actors connected with Strange's Men in the 1590s. Fleay's conjecture that the plot reflects one of the plays scheduled by the Queen's Men at court in 1585 as 'Five Plays in One' and 'Three Plays in One' depends on arithmetic that does not add up.[17] The Tarlton *Sins* play (which was never said to be in two parts) must be supposed lost.

Three Plays in One (lost). Scheduled for the Queen's Men at court, 21 February 1585, but not given. Not to be confused with the extant plot of 2 *Seven Deadly Sins*.

Valentine and Orson (lost). Stationers' Register entries of 23 May 1595 and 31 March 1600 indicate 'as played by the Queen's Men', but no printed text is extant. A play of the same title was played by the Admiral's Men at the Rose in 1598, but duplications of this sort were not uncommon.

Chronologies

There are two ways to think about the dates of the nine Queen's Men texts which we have settled upon. Their dates of composition and original perform-ance are one way, and their dates of publication – or, as we prefer to put it, their dates of first reaching the publishing industry – are the other. These approaches yield different results for the Queen's Men plays. Our preference will be for the less speculative chronology of when the plays first reached the publishing industry, but in order to give an outline of the standard guesses about the first chronology, when the plays might have been written and first performed, we will list them according to the dates estimated by Chambers in *The Elizabethan Stage*, vols. III and IV.

> *Clyomon and Clamydes. c.* 1570.
> *Famous Victories of Henry V.* Not later than 1588 for Chambers, who was
>   following the anecdote in Tarlton's *Jests* and the date of Tarlton's death.
>   But had Chambers known the date of Knell's death, which was
>   discovered later, his reasoning would have produced a date of before
>   mid 1587.[18]
> *Friar Bacon and Friar Bungay. c.* 1589.
> *Three Lords and Three Ladies of London. c.* 1589.
> *Troublesome Reign of King John.* Not earlier than 1587 or later than 1591.
> *Selimus.* Not later than 1594.
> *King Leir.* Not later than 1594.
> *Old Wives Tale.* Not earlier than 1591 or later than 1594.
> *True Tragedy of Richard III.* Not later than 1594.

There are many uncertainties here, and about all that can be said of the chronology by dates of composition is that these were among the earlier plays in the body of published Elizabethan drama. The other chronology, the more useful one from our point of view, is based on the dates when the texts are first recorded in the publishing industry – that is, either by entry in the Stationers' Register or by date on the printed title-page. This list benefits from being based on fairly exact dates, and it produces three groups of texts which will be strictly adhered to in subsequent chapters. The first group consists of the two plays published or entered before 1594: *Three Lords and Three Ladies of London* (1590) and *The Troublesome Reign of King John* (1591). The second group consists of five plays published or entered in 1594: *Selimus, The True Tragedy of Richard III, Friar Bacon and Friar Bungay, The Famous Victories of Henry V*, and *King Leir.* The third group consists of two plays entered or published after 1594: *Old Wives Tale* (1595) and *Clyomon and Clamydes* (1599).

By following the dates when the plays were first recorded in the publishing industry, this second chronology focuses on the transmission of text from acting company to printer rather than on the original composition of the text (or the transmission from author to acting company). The last play in the second chronology, *Clyomon and Clamydes*, for example, many would place first in time of authorship. Chronology is usually viewed by authorship, and in deviating from that practice we are both attending to necessity and making a case. Necessity tells us we cannot know much about the order of authorship for these plays, the identities of the authors themselves being largely unknown. Of the nine Queen's Men texts, only *Friar Bacon, Three Lords and Three Ladies of London*, and *The Old Wives Tale* gave indications of the author on their original title-pages: the first with 'Made by Robert Greene Maister of Arts' and the latter two, respectively, with the quieter 'By R. W.' and 'Written by G. P.' The position of *Friar Bacon* in Greene's career can only be guessed at. Perhaps it followed after Marlowe's *Dr Faustus*, perhaps it refers accurately to St James's Day falling on a Friday – these are the hints scholars have followed, and nothing certain can be told from them. Equally uncertain is the date of *The Old Wives Tale* in Peele's career. It shares some passages with Greene's *Orlando Furioso*, but the date of *Orlando* is itself not very precise (post-1588 because of a reference to the Armada). Mockery of Gabriel Harvey seems to occur in the role of Huanebango, but the satire cannot be pinned down to a specific date.[19] The only fairly precise date among the plays of known authorship is *Three Lords and Three Ladies of London*, which dramatizes the defeat of the Spanish Armada and refers to the death of Tarlton, both in the 'current events' mode of the play. Chambers's date of 1589 has to be correct, give or take a year, but such exactitude is owing to war, death, and publication rather than to anything we know about the career of Robert Wilson.

No one knows who wrote the other six plays. Later editions in the seventeenth century posted 'T. G.' for *Selimus* and 'W. Sh.' and then 'W. Shakespeare' for *The Troublesome Reign of King John*. Shakespeare's connection with the latter will be discussed in chapter 7 (see pp. 160–6 below), but the matter is obscure and certainly does not produce a firm date. The 'T. G.' for *Selimus* is sometimes taken to mean Thomas Goffe, who was at most four years old when *Selimus* was published. It seems unlikely he wrote it. Authorship usually leads to a blind alley when it comes to the plays of the Queen's Men, and a chronology based on dates of composition is bound to be virtually useless. The date of *c.* 1570 for *Clyomon and Clamydes* is plucked out of the air. Chambers is following the usual notion that an old-fashioned play like this, of which there is no sign anywhere before its publication in 1599, must go a long way back, and 1570 is chosen merely to seem primitive enough. 'Before 1594' for *The True Tragedy of Richard III* means that we know nothing about its authorship and must settle for saying that it was written before it was published.

The plays of this company are largely anonymous, but their printers and publishers are known: Thomas Creede, Edward White, Simon Stafford, John Wright, Adam Islip, Ralph Hancock, John Danter, Sampson Clarke, and Richard Jones, to name those involved in the nine texts we assume came from the company. When the printers made an entry in the Stationers' Register they were giving the kind of detail students of authorship would love to have: the date when a manuscript was in hand. It is on this point that necessity in regard to the two chronologies blends into a case to be made. The publication of texts may not be as important as the authorship of texts, but it ranks high, as every author of unpublished texts knows. To arrange plays by the order of their earliest publication records makes sense as a historical procedure even when the chronology of their composition can be determined, for the chronology of publication outlines a very special stage of a play's existence, one which most plays did not reach then and do not reach now, the transmission of the text from the theatre to the reading public.

We find the order of Queen's Men plays as they were recorded by the printers and stationers to be a precisely revealing chronology. In the chapter that follows we will use the second chronology as the basis for showing that this body of texts is a credible source of evidence for theatre history, especially on questions of the size of each play's casting requirements and its possibilities for doubling. Part of the excitement of studying a single acting company has been the discovery that patterns of evidence do take shape when play texts are collected according to their performing organizations. Casting and doubling reveal a pattern for the Queen's Men, but there is a bonus too. To find the pattern of casting and doubling is to find that the play texts in question can be trusted, even in the details. These texts have not been trusted very often before, and some have regularly been put into the category of 'bad' quarto by which Shakespearean textual studies have been influenced throughout the twentieth century. That the texts of the Queen's Men have a bearing on Shakespeare is an incidental matter, to be sure, but if we may venture an opinion based on our examination of these nine texts, the category of 'bad' quarto does not add up to anything. The printed texts do contain garbled passages and strange lineations, certainly, but for the most part they are accurately printed, as accurately as many sixteenth-century works which have never been called 'bad', and we believe they should be taken seriously as reliable indications of what the company performed and how they performed it.

5

Casting and the nature of the texts

Quartos good and bad

Our purpose in this chapter is to see what the nine published Queen's Men plays imply about the size and constitution of the company. We will also deal with the related question of the sources of the printed plays, in hopes that a fresh view of this long-standing issue will emerge from the study of an acting company's texts rather than of an author's texts. Elizabethan textual scholarship is almost entirely driven by Shakespearean interests. Our group of plays has the advantage of not having been written by Shakespeare – at least not to any great extent.

Shakespearean textual studies have been decisively influenced by the categories of 'good' and 'bad' quartos, terms invented early in the twentieth century as critical bibliography underwent the first of at least two modern revolutions. A 'good' quarto is thought to represent an authorial manuscript of some sort, and a 'bad' quarto is thought to suffer from some sort of corruption that an author would not freely introduce. The corruption of 'bad' quartos is usually said to originate in the theatre, perhaps with minor actors who recreated their own texts by writing down what they could remember from previous performances, or with play 'pirates' in the audience taking down the spoken text by shorthand, or, more regularly, by an acting company itself when there was some need to get together a new version of a play without worrying about the niceties. Shakespearean scholarship is currently in a phase of controversy over these labels and the issues that lie behind them – the second revolution is under way – but our nine plays have not come in for fresh examination during this invigorating period.[1]

The chapter that follows is based on an experiment we have conducted in the interests of theatre history. We have asked if these nine plays contain information about the casting practices and capabilities of the company they come from. With Elizabethan plays one has to be especially concerned with the practice of doubling, a widespread convention of the time. To distribute the 'traffic' of a play so that a company of between twelve and twenty performers could play twenty to forty speaking roles plus some walk-ons was an intricate business in which some decisions, especially the final decisions, would have been worked out in the theatre. This is one of the points where theatre history overlaps with textual study, particularly with the kinds of manuscript among which textual study seeks discriminations. Texts based on authorial papers would not reflect all the casting and doubling decisions unless they had been revised in rehearsals to the point of serving as what we call a prompt-book. Texts based on 'piracies' or the later 'reconstructions' that are thought to lie behind 'bad' quartos could hardly be trusted to have such details right. The details of casting and doubling – along with other phases of a play's production – ought to be evident, if they are evident anywhere, in texts based on a prompt-book.

Our nine Queen's Men texts have at one time or another been separately studied according to the categories of textual scholarship. Four have been regarded at one time or another as 'bad' quartos: *The Famous Victories of Henry V* and *The True Tragedy of Richard III* most frequently, and *The Old Wives Tale* and *The Troublesome Reign of King John* upon occasion and controversially. The other five plays have been called different kinds of 'good' quartos. *Friar Bacon and Friar Bungay* has been supposed to proceed from an authorial text that was marked up to some extent for production, *Selimus* from an authorial text that may never have been intended for the stage, *Clyomon and Clamydes* from a composite of author's foul papers and theatrical prompt-book, and *The Old Wives Tale* (when it is not being called a 'bad' quarto) perhaps from foul papers.[2] This is not a complete survey of the labels, and there is no reason to linger over the distinctions mentioned above, aside from observing that our texts have been thought to cover the range of possibilities according to the usual categories. Some are 'good' quartos, some are 'bad'. Some proceed from authorial papers fair or foul, some from prompt-books, some from 'memorial reconstruction'. When the texts have been studied separately, in other words, the results have been marked by variety.

When the Queen's Men plays are brought together as one textual group, however, sameness rather than variety is a leading characteristic, especially when it comes to such basic theatrical characteristics as casting, doubling, staging, and dramaturgy. Staging and dramaturgy will be considered in the following chapter. Here we take up questions of casting and doubling, in which regard the 'good' quarto/'bad' quarto distinction of Shakespearean textual studies turns out to have little bearing on the case. All nine of these texts seem to proceed from the source of the 'bad' – the theatre.

We should add a word about the clues that were once supposed to be 'marks of the theatre' in earlier textual scholarship. W. W. Greg and R. B. McKerrow thought the theatre was indicated by property calls, actors' names, exact specifications for number of attendants, etc., while, by contrast, vague calls for attendants, inconsistency in characters' names, and incomplete entrance and exit directions were signs of authorial papers.[3] Distinctions of this sort, which held sway for half a century (although there were always a few sceptics), have now lost much of their credibility. It appears that both types of writing were at the command of both types of writers, with supposedly vague playwrights sometimes being precise in their theatrical calls, and supposedly precise theatre-people sometimes thinking with the untrammelled imaginations of playwrights. Our approach has been to suspend Greg's and McKerrow's distinction between signs of the author and signs of the theatre, in order to proceed as follows.

Largest scenes

To gain a sense of a play's casting, the most obvious thing to look for is the largest scene, the moment in the text when the most characters are drawn together without possibility of doubling. This is the number of actors the play cannot do without, the bare minimum required to perform the text as we have it. This does not itself indicate the actual size of the company, but only the economic ground-level of the company – a limit below which the company cannot perform the play as it stands.

'Without possibility of doubling' is the important consideration, for the Elizabethan theatre was a fast-moving business in this regard. To be an Elizabethan actor was to be a quick-change artist, among other things, and if it is clear from playhouse evidence that an actor might be assigned between four and eight roles in one of the more demanding plays, it is also clear that he could, when necessary, change from one of those roles to another in a remarkably short time. What looks like a 'largest scene' in an Elizabethan play might be deceptive if there is time in the scene for actors to exit in their earlier roles and return in later ones. In looking for the largest scenes in these plays, we have counted the characters on stage together at one time, where doubling is obviously impossible, and have added to each group that leaves the stage together any characters who immediately enter (for instance, to begin the next scene). These combinations of departing and entering character we call 'immediate juxtapositions'. It would be possible, of course, for an exiting actor to change a cloak and swing round to enter immediately (a wonderfully theatrical trick, which enables the doubling, for example, of Theseus with Oberon and Hippolyta with Titania in some productions of *A Midsummer Night's Dream*).[4] The extant playhouse 'plots', which are outlines of the traffic of the plays, and which often show the doubling assignments of the actors, contain no example of such immediate doubling, however, and we have not taken the liberty of programming such a maneouvre into our casting outlines. As for splitting a role between two actors – that is, bringing a second actor on as a character whose first actor was needed to double another part – there is no Elizabethan evidence of such a practice (there is one post-Elizabethan case, in *Believe As You List*).

The largest groupings, then, are determined by characters who appear together or who appear in immediate juxtaposition with one another. The question of how to count extras – the lords, soldiers, attendants, who are rarely numbered in stage directions – can best be solved by sheer consistency, and we follow the lead of William Ringler and David Bradley in this regard by allowing for two in all cases where the text does not specify a number.[5] This is arbitrary, of course, but it does agree with most 'attendants' instances in the extant plots: there, as in our calculations, two seems to be the most economical way of representing a plural call for extras. Perhaps there was an immediate return of a doubling actor in one of these plays. Perhaps three attendants appeared on occasion. But such guesswork makes scholars into casting directors, and it is better for them to remain scholars, as any casting director knows. So we have tried to fix upon a reasonable system and remain consistent with it.

Here are the largest groupings in each play. The plays are set forth according to the chronology by which they reached the publishing industry – that is, according to the dates by which they were first entered in the Stationers' Register or were first published. This is the second of our chronologies in the preceding chapter, with the plays divided into three groups: entered or published before 1594; entered or published in 1594 (when there was a large group); entered or published after 1594. We have used the scene numbering of the Malone Society Reprints (MSR) or of Geoffrey Bullough's *Narrative and Dramatic Sources of Shakespeare* (Bullough), and the details of the largest gathering in each case are shown in the Casting Analysis (see pp. 189–93 below).

Pre-1594	Largest scene
Three Lords and Three Ladies of London	15
Troublesome Reign of King John	17
1594	
Selimus	14
Friar Bacon	14
True Tragedy of Richard III	14
Famous Victories of Henry V	14
King Leir	14
Post-1594	
The Old Wives Tale	10
Clyomon and Clamydes	10

It is clear at a glance that the largest groupings become smaller as the years go by. Equally noticeable is the consistency of the figures within each group, especially within the middle group, where the five texts which first reached the publishing industry in 1594 all attain a largest grouping of 14 characters. These will be important points in the discussion that follows, and we would like to prevent misunderstanding by repeating that the chronology is not necessarily the order in which the plays were published. It is the order in which they were first entered or published – that is, the order in which the texts reached the publishing houses. Some plays were entered in the Stationers' Register well before they were published. The '1594' group of Queen's Men texts, for example, were all either entered or published in that year, but two of those so entered were not published until later, as far as we know: *Famous Victories of Henry V* and *King Leir*, both entered in 1594, then published in 1598 and 1605 respectively. (These plays were entered on the same *day* in 1594, 14 May, along with *Friar Bacon* and other plays.)

The results for the 1594 group seem intriguingly consistent. The five texts represent plays of different scale. *The True Tragedy of Richard III* has 48 speaking roles and (counting two, again, for each case of unnumbered attendants, etc.) 68 roles in all; *The Famous Victories of Henry V* has 41 speaking roles, 47 roles in all; *Selimus*, 30 speaking roles, 40 roles in all; *Friar Bacon*, 32 speaking roles, 35 roles in all; *King Leir*, 26 speaking roles, 38 roles in all. There are 228 roles in all among these five texts. Yet there is no moment in any of the five plays where more than 14 characters appear together or in immediate juxtaposition, and a combination of 14 occurs in each of the five texts.

Perhaps, however, this phenomenon occurs often in Elizabethan plays. Heavy doubling was normal in the theatre, and perhaps many texts would 'scale down' to largest groupings of 13–15 characters. We may test this possibility by considering all other public-theatre plays published during 1594, for companies other than the Queen's Men were finding their plays in print that year. Ten other plays printed in 1594 are commonly assumed to come from public theatres.[6] Applying the same method to them that we have applied to the texts of the Queen's Men gives the following largest groupings:

1 Contention of York and Lancaster	23	(V.i)
Titus Andronicus	19	(I.i)
Wounds of Civil War	18	(III.ii–iii)
Battle of Alcazar	17	(I.i–ii)
Orlando Furioso	16	(IV.i–ii)
Cobbler's Prophecy	14	(xii–xiii)
Edward II	14	(xii)
Looking-Glass for London	12	(v)
Taming of A Shrew	11	(IV.i–ii)
Knack to Know a Knave	10	(ii–iii)

The range of largest gatherings is quite broad and denies the possibility that Elizabethan plays reduce to the same scale. It is true that the largest group of texts does collect around 14, for there are two plays on this additional list that join the five from the Queen's Men at that number; but *The Cobbler's Prophecy* is one of the 'possible' Queen's Men plays (because it was written by Robert Wilson – see p. 92 above), so it could be that its largest gathering of 14 is due to the possibility we are testing. Without pressing the question of *The Cobbler's Prophecy* further, we may suppose there is some significance to the facts we have turned up. The five plays which first reached the publishing industry in 1594 from the Queen's Men have largest moments of 14 characters in a range of possibilities of 10 to 23 derived from other public-theatre plays published in the same year.

Minimum casting: the 1594 group

The next step is more speculative. If five plays from one company in one year all have the same largest grouping of characters, the possibility arises that this phenomenon is owing to a practice of the theatre rather than to accident. The practice of the theatre most likely to have had the effect of consistency in the size of the largest scenes concerns casting and the economy by which Elizabethan companies operated. The Elizabethan theatre characteristically produced plays with more roles than there were actors to play them – a practice far from our working assumptions about the production of plays today. We tend to think in terms of one-to-one casting, in an economy that aims for trimness. That is not to say that doubling is never used in the modern theatre (the plays of Caryl Churchill and David Edgar use it extensively, for example) but that when doubling occurs in the modern theatre, it is an exception to the norm. The norm holds that an actor takes on a role, studies a role, plays a role, in the spirit of singularity and ownership – the role is his or hers. At the top of the Elizabethan acting companies, where star actors like Burbage and Alleyn were becoming identified with long title-roles, the modern way of thinking was taking hold, but in the rest of an Elizabethan company, the norm was to play a plurality of roles, more than one each day, often more than a dozen in a week. The Elizabethans did not think in terms of trimness when it came to the number of characters in their plays, which regularly call for more characters than there were actors to play them in a one-on-one casting scheme, and which frequently call for at least twice as many characters as there were actors to play them. The two-character or three-character play, which we are used to as a matter of our economy of trimness, did not belong to the Elizabethan professional theatre.[7]

In noticing that our group of 1594 Queen's Men plays all reduce to the same 'largest scene' of 14, we must ask whether all roles in each play could through doubling be played by something like this number of 14 actors. To put it another way, we are taking the maximum of 14 reached at least once in each play and ask-ing if that maximum distributes across the traffic of all the roles in each play.

The likelihood is that the distribution would prove impossible among the 228 roles in these five texts. Somewhere – perhaps in *True Tragedy of Richard III* with its 68 roles, or *Famous Victories of Henry V* with its 47 – the comings and goings of the characters would cancel the possibilities of doubling for 14, and a fifteenth actor, if not a sixteenth, would be required. And there can be no fiddling with the text. The 'immediate juxtaposition' rule still applies – no doubling when there is no time provided. Act intervals or musical interludes cannot be invented to make the casting easier. When the directions call for unnumbered attendants, two must be cast. When the directions specify a number, we must follow the specification. This last principle comes to the test with the odd call for 'six others' to try to rescue Buckingham at line 1360 in *The True Tragedy of Richard III*. Such a direction is usually read as a playwright's wishful thinking. Surely an acting company would cut *that* down in produc-tion. But the assumption behind our work is that the text means what it says about the comings and goings of characters, and it is necessary to be strict, literal, and consistent in this assumption. So, six 'others' must be cast.[8]

As it happens, the traffic of roles in all five 1594 texts is arranged so that it is possible for 14 actors to play all the roles. A casting and doubling scheme for each of the five texts is shown in the Casting Analysis (Appendix B, pp. 189–93 below). Moreover, the two post-1594 texts, which have largest scenes of 10, can be played by 10 actors, and these distributions are also shown in the Casting Analysis.

To illustrate here how the texts are arranged, we offer a discussion of the most improbable and difficult case. *The True Tragedy of Richard III* is the most demanding of the 1594 plays in terms of casting, and the biggest challenge in that play is a crowded stretch of action running from the beginning of xii through the opening entrance direction of xv. The largest grouping of 14 char-acters falls in this section, but there are other challenges too. Counting 2 for unnumbered groups of attendants, as before, we find 29 characters in this part of the play. (The 'six others' discussed above appear here, line 1360.) Can the 29 characters in this part of the play, including the luxurious 'six others', be played by the 14 performers who are required in the play's largest grouping?

The casting is possible, with all doubling being covered by at least 25 lines. Before charting the roles, however, we would like to raise the odds against this experiment by glancing at another series of scenes in the same play where the doubling is about equally heavy. From the beginning of viii through the end of

x, 22 characters appear – most of them different from the 29 we are considering
in xii–xiv. Can these 22 be played by our hypothetical 14 performers without
clashing with their possibilities of doubling the later 29 roles? It is intriguing to
discover that all these roles can be doubled by 14, and that all examples of
doubling are covered by more than 20 lines of text. Here is a listing for these
two crowded sections:

Beginning viii–end x	*Beginning xii–beginning xv*
1. Richard	Richard
2. Buckingham. Att. (line 895).	Buckingham. Richmond.
3. Mess. (ix). Att. (line 895).	Terrell.* Att. (Buck). Stanley.
4. Page.	Page.
5. Att. (Edw.). Card. Hastings.	Forest.* Att. (Buck). Oxford.
6. Grey. Noble (ix).	Slawter.* Herald. Mess. (xiv).
7. Vaughan. Att. (line 895).	Banister. Lovell.
8. Att. (Edw.). Catesby.	Brokenbury. Catesby.
9. Hapce. Noble (ix).	Douten. Att. (Buck). Landoys.
10. Att. (line 791, line 895).	Att. (Buck). Blunt.
11. Queen Mother.	Att. (Richard).
12. Prince Edward.	Pr. Edw. Att. (Buck). G. Stanley.
13. Duke of York.	Duke of York. Att. (Richard).
14. Elizabeth.	Att. (Buck).

* Quickest changes: approximately 25 lines.

(The lower end of the list is reserved for roles normally played by boys, a matter
to which we shall return. Boy actors hardly ever played adult male speaking
roles, but they did play adult male walk-ons.)

What makes this doubling possible is the same characteristic in both cases –
a segment, standing between the large groups, of 40 or 50 lines involving only
three or four actors. The large groups in viii and ix are separated by the small
beginning of ix. Three characters share 23 lines at the beginning of ix before
they are joined by a Messenger for 25 lines. The Messenger reports what we
have just seen in the preceding scene. Thus some 50 lines are provided among
4 characters before the heavy doubling begins. The heavy doubling arrives
with the Cardinal and an unnumbered group of 'ambushed noblemen', who
would enter sometime after line 840 and would be in place when the Cardinal
'notices' them at line 860. There is no entrance direction for the noblemen,
but their presence at line 869 is unmistakable, and it is virtually certain that
they surreptitiously take their places either during the Cardinal unit or the
Messenger unit of the scene. The 50-line segment, which might very well serve
other purposes too, and which certainly repeats an element of the plot, serves
the purpose of allowing doubling time for the performers from viii to change
for the Cardinal and the ambushed nobles of ix.

That impression is reinforced by the arrangement of xii–xiv. After the murder of the Princes in xii, when five actors leave the stage, a peculiar conversation occurs between Terrell and Forest – peculiar in that it recounts what has just been said. It is a small ending to a larger scene, just as the next scene, which will be larger too, opens small when Buckingham discovers Banister's treachery and threatens him with a knife. The scene builds from two to three with the arrival of a Herald to arrest Buckingham. Thus 40 lines elapse between the departure of the murderers and their victims in xii and the next entrance of a crowd, 'enter six others to rescue the Duke' in xiii. It happens that exactly 6 actors would be available for the 'others' at this point according to our hypothetical casting for 14.

This pattern of alternating large and small groupings of roles runs through the 1594 text and is the device that allows all 68 roles to be played by 14 performers. The casting is heavy, judging from the extant playhouse documents and what they tell us about practices in other companies, but the signs of strain are in fact reflected in the other evidence. Our chart assigns seven parts to several actors, for example, and it has boy actors doubling as mute attendants. The plot of *1 Tamar Cam* assigns eight parts apiece to two actors, and the plot of *The Battle of Alcazar* has a boy actor doubling an attendant role.[9] Our chart has several actors forced to 'redouble' – return to roles previously played after picking up other parts – yet this happens on the plots of *Frederick and Basilea* and *Battle of Alcazar*. It is the *combination* of strains which seems unusual in casting the *True Tragedy of Richard III*. Nearly the entire company is straining. It is not typical for all of the boy actors to double, or for as many as four adult actors to have seven roles apiece. There is no doubt that 14 actors *can* double the 68 roles in *True Tragedy of Richard III*, but by itself it does not make the case that this possibility was intentional.

The other four 1594 texts keep the issue alive, however, for they all match up to *The True Tragedy of Richard III* in arranging the traffic of roles so that a hypothetical casting for 14 performers is possible. Moreover, they contain signs that some roles were dropped out of scenes where they would normally appear, as though some measure of revision were involved to bring the casting down to the minimum level. *Friar Bacon and Friar Bungay* would have been a large-cast play in its original design, for example, because it brings large groups of characters into immediate juxtaposition. It does not follow *The True Tragedy of Richard III*'s method of interspersing small groups among the larger ones, in other words, but replaces one large group with another, as though heavy doubling were not a consideration in the general planning of the action. What allows *Friar Bacon* to be played by 14 performers throughout is the 'disappearance' of characters where they would normally be expected. As some editors of the play have noticed, one character has disappeared entirely.[10] Two references to a 'Saxony' in the dialogue show that originally a Duke of Saxony travelled in company with the royal party of Henry III, and that his character was written out of the play at some point (there are no speeches for 'Saxony' and he is not mentioned in stage directions). The phenomenon of the 'disappearing character' also occurs with some roles which belong to the play but which do not occur in scenes where they normally would. Warren and Ermsby, for example, normally accompany Prince Edward and Lacy, but in one Edward–Lacy scene, xi, they do not appear in the stage directions, have no speeches, and are not referred to. Ralph Simnell, the jester, also travels with this group, but there is no reference to him in scenes viii and xv. And what happens to Friar Bungay in xv? This is the concluding scene, where one would expect a title character to appear, but he does not. It happens that these are the most crowded scenes in the play. The beginning of xv is when our largest grouping of 14 characters occurs, and Ralph Simnell and Friar Bungay are not among them. In line with the assumption that the text means what it says about the appearances of characters, we omit Ralph and Bungay from the final scene (see the Casting Analysis, p. 190), drop Warren and Ermsby from xi, drop Ralph from viii – and suddenly a play that would have required some 16 or 17 performers at a minimum can be doubled by 14.

Famous Victories of Henry V uses both methods – interspersing small groups among the large, and removing some characters from scenes where they would be expected. The most important 'disappearance' is that of Oldcastle in scene iv, the famous scene where the Prince of Wales strikes the Lord Chief Justice a blow on the face. 'Jockey' Oldcastle (as he is called) appears in the other three scenes which involve the Prince and his reprobates, but he does not appear with them in the Chief Justice scene. No explanation is given for his absence. The Chief Justice scene is a difficult one to cast, for the sixteenth, seventeenth, and eighteenth speaking roles of the play are added here, just after four others have been added in the previous scene. It appears that the actor of Oldcastle was freed to play the Chief Justice – a point which Falstaffians will want to ponder. For the anecdote about Tarlton's doubling the Chief Justice, see our discussion in chapter 4 (pp. 89–90 above). Tarlton almost certainly played the role of Derick, not Oldcastle, and Derick appears in the scene in question. But the anecdote actually rings true, because it says that Tarlton's doubling the role was unusual. The text would have to be revamped to double Derick and the Justice. As it stands, the text implies that the normal manoeuvre was to double Oldcastle and the Justice.

Another aid to casting this text for 14 is that it spares the walk-ons. Nearly every character mentioned in entrance directions also speaks. And the technique used in *True Tragedy of Richard III* is evident: the largest scenes are tapered down at either end by small groups, who provide time for costume changes. The victory at Agincourt is handled in a wordless scene simply called 'The Battell', in which soldiers must have been as plentiful as possible. Only three speaking roles occur just before and just after 'The Battell': Henry V, Oxford, and the French Herald in each case. The rest of the company must have been dressed for battle and for crying 'S. George and God and S. George helpe us' at the end of Henry's battle speech or, speaking offstage for the other side, 'S. Dennis, S. Dennis, Mount Joy, S. Dennis' before the fighting begins.

Selimus and *King Leir* can also be played by 14 performers without clashes in the doubling assignments. Again, the 'disappearance' of characters from scenes where they would normally be expected enables the doubling. In *Selimus*, the absence of Sinam Bassa from the Selimus group from vi to mid-way in xviii appears to be a casting manoeuvre, as does the absence of the bashaws, Hali and Cali, from the Bajazeth group in i–viii and in xiv. These absences, together with the insertion of small scenes in the more crowded stretches of action (in *Selimus* the gradual reduction of the last half of xiii followed by the gradual increase at the beginning of xiv, for example, and in *Leir*, Ragan's soliloquy just before the beginning of the climactic battle scenes), allow a pattern for 14 performers to be maintained.

We have also divided the roles in each of the 1594 texts into those customarily played by men and those customarily played by boys, in order to see if this division remains the same across the five plays. To count the roles for boys, we have included all female roles and all roles for males who (as far as one can tell from the text) have not reached puberty. One of the unusual characteristics of these five plays is their emphasis on younger male characters who are anything but boyish: youths, let us say. The title character in *Selimus*, for example, is identified as a 'youth' several times, but he is a youth who poisons his father and strangles his two brothers while setting out to start a family of his own, and it would be a mistake to think him pre-pubescent. The Prince of Wales in *Famous Victories* is not of the same character, but he may well be the same age – deceptively youthful, one might say. The cynical Page who appears in both *Selimus* and *True Tragedy of Richard III*, and who knows where to find the murderers of the young Princes in the latter, would not have been played by a boy, we assume, although boys would have played the young Princes, whose innocence and helplessness are stressed. The distinction between boys and youths can usually be made on the basis of epithets in the text, and in our hypothetical casting, the youths' roles mentioned above have been distributed to the adult actors.

In the five 1594 texts, we count the following roles for boys: *Famous Victories*, 5 (includes two walk-on attendants); *King Leir*, 5 (includes two walk-on attendants); *Friar Bacon*, 5; *Selimus*, 5; *True Tragedy of Richard III*, 7. In all the plays except *True Tragedy of Richard III*, no more than three of these roles are brought together at one time in the largest-grouping method of counting; in *True Tragedy*, four appear together. It happens that three boy actors can double the other roles for boys in all five texts, with the single exception of the largest grouping of roles for boys in *True Tragedy*, where four are required.

In other words, all five of the 1594 texts, no matter how large their casts of characters, can be staged by the 14 actors who are required in the largest group-ings of each play. All of the roles normally assigned to boys can be played by four of those performers – and all but one of *those* roles can be played by three boys. We find it unlikely that such consistency is an accident. The 1594 texts seem to be designed – very tightly designed – to be playable by a cast which by our index would number 14. We must continue to note that 14 is an index because we count two by rule for all cases of unnumbered attendants. In this, we would not be far from the historical fact, for two attendants save a costume over three, but of course the companies were not bound by such a rule. There-fore, we do not say these plays *were* performed by the minimum of 14, but that they could have been. The consistency with which the 'could have been' comes out to 14 makes us think we are not far from historical fact in this estimate, however.

Several of the texts have 'disappearances' of characters who would be ex-pected to appear, leading us to think that the published texts have been cut down from larger versions. We know that the Queen's Men were dividing into two branches from early in their career. Yet they were formed as the largest company to date in the professional Elizabethan theatre, and their size gave them the opportunity to stage a new kind of play, a kind demanding their unique numbers. This was the 'large-cast' play, to put it simply, and it appears to have caused other companies in the 1590s to build up their numbers and stage their own 'large-cast' plays.[11] The most important kind of 'large-cast' play staged by the Queen's Men was the English history play. Plays first written for the largest acting company would have been rearranged for lesser numbers of actors when the company divided into branches, and this kind of tailoring is very likely to lie behind the 1594 and post-1594 groups of Queen's Men plays.

The implication is that the Queen's Men texts result not from various kinds of manuscripts authorial and theatrical, but from the kind of planning that must be carried out as a play is put into production. The traffic of the roles seems to have been carefully planned, with special attention being given to the vital question of doubling large plays for a limited number of actors. In this respect, the texts are not at all slapdash or errant, no matter how strange the dialogue may seem at times. They are not 'good' quartos and 'bad'. They are plays designed for the professional theatre.

Minimum casting: the remaining plays

The casting evidence for the two plays published before 1594, *Three Lords and Three Ladies of London* and *The Troublesome Reign of King John*, shows a different situation. The largest groupings run higher than in the 1594 plays – 15 and 17 characters respectively – and in each case the rest of the play cannot be doubled by that group of actors. In *Three Lords and Three Ladies*, the final procession draws 15 roles together, 7 of these being roles for boys. There are 3 other roles for men in the play that cannot be doubled by the adult actors of the large procession or with one another: Fealty, Simony, Usury. So the large-scene must be expanded by 3 adult actors, producing a revised minimum figure of 18 actors in all for *Three Lords and Three Ladies*.

The 17 actors required in the large-scene test of *Troublesome Reign* cannot handle the 'many Priests' (rated at two) called for in Part II, line 632, along with 'all the Lords from France and England' (two again) a few lines later. By increasing the casting of *Troublesome Reign* to 18 and assuming steady doubling for the players of the female roles, we could provide the 'Priests' and 'Lords', but the real point is that both of the earliest-published plays from the Queen's Men run beyond their large-scene casting, call for more than 17 performers according to our method, and suggest a large company relatively unconcerned about matters of doubling and economy of casting. These characteristics fit with the formation of the Queen's Men as the largest of the London professional companies to date, while all the other plays, the 1594 group and the post-1594 group, appear to have been tailored to a smaller company of Queen's Men. We have noted in chapter 3 the slight possibility that the Queen's Men had become a smaller company overall by 1588, when nine sharers appear on what may be an incomplete subsidy list. That is one possibility for requiring smaller plays. The clearer possibility lies in the company's practice of dividing themselves into smaller groups for purposes of touring, also discussed in chapter 3 (p. 44).

A further word should be said about the final group, the two plays first entered and/or published after 1594: *The Old Wives Tale* and *Clyomon and Clamydes*. These two plays are not often considered together, and their resemblances deserve to be noted. Both call for the same largest grouping, 10, with three of those roles being female in each case. Both plays can be entirely doubled by a company of 10.[12] Both use the special effects of magician's tricks, both depend on the theatrical device of 'exchanged identities', whereby the plot turns on one character's stealing away the appearance of another, both involve the slaying of an evil character, both involve a burial scene, and both require music and singing (very prominent in *The Old Wives Tale*). The theme of stolen identity is related to doubling and casting. To double is, in a sense, to steal an identity, with two (or more) persons being represented by the same actor, and in these magic-charged romantic comedies from the later Queen's Men, doubling becomes thematized when the actor playing Brian Sans Foi fools everyone into thinking him Clamydes in scene xxiii of *Clyomon and Clamydes*, and when Sacrapant is discovered to have been Erestus all along at the end of *The Old Wives Tale*. This latter point has been misunderstood by earlier commentators, who assume that the actor playing the old man Erestus would appear as 'Erestus' in the final scene.[13] On the contrary, since the point is that the old man is finally being restored to his youthful appearance, which had been stolen and worn by the sorcerer Sacrapant throughout the play, it would be the actor of Sacrapant who enters at the conclusion dressed in Erestus's costume and looking young. Sacrapant is now 'doubled' with Erestus – only this is a point of the magical plot in addition to being a casting device of the playhouse. That is why our list of characters for the largest moment in the Casting Analysis shows 'Sacrapant' in the final scene.

The largest moment in *Clyomon and Clamydes* is scene xxii combined with the immediate juxtaposition of female roles between scenes xxii and xxiii (see Casting Analysis, p. 192 below). This group of 10 can also fill all of the supernumerary parts if these are counted as two each time they are not numbered. The doubling is possible because of frequent soliloquies, which occur at nearly every clearing of the stage and are a distinct mark of the dramaturgy: these people talk mainly to themselves until the very end, and this is one way in which the play differs from *Old Wives Tale*, where people converse – sometimes in strange ways, but they converse. It is possible for this implied cast of 7 men and 3 boys to play all the roles in *Clyomon and Clamydes*, as David Bevington and Arleane Ralph have shown.[14]

In *The Old Wives Tale* the largest gathering of 10 occurs in the final scene. Ten can play all of the roles, but the casting is extremely heavy and some of the costume changes are so quick – under 10 lines in two cases – that they would certainly call attention to themselves. The 'frame' story is what allows the swift changes to take place, for the dialogue among the Old Wife (Madge) and her listeners, Frolic and Fantastic, provides brief spaces before the singing Harvest-men make their two appearances, and the Harvest-men are the figures most difficult to cast among a group of 10. The hardest stretch of action as far as casting is concerned is the combination of the churchyard scene, which introduces three or four characters who do not appear elsewhere in the play (the reason for the ambiguity between three and four will be apparent in a moment) and the entrance of the singing 'Harvest-men' with 'women in their hands' at line 561 (Revels edition). Seven lines between the frame characters are all that separate the exit of the churchyard characters and the entrance of the 'Harvest-men', yet at least one piece of doubling must occur between these groups if the play is to be entirely performed by its largest gathering of 10 performers.

We think it clear that this is exactly what happened. For when one stops to think about it, *The Old Wives Tale* does call attention to the rapid changes of costume that would be required for 10 performers to do the entire play. It has long been recognized that the final scene fails to draw all the strands of the plot together, because two of the happy couples expected in the final grouping do not appear: Huanebango and Corebus are missing, along with their mates Zantippa and Celanta. Their presence would bring 14 characters into the largest moment, so possibly the longer text matched up to the 1594 group. Harold Jenkins (1939) was the first to note that the absence of the quartet of lovers at the end resulted from considerations of casting.[15] But the matter is more intriguing than has been realized. Jenkins argued that the Corebus who is missing from the final grouping is also subject to an earlier textual confusion. Earlier, Huanebango's clownish servant, called Booby in his first appearance, takes on the name Corebus in his later scenes, after a character named Corebus – apparently a different character originally – appeared in the churchyard scene. Jenkins thought the earliest Huanebango scene (lines 254–317) was meant to be cut, but the job was not carried out carefully enough for the printing-house compositors to realize that an omission was intended. By this line of reasoning, Booby would have disappeared and the roles of Corebus and the Clown could have been merged into one, saving an actor but making it impossible to carry the full Huanebango quartet into the final scene. (If one of the four cannot appear, it is pointless for any of the four to appear.)

We cannot follow Jenkins in regard to cutting the first Huanebango scene (it is there and has to be dealt with), but his point about a merging of the Clown and Corebus seems right. The reason for ambiguity between three and four new characters in the churchyard scene can now be explained. The original Corebus, a separate character from the Clown, would have joined the Churchwarden, the Sexton, and Wiggen to make four new characters in the churchyard. If Corebus *became* the Clown to save an actor (and a costume), there would only have been three new characters in the churchyard: the Churchwarden, the Sexton, and Wiggen. The churchyard scene contains another textual anomaly: the speech prefix for the Churchwarden is once given as 'Simon'. This has long been taken for an actor's name, although the previous guess that the actor was John Symons (the famous tumbler who toured with the Queen's Men in the late 1580s) now seems less attractive than the possibility that he was Simon Jewell, whose will (discovered in the 1970s) shows that he was probably a member of the Queen's Men.[16] Together with the apparent merger of Corebus into the Clown, the use of an actor's name as a speech prefix indicates that casting was a special concern in the churchyard scene.

Such manoeuvres make it possible to double *The Old Wives Tale* with 10 actors. We wish to stress that this doubling scheme is the tightest and most difficult of all the Queen's Men plays, and we also wish to stress that this tight doubling is built into the dramatic meaning of the play. *The Old Wives Tale* is about doubling. That is what we have noticed about the conclusion, when the actor of Sacrapant comes on as Erestus. The entire play can be read (and produced) as a thematization of this idea, that identities arise in doubled and miraculous ways if one has faith in maintaining relationships rather than in seeking one's own advantage. This is not the place to elaborate on an interpretation, but we might mention that in the churchyard scene, where a particularly tight doubling has to occur between at least one of the characters involved in the burial of Jack and one of the singing Harvest-men who enter after a gap of only seven lines, this doubling is meant to be noticed, meant to be obvious. All doubling in the Elizabethan theatre was 'obvious' to the sharp-eyed observer (for doubling is difficult to hide without artificial lighting), but the suspension of disbelief would normally have prevented such a convention from becoming a distraction. With the churchyard characters turning into Harvest-men in seven lines, however, distraction would be hard to avoid and just what the scene needs. Having churchyard characters who talk about burial turn suddenly into Harvest-men who sing about fruition is part of the play's beauty.[17]

'Bad' quartos and the transmission of text

To summarize, the published Queen's Men texts form a pattern when they are studied for their casting implications. The earliest two plays to reach the publishers are approximately twice as heavy in their casting demands as the last two. In between falls a group of plays first entered or published in 1594, and these all fit a minimum casting pattern of 14 performers, approximately midway between the large pre-1594 plays and the small post-1594 plays. We do not believe that consistency of this sort can be accidental. The early Queen's Men were an unusually large company, and we know that they divided into branches as a way of spreading their influence (and increasing profits). They must have had different versions of their plays for these different circumstances. The casting evidence we have presented matches this difference. The pre-1594 plays probably represent the sort of 'large-cast' play the original company would have specialized in, and the remaining plays probably represent revisions for smaller numbers.

The implications of our findings for textual studies are important. The texts of the presumed 'bad' quartos among these plays are usually thought to be filled with error, indecently printed, and virtually unreadable, yet we have seen that the details of their stage traffic fall into the same patterns as do the details of 'good' quartos. We believe that theatrical coherence is the basic characteristic of these texts, not just in casting implications but in all phases of dramaturgy, and yet the opposite opinion circulates widely. There are errors and garbles, to be sure, but these have been seized upon as the basic characteristic and the texts have sometimes been ostracized from the realm of the believable. *The Famous Victories of Henry V* seems to drive some readers wild: it has an 'almost imbecile nature', according to an edition of one of Shakespeare's corresponding plays on Henry IV and Henry V, and according to another, it is 'so corrupt that it may even have been reconstructed from an author's plot of the kind represented by the so-called *Philander, King of Thrace*'.[18] W. W. Greg introduced his Malone Society Reprint of *The True Tragedy of Richard III* by calling it a 'strangely amateurish composition' which, even so, could not have been anything like its printed version originally. Debased, corrupt, chaotic – how could texts deserving such opprobrium provide accurate details about the casting procedures of the company that produced them?

One characteristic does stand out in the two texts most often thought to be 'bad' quartos. It is specific, it contains a puzzle, and solving the puzzle may answer the question posed above. Both *Famous Victories of Henry V* and *True Tragedy of Richard III* are printed with long stretches of mislineation – verse printed as prose, or (the more interesting case) prose printed as verse. The former of these, verse printed as prose, presents no puzzle, for it can be readily explained as a way of saving space, either in the printing house or in the theatre manuscript. Turning verse into prose, which runs to wider margins, would be an economical move for either a printing-house compositor or a playhouse scribe. (The manuscript play called *John of Bordeaux* shows verse being written out as prose, apparently by a playhouse scribe.)

The puzzle concerns prose being turned into verse – a certain way to lose space. Losing space was sometimes desirable in the printing house, of course, where a miscalculation in counting off could be corrected by expanding the text. This would explain short stretches of prose lined as verse at strategic points. But the examples before us consist of page after page of prose set as verse: in *True Tragedy of Richard III* such mislineation begins on A4r and continues seriatim through B4v, over nine pages. Another burst of over a page runs from the final 21 lines on F3v through F4r, and there is another complete page on G1a. *The Famous Victories of Henry V* is written entirely in prose, but the quarto has 34 pages set as verse, running in two segments: A2v through A4v, and C4v through G2v. Mislineation is the leading characteristic of these two Queen's Men texts, and the puzzling form of mislineation turns prose into verse for long stretches at a time – to the advantage, it would seem, of no one. How could this have happened?

Both texts were printed by Thomas Creede. Creede's other two plays for the Queen's Men, *Selimus* and *Clyomon and Clamydes*, have no prominent mislineations. Prose is very rare in these two plays in the first place, so the puzzling prose-into-verse mislineation hardly has a chance to occur. (Bullithrumble speaks prose in *Selimus*, sometimes in scenes otherwise in verse, and his speeches are set correctly.) A recent study shows that normally two compositors were at work in Creede's shop, and in our texts it does appear that one compositor was responsible for the extensive prose-as-verse mislineations, another for the correctly lined pages.[19] The difference in compositors can be seen sharply in *True Tragedy of Richard III*, where the mislineation ends with F4r in mid speech and a correct setting of prose as prose picks up the same speech at the top of F4v.

How could a compositor in Thomas Creede's shop go to the trouble of turning page after page of manuscript prose into page after page of printed verse, wasting space as he went along, especially when another compositor was apparently doing things right? Roughly half of each text is correctly aligned.

The answer may depend on rephrasing the question. Is it possible that the turning of prose into verse occurred not in the printing house but in the theatre? The difference between the compositors in Thomas Creede's shop, in other words, may have been between one who corrected the mislineation of his copy as he worked and one who did not.

Does it make sense to suppose that a playhouse scribe would sometimes write long sections of prose as verse? The answer to that question is yes, if the scribe can be imagined as working not from manuscript copy but from dictation. For when one is listening and writing, one might very well not know at the beginning of a speech which cadence it is going to fall into. One might not even care. One would care about keeping up with the dictation. Dictation has long been suspected as a possible factor in 'bad' quartos – by D. L. Patrick for the quarto of Shakespeare's *Richard III*, by Greg for the quarto of *Orlando Furioso*, and by G. I. Duthie for the quarto of Shakespeare's *King Lear* – and there is evidence from the Jacobean theatre that the practice did result in garbled texts.[20] Thomas Heywood complained in 1608 that imperfect versions of his plays reached the press from the acting companies, apparently by means of transcriptions 'coppied onely by the eare'. Yet there is no general agreement on how extensive the practice of dictation may have been in the playhouses, and the idea has not entered prominently into Shakespearean textual theory.

We propose that our two mislined Queen's Men texts were prepared by dictation in the playhouse, with actors reciting their parts after they had memorized them, and with a scribe recording those recitations in order to have a temporary copy of a revised play. In this connection, we note that these two texts have a number of apparent 'mishearings'. Greg's introduction to the Malone Society Reprint of *True Tragedy of Richard III* noted that the references to a 'Lord Marcus' in scene ii must be mishearings of 'Lord Marques', i.e. Dorset. We would apply the same explanation to 'Casbe' or 'Casbie' for 'Catesby', 'Hapc' for 'Hapce' (scene viii but not scene v), 'cresse' for Latin 'cresce' (lines 4–5) and 'dissent' for 'descent' (line 20). In *Famous Victories of Henry V* the following apparent mishearings occur: 'a narrant whore' for 'an arrant whore' (line 589), 'bollion' for 'bullion' (line 681), 'Burgony' for 'Burgundy' (line 798), 'broad seale Emanuel' for 'broad seal manual' twice (line 855 and line 863) and 'wronfull' for 'wrongful' (line 1061). Moreover, the bizarre arithmetic by which the French and English forces are estimated before Agincourt (scene xiv) becomes more secure when it is realized that the text's 'forty' is a mishearing for 'fourteen'.[21]

One cannot be sure about mishearings, of course. Elizabethan spelling was a practice imbued with variation, and even if the examples above do seem to be aural, perhaps the dictation occurred in the printing house, with a compositor setting type as he listened to someone read copy aloud. Yet it does seem to us that the theatre is the most likely place for dictation to have occurred, and it does seem to us that the vast mislineations of prose as verse are best explained on this hypothesis. The key item to think about is the preparation of a new prompt-book if an acting company found it necessary to reduce a play – as the Queen's Men must have done, when they divided into branches. When would the new prompt-book have been made? Considering the many adjustments that would have been necessary to rearrange a 'large-cast' play for a smaller number of actors, we think the prompt-book would have been prepared late in rehearsal, probably as the final stage in the revision. A company that had once consisted of, let us say, 18 actors doubling across some 40 or 50 roles in a history play would have had an intricate task in rearranging that play if the company were reduced to, let us say, 14 actors. The new and heavier doubling assignments would have been especially problematic. The revision would have to be worked out as a company venture during rehearsals, and there would be no sense in writing a prompt-book in advance of those rehearsals. The original actors' 'parts' might have to be worked over in the first place, for 'learning the cuts' is the hardest thing for an actor to do with a role he already knows, but writing the new prompt-book would be delayed as a matter of common sense until after it was clear how many new roles each actor would have to double, which characters would have to be cut out altogether for the doubling to be possible, and where patches of additional dialogue would be necessary to provide time for the new doubling to be possible in each case. New patches of dialogue would almost certainly have been necessary here and there, just to create extra time for costume changes backstage.[22]

Once the theatrical revisions were complete, a new prompt-book would have had to be made. It would not be the permanent prompt-book, and it would not have to be submitted for licensing. The licence had already been obtained on the original book. How was this new prompt-book to be made? Would the scribe (or author) have been following the rehearsal/revision process, crossing out passages in the original book, writing additions in the margins, cutting roles here, even adding some there? That would have been a quick way to ruin the original book, the one that carried the licence from the Master of the Revels. It seems more likely that a new prompt-book would have been prepared, and the most efficient way to have prepared a new prompt-book would have been for the actors to say their lines, slowly and from memory, while a scribe listened and copied. Working in this fashion, a scribe would get most of the text right, but he might very well mishear some names and words, and he might introduce garbles. But he would have a record of the revised ordering of the play for purposes of regulating performances backstage. (We venture to suggest that when the problem of 'bad' quartos finally comes to be settled in Shakespeare studies, the breakthrough will be the recognition that the prompt-book for a revision would have come last, *after* the actors knew their revised parts, and sometimes would have been made by dictation by actors who had memorized their text. It is usually assumed that the prompt-book was prepared earlier and that the actors' parts were copied from it.)

We have used the term 'prompt-book' until now, for that is the usual designation among textual scholars. It is not historically sound. The document used for regulating performances was called the 'book of the play', and the figure in charge of that book, whose role was more like that of a modern stage-manager than a modern 'prompter', was the 'book-keeper'. The book-keeper's main task was to make certain that the actors were ready for their entrances and that the necessary properties were on hand. The actor who dried might hope that the book-keeper would prompt him, but he might hope in vain – the book-keeper had other duties to attend to, and he was not well positioned for prompting anyhow. (One of the discoveries made at the new Globe playhouse in Southwark is that prompting is impractical in the configuration of the Elizabethan theatre.[23]) The book-keeper was busy regulating the traffic of the actors and their properties. 'Books of the play' with the careful arrangements for doubling that we have detected behind the printed texts of the Queen's Men would have given the book-keeper what he needed, and if some of the dialogue in some of the books was garbled, that would not have been his first concern. The length of the speeches would have mattered to him more than the content, for length was a matter of timing, and timing was crucial to the backstage arrangements of doubling.

A scribe taking down a play from the dictation of actors would have faced a special problem in regard to doubled roles. He would have listened to the actor, not to the character, and listening to an actor who plays three or four different roles in the same play might lead him to assign the name of the wrong role to a speech. That seems to have happened in *The True Tragedy of Richard III*, scene ix, when a messenger who is said to be 'servant to the Arch-Bishop of Yorke' suddenly gains the speech prefix 'Cates'. There is one good explanation for this mistake. As Greg pointed out in his introduction to the Malone Society Reprint, Catesby and the Messenger must have been doubled roles. Who would have mistaken one for the other? A scribe listening to dictation would have had to think for himself which of an actor's several roles was now being spoken, and it seems virtually certain that he would sometimes get things wrong – Catesby one minute, a Messenger the next. Who else would make this mistake? Playwrights are sometimes thought to have planned for certain combinations of roles for one actor as they wrote. But a playwright would not be very likely to mistake 'Catesby' for 'Messenger' – he would be misunderstanding his own plot to think that Catesby was a servant to the Archbishop. A scribe taking dictation from actors who played several roles, however, would face this confusion as an occupational hazard.

Let us imagine a scribe listening to actors recite their lines at the beginning of *The True Tragedy of Richard III*. This is the scribe who will later mishear 'Lord Marques' as 'Lord Marcus', 'Catesby' as 'Casbie', and will confuse Catesby with the Messenger. The opening scene consists largely of a figure named Truth giving out historical information in the kind of blank verse that is characteristic of the Queen's Men – insistently end-stopped blank verse. This is not hard for a listener to get right – our hypothetical scribe knows to listen for the pause at the end of each line and to supply punctuation at those pauses. Nearly every line in Truth's correctly-lined summary ends with a mark of punctuation (46 of 51 lines).

In the next scene, however, the scribe continues to listen for pauses but the actors are speaking prose. Here is trouble for the scribe – the pauses do not mean what he hears in them. He hears the end of a line, but the actor is only pausing in the syntax of prose. As a result, the scribe writes a blank verse that is not being spoken. Here is how he writes the King's speech beginning at line 82, listening for the pauses, inserting the punctuation to mark the end of the line, and beginning a new line with a capital (these quotations are in the original spelling):

> *King.* Why Nobles, he that laie me here,
> Can raise me at his pleasure.
> But my deare friends and kinsmen,

> In what estate I now lie it is seene to you all,
> And I feele my selfe neare the dreadfull stroke of death:
> And the cause that I have requested you in friendly wise
> To meete togither is this,
> That where malice & envy sowing sedition in the harts of men,
> So would I have that admonished and friendly favours,
> Overcome in the heart of you Lord Marcus and Lord Hastings
> Both, for how I have governed these two and twentie yeares,
> I leave it to your discretions,
> The malice hath still bene an enemy to you both,
> That in my life time I could never get any lege of amity betwixt you,
> Yet at my death let me intreate you to imbrace each other,
> That at my last departure you may send my soule
> To the joyes celestiall:

In the original manuscript, this must have been written as prose and would have looked something like this:

> *King.*   Why, Nobles, he that laie me here can raise me at
> his pleasure. But my deare friends and kinsmen, in
> what estate I now lie it is seene to you all, and I feele
> my selfe neare the dreadfull stroke of death. And the
> cause that I have requested you in friendly wise to
> meete togither is this, that where malice and envy
> sowing sedition in the harts of men, so would I have
> that admonished, and friendly favours overcome in the
> heart of you, Lord Marques and Lord Hastings both. For
> how I have governed these two and twentie yeares I
> leave it to your discretions.

And so on. There is a layer of garbling along with the mislineation, and one cannot be sure whether this comes from the speech of the actor or the mishearing of the scribe. But those are the two likeliest sources of the phenomenon in question. On the printed page, this is mislineation to our eyes, and it may look like incompetence, as though amateurs were hacking about, or pirates were stealing a text. But the prompt-book that resulted from dictation would have been a record of the text – not a perfect record, but serviceable – and the book-keeper could have followed the text during performance. Prose mislined as verse is actually easier to follow than prose itself.

The same phenomenon appears in *Famous Victories*, written in prose throughout but printed with occasional outbursts of false-poetic lineation. Here is an example of the mistaken lineation:

> *Hen. 5.*   Most soveraign Lord, and welbeloved father,
> I came into your chamber to comfort the melancholy

Soule of your bodie, and finding you at that time
Past all recoverie, and dead to my thinking,
God is my witnesse: and what should I doo,
But with weeping tears lament the death of you my father,
And after that, seeing the Crowne, I tooke it:
And tel me my father, who might better take it then I,
After your death? But seeing you live,
I most humbly render it into your Majesties hands,
And the happiest man alive, that my father live:
And live my Lord and Father, for ever.
Hen. 4   Stand up my sonne,
Thine answere hath sounded wel in mine eares,
For I must need confesse that I was in a very sound sleep,
And altogither unmindful of thy comming:
But come neare my sonne,
And let me put thee in possession whilst I live,
That none deprive thee of it after my death.

Here the first line, with its pause after the eleventh syllable, sounds like blank verse, and the scribe sets that pattern into place with a comma and capitalizes the beginning of what he takes to be the next line. But the next 'line' confuses him, for there is no end-stopped pause, so after writing for a hexameter and then some, he goes to a new 'line', which also refuses end-stopping. Finally the next 'line' gives him a pause about where one should fall, so he marks a comma, and is then able to end-stop the remaining 'lines' of the exchange. But the actor was speaking prose all the while.

Our hypothesis is that these two texts, *The True Tragedy of Richard III* and *The Famous Victories of Henry V*, often suspected of being 'bad' quartos, but showing the same casting pattern as the other Queen's Men texts first entered or published in 1594, faithfully record the order of the speeches but carry an extra element of error introduced by transcription from dictation, which, we propose, was one way the company put together a new book when they divided into smaller units. Books created in this fashion would have been imperfect. They would have suffered from aural mistakes, but they would have served their purposes in performance. Perhaps others of the Queen's Men plays were dictated too, for signs of mishearing have been noted in *Old Wives Tale*, *Clyomon and Clamydes*, and *The Troublesome Reign of King John*.[24] These texts do not have lengthy mislineations – perhaps the scribe was better at his business, perhaps the mislineations were caught in the printing house. Possibly, in other words, the relative 'goodness' of the other quartos is not a sign of a different textual origin (author's papers, for example) but of the same textual origin being conducted in a different – i.e. better – fashion.[25]

We do not pretend to be certain. We have the distinct impression that the nine texts from the Queen's Men are like one another in many respects, and that their underlying coherence in regard to casting and doubling makes a theoretical division into 'good' quartos and 'bad' quartos unwarranted. In the next chapter, we will show that some of the conventions of dramaturgy which seem strange to modern readers in plays like *The True Tragedy of Richard III* and *The Famous Victories of Henry V* run through the other texts as well and are to be understood as a kind of playing at which the Queen's Men were specialists. In their possible casting patterns, we find a very strict consistency in groups of texts divided according to the dates when the texts are first recorded in the printing industry. There are abundant mistakes of other kinds in the printed texts, but in the two plays where these are most abundant, we can imagine a reasonable procedure of the playhouse which could give rise to many of the errors, and we see no reason to resort to theories of play-pirates, low-down publishers, dishonest actors, and whatever other reprobates have been summoned to the bar in the annals of 'bad' quarto scholarship.

6

Dramaturgy

Plays on the bookstalls in 1590

Let us look further at what we earlier called the 'defining moment' of 1590, when the stationer Richard Jones published two plays, *Three Lords and Three Ladies of London* from the Queen's Men and Marlowe's *Tamburlaine* from the Admiral's Men. The two titles rest strangely together today: we know that one of them changed English drama while the other virtually disappeared. To a playgoer of 1590 they would have seemed equally interesting, Robert Wilson's lively compendium of the old allegorical devices set beside Marlowe's astonishing study of conquest and the power of the individual will. One would have cared about the contrast between the old and the new without feeling certain that the old was virtually exhausted or the new about to become permanent, and one would have noticed the innovation of seeing plays from the Queen's Men or the Admiral's Men on the bookstalls in the first place. Neither company had published its plays before. These were among the first plays to reach print from the new and large companies that had been thriving and expanding in the permanent playhouses near the city and building their fame with tours throughout the country. These were big, gorgeous plays on the stage – crammed with incidents, dazzling in their costumes, played by the best actors ever seen in London – and now they were in print.

The two plays would have seemed alike in some ways, that is to say. For all its verbal innovation and nerve, *Tamburlaine* is set forth in highly pictorial staging. The hero's change from shepherd's weeds to conquerer's armour, the humiliation of Bajazeth when he must serve as 'footstool' to his adversary, the whipping of Trebizon and Soria in the 'pampered jades of Asia' scene – moments like these give an emblematic quality to the play which puts it in the kind of theatre where *Three Lords and Three Ladies of London* also belonged. The revolutionary content of Marlowe's play is embodied in pictorially controlled forms. The action ranges over a vast geography, but at the centre of all this movement and range stands Tamburlaine's tent, which in its colour symbolism represents the growth of his power in Part 1, and which contains the

reversal of his career when Zenocrate dies there in Part 2.[1] It is the kind of
standing property the Queen's Men found conformable to the conservatism of
their plays. Richard Jones claimed that he removed some comic bits from
Tamburlaine, and these would have made this play look a little more like the
style of the Queen's Men too.

Jones did remove the comic bits, however, and it is hard to imagine this
happening to a play from the Queen's Men, where clowning is at the centre of
the dramaturgy. The sneer against 'rhyming mother wits and such conceits as
clownage keeps in pay' in the prologue to *Tamburlaine* seems aimed at the
Queen's Men, and Marlowe's 'mighty line' is a dominating blank-verse style
which proclaims a basic difference from the dramaturgy the Queen's Men
practised. We will discuss this contrast more fully in the next chapter, but here
are three passages from *Three Lords and Three Ladies* which show Robert
Wilson's style and how far it stood from the style of Marlowe. The passages are
chosen to represent Wilson's style in different kinds of writing – rhymed dialogue, prose, iambic pentameter. One can zero in on the difference from
Marlowe's style by noting the passivity of language in each case – more particularly, the dependence on forms of 'to be' in the verbs, a linguistic passivity
which it is the actor's business to enliven. The first is the lament for Tarlton,
conducted by Simplicity and Wealth as they look at the dead clown's picture:

> *Sim.*   O it was a fine fellow as ere was born,
> There will never come his like while the earth can corn:
> O passing fine Tarlton, I would thou hadst lived yet.
> *Wea.*   He might have some, but thou showest small wit.
> There is no such fineness in the picture that I see.
> *Sim.*   And thou art no Cinque Port man, thou art not wit free,
> The fineness was within, for without he was plain,
> But it was the merriest fellow, and had such jests in store,
> That if thou hadst seen him, thou wouldst have laughed thy heart sore.
>
> (CIV)[2]

The second example comes from one of the many explanations of impresa, in
this case the emblem of the lily,

> whose glory is without comparison, and beauty
> matchless, for Solomon, the most sumptuous king that
> ever was, was never comparable in glory with the Lily,
> neither is there any cities matchable with the pomp of
> London, mistake me not good boys, that this pomp
> tends to pride, yet London hath enough, but my Lord
> pomp doth rightly represent the stately magnificence
> and sumptuous estate without pride or vainglory to

London accommodate, and therefore the word is well
applied to the impresa (*Gloria sans peer*) for that the
Lily is neither proud of the beauty, nor vainglorious of
the pomp . . .

(B3r)

And finally, a description of the approaching Spanish forces:

I need not tell thee, they are poor and proud,
Vaunters, vainglorious, tyrants, truce-breakers,
Envious, ireful, and ambitious,
For thou hast found their facing and their brags,
Their backs, their coffers, and their wealth, their rags,
But let me tell thee what we crave of thee,
To scan with judgement what their leaders be,
To note their presence and observe their grace,
And truly to advertise what they seem . . .

(F4v)

What these passages share – and they are typical of the writing throughout
– is a concentration upon the status of persons and objects. To show things as
they *are* is the fundamental dramatic conception of the plays of the Queen's
Men. Language serves as a gloss upon the visual items of the play, and the
visual items of the play, glossed by necessary words, become the primary means
of revealing a characteristic status. Marlowe's play concerns activity, what characters do rather than what they are, and his language generates a sense of that
activeness at every turn. Compare the final example given above with a speech
of similar purpose – the description of a threatening figure who has not yet
appeared – from the beginning of *Tamburlaine*:

Oft have I heard your majesty complain
Of Tamburlaine, that sturdy Scythian thief,
That robs your merchants of Persepolis,
Treading by land unto the Western Isles,
And in your confines with his lawless train
Daily commits uncivil outrages,
Hoping (misled by dreaming prophecies)
To reign in Asia, and with barbarous arms,
To make himself the monarch of the East.[3]

This is an ordinary passage by a minor character, chosen to show that even
in plain exposition the language takes form from a dramatic conception different
from Wilson's. Something is happening even in the words of Marlowe's play;
the characteristic action of the drama is beginning to occur in the urgency of

those active verbs, pressing the syntax past the trim end-stopping of Wilson's lines to the variability of the verse-paragraph, and the essential status of the described figure, which Wilson could reveal in an emblem and an accompanying comment, cannot be known until the activity of speech and stage imagery accumulate to a sense of an ending.

'Medley' as style

Wilson had his own word for the genre he fancied most: the 'medley'. Thinking about 'medley' acting is the best way to grasp the style of the Queen's Men, and to gain a sense of this style, we would call upon the play that is before us, *Three Lords and Three Ladies of London*. It cannot be thought of as history, tragedy, or comedy – it is medley or it is nothing.

Three Lords and Three Ladies of London is an up-to-date collection of the most topical items for Londoners of the late 1580s. Its one quiet moment is the gentle lament for Tarlton, whose death was recent. Otherwise the play is filled with exuberance, celebrating the victory over the Armada, defending pastimes like playing in the face of puritan opposition, glorifying the rule of Elizabeth, and praising the cosmopolitanism of London over the bumptiousness of provincial towns like Lincoln. All of this is wedged into the framework of an old-fashioned allegory which revives the personifications of Wilson's earlier *Three Ladies of London* (which probably goes back to Leicester's Men). It is a rarity among Queen's Men plays for being so London-centred, although the centralizing theme of the Armada would have played well enough on tour, especially along the south-east and south-west routes. The play can hardly be called forward-looking. It summons the theatrical characteristics of the past and uses them flamboyantly to convey the present news of the day.

The heart of the dramaturgy lies in the interplay between the lowly and the powerful. A 'pleasant and stately moral' is how the title-page of the 1590 edition puts this combination. The stately manner comes from the solemn conduct of the three lords and ladies, along with the abstract figures associated with their affairs; the pleasant manner is provided by the lowly characters – particularly by the clown Simplicity, who (when he is not under a scolding by his wife Painful Penury) must confront the deceptions of Fraud, Usury, Simony, and Dissimulation. As in all of Wilson's medleys, the histrionic interest develops from an alternation between these two modes, so that alongside the stately affairs of the lords and ladies there is always something of plain simplicity or lurking knavery ready to take hold. The solemn marriage between the lords and ladies is attended by Fraud and Dissimulation, dressed for all the world as honest serving-men, and it takes Simplicity to spy them out and attempt to bring them to justice with a comic turn (they escape – they always do). At the beginning of the play, after the lords have placed their shields on the stage as chivalrous challenges, Simplicity enters with *his* impresa, which is a picture of Tarlton, and begins to move the lords' shields: they are blocking the stall from which he tries to wring subsistence by selling ballads. This kind of interplay between the lowly and the exalted lies at the centre of all of the plays of the Queen's Men, and in its reliance upon earlier Tudor acting and visual traditions, it provides as lively an example of a continuing popular tradition as one can find in English drama.

The style of performance is predominantly visual. Attention focuses on objects, costumes, the gestures of actors, and patterns of stage movement; to these elements, spoken language tends to be subordinate. When the three lords of London enter at the beginning, their statements (that each intends to marry one of the three ladies) are less the focus of theatrical attention than the formality of the entrance, the relation of each lord to his page, the costumes, and the heraldic shields which they place in view – all of which can be seen at a glance. The statements of intended marriage are routinely informative, and the suggested conflict over who will marry which lady eventually dissolves without much emphasis. But the shields and costumes are there to be seen and used, exactly the sort of properties on which a dramatist like Wilson lavished his care:

> Enter the three Lords and their pages: First,
> Policy with his page Wit before him, bearing a shield: the
> impresa, a Tortoise, the word, *Providens securus*. Next
> Pomp, with his page Wealth bearing his shield, the
> word, *Gloria sans peer*: the impresa, a Lily. Last,
> Pleasure, his page Will, his impresa, a Falcon, the word,
> *Pour temps*: Policy attired in black, Pomp in rich
> robes, and Pleasure in colours.

Nothing in the text is written with more care. These shields are part of the text of the play. They speak in emblem and word, they represent the authority of the absent three lords for a long stretch of action, and they form the centre of the contest in the climactic Armada scene, where the three Spanish lords have textual shields too, and the battle is marked out by the advance and retreat of these blazons. They are part of a ballet in which England defeats Spain – virtually a dance of herald against herald, page against page, lord against lord – which ends when the Spanish shields can be battered apart and the English held up in triumph.

This concentration upon visual emblems is maintained throughout the play, forming such tableaux as the three ladies, ragged and dirty, seated upon their stones of Care, Remorse, and Charity, or the contrasting scene of the marriage procession of these ladies, gorgeously attired now, and their lords. Parts of these major moments of battle, penance, or marriage are conducted wordlessly, the pageant conveying a full meaning to the eye. That is not to say that the play lacks a fully composed text (we shall consider Wilson's elaborate verse forms in a moment) but that the verbal serves the visual and rarely asserts an intrinsic interest. It requires the visual for its completion, as anyone attempting to read the printed text will quickly know. A great tradition of Tudor showmanship lies behind this play. For generations the festive days of city, town, and court had been highlighted by the kind of pageantry on which *Three Lords and Three Ladies* is founded. Elizabethan amateurs were good at this kind of display, but for the players in the Queen's Men and their predecessors, it was a highly-developed professional skill – which did not translate into the medium of print. *Three Lords and Three Ladies of London* was in trouble the moment it reached the bookstalls.

The acting style required by *Three Lords and Three Ladies* had taken generations to develop. It placed a premium on the sharply etched characteristic that would match up to an allegorical name – the peculiar gesture, the odd inflection, the idiosyncratic bit of costuming, something that says Honest Industry or Fealty at a glance. In *Three Lords and Three Ladies*, the ballad-seller's wife is bent over a little from carrying the water she sells in the streets of London. She has to make up the money her gullible husband loses at selling ballads – not for nothing is he called Simplicity. Her voice is raspy with anxiety, and her clothes are getting ragged. She could some day appear in a novel by George Gissing, but here her name is Painful Penury, and she is played by a boy actor who does not think in terms of social realism and the psychology of the poor. He thinks in terms of the bent-over body and the raspy voice, in order to demonstrate his own name instantly. Names are the one kind of text that ranks with the visual in this play, the allegorical abstraction giving the actor something to aim for in body and voice. The boy in this case would have sought the quick visual sign of an impoverished woman burdened with work, so Penury is bent over to be Painful. That is where Painful Penury comes from first of all, from the boy actor's need to give immediate demonstration to the abstraction.

Let us imagine this boy doubling another female part in *Three Lords and Three Ladies*, for this play has an unusually high number of roles for boys and some doubling is a likelihood. He might well double London, who speaks the prologue and never reappears. London is richly attired, guarded by angels, and proclaiming what the costume and angels have already made clear to the eye, that this city is looked after by God and bears herself with serenity. If the boy comes back as Painful Penury, he will not quite have laid his image as London to rest. Doubling was an expected practice, and in the daylight of Elizabethan staging, one could see it was the same actor. Robert Wilson, a shrewd social commentator, would not have minded the audience's seeing something of Painful Penury follow from this London of divine protection, for he knew that God's business with London was not so advanced as London claims in her prologue. There is no reason to suppose that a primarily visual theatre does not convey complications of this sort – these plays do work around to social realism and the psychology of the poor in the long run. But the first thing the boy actor has to be able to do is to demonstrate Painful Penury at a glance, London at another glance, with the difference between his demonstrations being immediately apparent to the audience, who might also notice the similarity. All actors in this style of performance knew how to double, and all actors knew how to convey Usury, or Pomp, or Love, or Simplicity upon entering – how to render the signs of abstraction in the balance and grace of the trained body. These actors had to be agile and quick. Their style had to encompass the unmistakable characteristics for all the social and moral types the age could recognize, and the Tudor age was abundant in recognized types.

Behind the Queen's Men, in other words, lay a system of acting by brilliant stereotype. They were the largest professional company England had ever known, but there is not a hint that they sought to reduce the system of doubled roles. Instead, as we have seen, their texts continue to be designed according to the doubling system, and the doubling system is congruent with the allegorical dramaturgy of a play like *Three Lords and Three Ladies*. The unmistakable sign is crucial to this system – the gesture no eye can misread, the accent no ear can misunderstand. Tudor actors sometimes doubled a half-dozen parts in a single play, and their repertory of standard techniques for playing a character type must have been extensive, their artistry at the quick-change superb.

Like the visual concentration, this traditional acting style creates its effects in the absence of an intrinsically interesting text. The real interest of the style lies in the way the stock gestures and routines are offered to the audience as old things newly found and worth sharing. The playmaker's business is to set up the situation for the performer to exploit. And when the situation itself promises nothing, the actor must resort to the solo devices which had sustained Tudor performers for generations, making an unreadable jest amusing, turning a silly ditty into a song, drawing pathos from routine sentimentality. Frequenters of vaudeville or the music hall know these things well. When Simplicity asks a member of the audience to judge his singing contest with another character, he is not violating the decorum of the scene; he is acknowledging his role as a performer before spectators, making explicit the histrionic assumption that runs throughout this play about London presented to Londoners, English victory presented to Englishmen, with the queen's own men doing the presentation.

Literalism of the theatre

This visually-oriented style of acting runs through all of the Queen's Men published plays. It can be called a 'literalism of the theatre' in order to set it apart from the plays of Shakespeare, Marlowe, and Kyd, which selected some elements of literalism, transformed them by means of an astonishing advance in dramatic poetry, and eventually marginalized the older style (although it makes prominent returns, as in silent film). Theatrical literalism assumes that the real language of showmanship is objective and visual. It consists of the figures and costumes of the actors, the objects they handle, and the properties and structures which frame their acting space. The clown is a literalist of the theatre. He is funny the minute he is seen, and he builds his role by visual gags and routines. He is the object-ridden man, the man whose identity is more readily apparent in his over-size shoes and baggy trousers, or his bulbous nose and reddened eyes, than they are in the language he speaks. There is always room for clowning in the plays of the Queen's Men, and when the picture of their most famous actor was shown in *Three Lords and Three Ladies*, the audience would have found it as familiar as the image of Chaplin is today. The first thing spectators remembered about Tarlton was his flat-nosed face and his props: the pipe and tabor with which he was pictured, the sword and longstaff with which he fought hilariously against the queen's little dog. Tarlton could make you laugh by peeping out from behind a curtain, nothing more than that. And he was famous for extemporal rhymes, a sort of anti-poetry improvised on 'themes' called out from the audience after the play ended. Tarlton actually wrote poetry and plays, but the stance of the clown is to toss these things off as doggerel, while others bite their pens and tell themselves to look in their hearts and write. The clown's rhymes turn poetry into a joke against itself:

> Sith verse and I so different are,
> I'll press in ragged rhyme
> To manifest the more goodwill
> That I to learning owe,
> No painted words but perfect deeds
> Shall my invention show.[4]

Tarlton was the most famous clown of his day, but the Queen's Men also had Adams, Wilson, Singer, Garland, Lanham – all of them known for their comic acting, jigs, and improvisations. Their plays bring the clown into any situation. Into the midst of the Turkish tribulations of *Selimus* – just after the most pathetic scene, where the royal father is poisoned by his son – there trots one Bullithrumble, an English shepherd who has slipped away from his shrewish wife and seventeen children long enough to enjoy a snack in the (Persian) countryside. The Tarlton tradition of turning language to comic gesture is alive in Bullithrumble. When his wife beats him, he is

> fain to run through a whole Alphabet of faces: now at
> the last, seeing she was so cramuk with me, I began to
> swear all the criss-cross row over, beginning at a
> great A, little a, til I came to w, x, y.

(HIV)

He is like Miles in *Friar Bacon and Friar Bungay*, who turns his master's Latin phrases into bawdy jokes and cannot fathom the significance of the Brazen Head's seven words. The clown is a stranger to deep language, and in the Queen's Men he makes his way by running, darting, slipping away: 'Enter Bullithrumble, the shepherd, running in haste, and laughing to himself.' 'Enter Derick, roaming' (*Famous Victories*). 'Enter Subtle Shift, running' (*Clyomon and Clamydes*). 'Exeunt all, but Bullithrumble stealing from them closely away' (*Selimus* again). How the clown moves across the stage is as important as what he says.

The pure form of literalist theatre, however, is the pantomime, and there are stretches of pantomime in nearly every play of the Queen's Men. Battle scenes are a case in point. One entire scene in *The Famous Victories* consists of the stage direction 'the Battle enters' – the 'Battle' suggesting the degree of autonomy such scenes had attained. Much the same thing happens in *The True Tragedy of Richard III*: 'The battle enters, Richard wounded, with his Page' (line 1984). 'The battle enters' must be the shorthand description for the staging of the fight in which Richard is wounded, but because the scene is wordless, the wounding is not conveyed in the text: the entrance direction's 'Richard wounded' names what will happen during the wordless battle. Then the wounded Richard does speak – he cries for a fresh horse and defies his fate – but this speech ends with his exit. Why should he exit when the next scene has him fighting against Richmond? 'Enters Richmond to battle again, and kills Richard.' The action seems strangely segmented, with wordless battles set apart from moments of speech, as though the battles were thought of as having a text of their own. We suggest that this is exactly how the Queen's Men thought of battle scenes. There is little sign in their extant repertory of the experiments that were being tried in Shakespeare's plays on Henry VI, where battle scenes ebb and flow with full-fledged dialogue among the contenders. Only in *Selimus*, scenes vi and vii, does the rhetoric of battle and loss combine with the staging of battle scenes themselves among the plays of the Queen's Men. There is also a parody of a battle scene in *The Famous Victories*, where the clown and a French soldier have enough patter to set up a joke with a sword.

We must remember that these were the plays that were published and therefore probably no longer played — they were outdated by that time.

THE QUEEN'S MEN AND THEIR PLAYS

But the serious battles tend to be wordless. Some readers have probably taken stage directions like 'enter the battle' as signs of 'corruption', further evidence of 'bad' quartos, on grounds that a 'pirate' or a minor actor could not remember the lines at this point. The pirate cannot remember, according to this view, and in exasperation says 'Enter the battle.' But this is the way the Queen's Men worked out their battle scenes, by pantomime and wordlessness. *The Troublesome Reign of King John* has wordless battles at the beginning of scenes iii and viii. Of course some think that a 'bad' quarto too. Bad quartos are all around us. *Three Lords and Three Ladies of London* has never, to our knowledge, been called a 'bad' quarto. Here is how the decisive battle is won there: 'Let the Three Lords press towards the Spaniards, and the Spaniards make show of coming forward and suddenly depart.' Not a word.

That is not to suggest that the ballet-like battle of Wilson's play was repeated in the other plays. We doubt if 'the battles' called for in the plays on John, Henry V, or Richard III were dance-like. All of the Elizabethan companies were driving toward realism in the staging of history plays by the time these texts were published, and we assume that the Queen's Men depended on the same combination of fencing and acrobatic prowess that Shakespeare and Marlowe obviously counted on to create the illusion of real fighting. But Shakespeare and Marlowe were also trying to penetrate the visual sensationalism of the battle scene with a rhetorical analogue, and the Queen's Men for the most part were not. The dance-like battle scenes of *Three Lords and Three Ladies of London* are stylistically different from the wordless battles of the history plays, but the entire group has a consistent theatrical attitude behind it: battles for the Queen's Men have a language of their own, a language of bodies in contest, and it is the literalist theatre's business to let that language be witnessed by itself.

Another form of mime which the Queen's Men obviously specialized in was the procession. The same care that Robert Wilson lavished upon impresa, costumes, and properties throughout his plays can be seen at the end of Greene's *Friar Bacon*:

> Enter the Emperor with a pointless sword; next the
> King of Castile, carrying a sword with a point; Lacy,
> carrying the globe; Edward; Warren, carrying a rod of
> gold with a dove on it; Ermsby, with a crown and
> sceptre; Elinor, with the Fair Maid of Fressingfield on
> her left hand; Henry; Bacon, with other lords attending.

(11r)

This is not an easy piece of writing. It requires working through a host of details about staging and it requires confidence that the company involved knows how to bring off the pompous and swollen scene. Greene and Wilson knew, we submit, that the Queen's Men were specialists in that kind of theatrical literalism, and so did the anonymous authors of most of their extant plays, although they did not always write out the detailed processional stage directions. Both *Selimus* and *The True Tragedy of Richard III* have scenes which begin with processions which are instantly dismissed. These seem very peculiar in the text. Here is the *Selimus* example:

> *Enter Bajazeth, Emperor of Turkey, Mustapha,*
> *Cherseoly, and the Janizaries.*
> *Baj.* Leave me my Lords until I call you forth,
> For I am heavy and disconsolate.
> *Exeunt all but Bajazeth.*

> (A3r)

This is a strange way to get a character alone on a stage, but we should realize that the economy of the Queen's Men was not best served by getting directly to the important speech. The procession is a speech too, and it is the kind of speech in which the Queen's Men were eloquent.

The real challenge for readers of these plays from the Queen's Men is to see that the unwritten text of mime, fairly obvious in the wordless scenes, also runs alongside the spoken text too. The dialogue of these plays often seems naïve and abrupt until one realizes that its sense, and even its sophistication, is completed by the accompanying visual action. *The True Tragedy of Richard III* is as nearly unreadable a play as one can find from the Elizabethan drama if one expects the dialogue to tell its own story, and Shakespeare made a joke out of one of its more bizarre lines (see *Hamlet*, III.ii.254, 'the croaking raven doth bellow for revenge'). Its style is lost to us today unless we picture the visual literalism of the dramaturgy. One scene is pure pantomime: '*Enters mother Queen and her daughter, and her son, to sanctuary.*' That is the entire scene. Some emblematic sign of church sanctuary has been established on the stage, its purpose being made clear by the reception of the Queen and her children into it. It is supposed to be a place of safety. The point is to show how easily and repeatedly the forces of Richard's tyranny can enter and occupy the places of safety. Two scenes later the Queen and her children reappear in the sanctuary space and are visited by the Archbishop, who pretends not even to know that sanctuary is involved. While he ever so kindly tries to 'persuade' the Queen to give her young son to him, an ambush of Richard's noblemen is gathering on the edges of the sanctuary space. No stage direction reveals this silent ambush, but it is clearly in place and visible by the time the Archbishop changes his tone and says: 'see, the ambushed nobles are at hand to take the Prince away from you by force, if you will not by fair means let him go' (lines

869–71). In a moment, the young Duke of York is in the hands of Richard's agents.

This motif of penetrating safe places is repeated in a later scene involving pantomime – the arrest of Hastings in the council chamber. Again the pantomime is not noted in the text, and readers must visualize the silent action which accompanies this text:

> Page   . . . Now there is court held today by diverse of
> the Council, which I fear me will cost the Lord
> Hastings and the Lord Stanley their best caps: for my
> Lord hath willed me to get half a dozen ruffians in
> readiness, and when he knocks with his fist upon the
> board, they to rush in, and to cry treason, treason,
> and to lay hands upon the Lord Hastings, and the Lord
> Stanley, which for fear I should let slip, I will give
> my diligent attendance.
> *Enter Richard, Catesby, and others, pulling*
> *Lord Hastings.*
>
> (lines 934–42)

Obviously the plan the Page reveals to the audience has already occurred when Hastings is haled onstage at the end of the speech. What the text does not make clear – because the action is wordless – is that each item of the plan is enacted as the Page names it, so that his narration is co-ordinated with a mime of the ruffians gathering onstage, hearing their signal and breaking into the Court (offstage), and then re-entering (as 'others') with Hastings in their grasp. The staging suggests the slickness of Richard's machinery. Committing the act is no more difficult than the Page's naming of it, and there is no delay. The well-oiled machine works quietly, and there is no place it cannot reach.

All theatre contains an element of visual literalism, of course. The Queen's Men made it their foremost technique. To dramatize the 'five moons' episode that attends the second coronation of King John, the Queen's Men manufactured from their array of visual devices the five moons themselves – 'there the five moons appear' (line 1583). To be theatrically literal, one makes the obvious idea visibly unmistakable, and thus precludes misunderstanding and subtlety at a stroke. When Prince Hal visits his father in *The Famous Victories of Henry V*, he wears a cloak crammed with needles, as 'a sign that I stand upon thorns, till the crown be on my head' (lines 487–8), and he carries a dagger as though he might kill the king: 'for the breath shall be no sooner out of his mouth but I will clap the crown on my head' (lines 479–80). It is bold and unimaginative characterization to present England's hero as absolutely base, and when his transformation comes there is no fussing over careful language and psychological shadings. It is sudden and complete: 'even this day I am new born again' (line 581).[5] Literalist staging softens no edges: it is capable of maintaining a stark melodramatic effect, as when the would-be murderer in *King Leir* stands between his two intended victims, quaking at the thought of hell-fire, the thunder rumbling behind him, and lets the daggers fall from his hands one by one; and it is capable of toppling into the bathos of the repeated kneelings in the reconciliation scene of the same play.

This organization of important effects around visual emblems in the Queen's history plays is joined by other routines of literalist theatre. The wordless battle scenes in *The Famous Victories* and *The Troublesome Reign of King John*, the pantomime of the Queen Mother's retreat to sanctuary in *The True Tragedy of Richard III* (scene vii) or of the king's second coronation in *The Troublesome Reign* (scene xiii) come from the same theatrical conception as the Armada scene in *Three Lords and Three Ladies*, although the manner would be less choreographical. The rhymed clowning of the friars and nuns in *The Trouble-some Reign*, the knockabout fussiness of the drunken watchmen in *King Leir*, and the unexpected appearance of a beshrewed Cotswold rustic in *Selimus* (the one non-English historical play extant from the Queen's Men) remind us that the Tarlton tradition lingered in the later plays of the company. Indeed, the interplay of stately and comic elements, central to the dramaturgy of Wilson's medleys, is the principal organizing device of *The Famous Victories*. When Derick and John Cobbler enter hard upon the scene in which the Prince strikes the Chief Justice and enact a comic version of the same thing, the clown's roles are being turned to exactly the parodic gesture employed in *Friar Bacon and Friar Bungay*, where Rafe Simnell the Fool impersonates Prince Edward, and Miles the poor scholar mimics his scientific master (see scene vii). In short, when one thinks of the dramaturgy of the Queen's Men history plays, one is reminded of the dramaturgy of the rest of their repertory. That is how they 'came upon' the English history play – with the same sense of style by which they did all their plays.[6]

Narrative overdetermination

We have noted that the Queen's Men were displaying the 'truth' in their his-tory plays, and that their emphasis on such plainness, set against something more ornamental called 'poetry', or 'forged tragedy', was a function of the purposes they served in the Protestant politics of the 1580s. There is something to be added about their conception of 'truth' in their chronicle plays. An anxi-ety for narrative completeness runs through their plays, at times contradicting the visual design of their staging and insisting on a kind of plotting that it is hard to call sophisticated. It is as though the absence of an intrinsic interest in dramatic poetry created a vacuum which was normally filled with the brilliant stagecraft of literalist theatre, but was sometimes filled with a surplus of narrative explanation. It should be added that the exception to this generalization is Greene's *Friar Bacon and Friar Bungay*, which uses all the devices of literalist theatre but also joins these to what is unusual in the Queen's Men plays, a fully articulated blank-verse style, and a willingness to let metaphorical statement take the place of narrative explanation. More will be said about this trait below.

The climactic speech in *King Leir*, occurring at the centre of the reconciliation scene between father and daughter, is Leir's forty-line recapitulation of the plot, every bit of it having been witnessed by the audience earlier. This tale is intended to bring tears to the eyes of Cordella, but she is already weeping before the speech begins. This is a dead scene, and no one would know it more sharply than the boy actor playing Cordella, who has nothing to do during Leir's recapitulation but go on weeping. When Leir finishes his recapitulation, Cordella reveals her true identity (she has been in disguise), and they argue over who should kneel to the other. The well has run dry for the Queen's Men at this point, but the motive to tell the story plainly, and to tell it again, and to tell it so that no one can possibly miss it – this motive runs through many of their plays and fits naïvely into their conception of truth and plainness.

It also affects the logic of their historical plots. The requirement for narrative completeness can lead, as it does in the flurries of short scenes which make up much of *The Famous Victories of Henry V*, to the effect of referring to an incident instead of dramatizing it. Some have thought *Famous Victories* a 'pirated' text because of this phenomenon, but the chronicle plays of the Queen's Men often run into patches of short scenes which fill in the plot in a pedestrian way. *Selimus*, a history play on a non-English subject, is a case in point. The prologue disavows 'forged tragedy' in favour of what has been acknowledged 'true', and then proceeds to offer some thirty scenes of chronicle piece-work about dynastic warfare in post-Tamburlaine Turkey. The play has brilliance when one realizes it is *about* Tamburlaine's style (we will discuss this in the next chapter, in reference to Marlowe), but its achievement is not related to its chronicle plotting, which is both naïve and thorough-going. The incidents of the play are joined together by nothing more than a pattern of prediction, in which nearly every scene concludes with an announcement of action to follow, followed by, sure enough, that action at the beginning of the next scene. When at the end of scene xxiii a messenger is sent to warn Aladin and Amurath of approaching danger, scene xxiv is bound to show Aladin and Amurath being warned, although they have no other role in the play. This is the 'see, my lord, where he comes' phenomenon, where my lord asks where is X who was sent to Y to learn Z, and upon someone saying 'see, my lord, where he comes', X arrives from Y to report Z. This routine can be seen most clearly in *True*

Tragedy of Richard III, lines 1570 ff., throughout *Three Lords and Three Ladies of London*, frequently in *Selimus*, and always in *Clyomon and Clamydes*. There is a narrative overdetermination about the plotting of these plays which is consistent and which has sometimes been misunderstood as one of the textual anomalies thought to lie behind 'bad' quartos. It is not a textual anomaly. It is the Queen's Men telling the 'truth' at their worst.

At their best, they were engaged in what modern criticism calls 'double plots'. In *Some Versions of Pastoral*, William Empson praised *Friar Bacon and Friar Bungay* for having one of the earliest 'double plots' in Elizabethan drama and for being the progenitor of more significant examples in *King Lear* and other later plays. This is actually a misnomer for *Friar Bacon*, which does not have a 'double plot'. *Friar Bacon* is like other plays from the Queen's Men in having multiple 'strands' of plot woven together. This is the 'medley' style of narration at its finest: *Old Wives Tale* has five or six strands (six including the frame story), *Three Lords and Three Ladies of London* has four, *Clyomon and Clamydes* has at least two (the Clyomon–Neronis romance and the Clamydes–Juliana romance, but each romance proliferates with other narrative elements), and *Friar Bacon* has three. It is simply not true that *Friar Bacon* has a new kind of plot. It is an old kind, which comes from the 'medley' style of mixing elements together.

The history play does present a problem to the 'medley' style, however, in that one strand must necessarily bear the weight of dynastic chronicle. This is the problem the Queen's Men solved by resorting to narrative overdetermination: the operating principle seems to have been that if there is a story to tell, just tell it – and tell it so as to save time for the other strands of literalist theatre, especially for the clowning strands. Their history plays always make room for comic strands to run alongside dynastic strands. *Famous Victories of Henry V* is the most interesting example. Its clowning scenes become a parody on the heroic scenes they follow and imitate, with the heroic scenes being weakened by the tendency toward narrative overdetermination and the clowning scenes being strengthened by the comic conventions in which Tarlton and his fellows were expert. It is not a pious play. It shakes loose from the element of Tudor apologia which runs through the Queen's Men repertory, and raises questions about the 'famous victories' which its narrative strand wants to set forth. Shakespeare knew this play well when he wrote his series of three plays on the same material. You betcha!

But piety usually prevails in this repertory. The narrative that counts most for the Queen's Men is the narrative that culminates in their patroness. Their other English history plays seek the concluding prediction of the lineage that will follow from the troublesome reign or the true tragedy we have just seen. *The Troublesome Reign of King John* loses contact with the interesting characterization of the king, whose potentially tragic recognition of his own failure in resisting Rome is deflected to the pious prediction that Henry VIII will emerge to win the battle: 'But in thy seat, if I may guess at all, / A King shall reign that shall suppress them all.' The inertia of such an ending can be appalling. The final seventy lines of *The True Tragedy of Richard III* give us, 'as writers truly say', a potted history of the English monarchs from Henry VII ('who was for wit compared to Salomon, / his government was vertuous every way, / and God did wonderously increase his store, / he did subdue a proud rebellious Lord, / that did encounter him upon black heath' *etc.* – nine lines in all), Henry VIII (eleven lines), Edward VI (five lines), Mary (no details here! – three lines), and then thirty-two lines on Elizabeth, breaking out into rhymed couplets, including the astonishing 'Then England kneel upon thy hairy knee, / And thank that God that still provides for thee.'

Friar Bacon and Friar Bungay brightens the genealogical picture. It is an English history play too, in the company's method of twining together chronicle material, countryside romances, and clowning elements, and its ending is a masterly combination of two of the strands, the romance and the chronicle. Bacon's mystical speech about the horticulture of 'Diana's rose' celebrates the lineage of Elizabeth from a magician's point of view, but it is also (the point does not seem to be noticed often) the concluding reversal of the romance action. The plot has passed through twin crises involving Margaret and Bacon, for the one has vowed to spurn her beauty and enter a convent, while the other has vowed to spurn his magic in favour of 'pure devotion'. Beauty and magic, rightly understood and employed, are the chief qualities of all romantic comedies. Friar Bacon's necromancy has been the wrong sort of magic, and his recognition scene is posed as a deliberate reaction to *Dr Faustus* – Bacon will repent, accept mercy, recognize the blood of Christ, all of this being a reversal of Faustus's despairing final soliloquy. But it is flatly impossible for him to spend the rest of his life praying to God, just as it is impossible for Margaret to enter the nunnery. Each considers an ascetic withdrawal and each comes back to the world of romance. So Margaret undergoes a change of heart, agrees to marry her lord after all, and brings the charm of her beauty into the concluding court scene. Bacon's mystical speech is the counterpart to Margaret's decision, for he shows that he has not abjured his magical power but has turned it to such beneficial uses as the prophecy about the growth of the Tudor dynasty. The restoration of beauty and magic to the romantic world of the play is complete with Bacon's speech, and the celebration of Queen Elizabeth belongs to this concluding reversal.

In comparing the ending of *The True Tragedy of Richard III*, with its hapless narrative device of telling the 'true' facts about Elizabeth's lineage, to the ending of *Friar Bacon*, with its lush metaphorical rendering of the same material as the resolving gesture of the romantic plot, we are observing the nadir and zenith of narrative overdetermination in the Queen's Men. Yet neither example contains the most vivid element of the company's style, the visual realization of a scene. Greene's ending for *Friar Bacon* is an exception to the company's normal style: the metaphorical elaboration of the garden imagery contradicts the plain utility of most of their verse. The literalism of the theatre gives way to poetic drama in the ending of *Friar Bacon*, and one senses that although in this case the Queen's Men are far removed from foolish writing about England's hairy knee, they are also engaged in a lushness of dramatic speech which is not their true element. There are wonderful scenes for the clowns of the company earlier in *Friar Bacon*, but Miles has been carried off to Hell by the end (willingly – he will be a tapster there, where men are really thirsty), and Rafe Simnell has no part in the final scene either. It is a complex moment in the plays of the Queen's Men, for it is not quite typical of their style. It does combine the romance strand with the dynastic strand of 'medley' drama, but the most obvious literalists of the theatre, the comics, have disappeared, and the climax is given over to a big rhetorical moment for the leading actor.

More typical are moments where theatrical literalism and narrative overdetermination work together. The scene from *The True Tragedy of Richard III* in which the Page announces the arrest of Lord Hastings as it is pantomimed before our eyes combines these traits, the Page's narration predicting what is *already* happening. Tyranny can be thought of as the firstlings of a ruler's thought becoming the firstlings of his hand, but here the tyranny is more systematic. A Page can tell us that the king will do what the king is already seen to be doing – the firstlings of a boy's thought are the firstlings of the tyrant's hand. The two Jane Shore scenes in the same play form another expert combination of the narrative and visual elements. In the second scene, the three men who earlier promised aid to the wretched mistress of Edward IV find they must spurn her pleas, because the king has decreed that none may help her. As the three men enter one after another, there is a 'see where he comes' feel to the arrangement, and each man comes bearing bits of narrative information: the king's consolidation of power, the imprisoning of the Princes, and the rebellion of Buckingham. But in this case the narrative information comes to bear on the visual image of the king's tyranny, Jane Shore herself, her rich garments of the earlier episode now turned to rags, her former beauty now covered with grime. (Turning women from rags to riches, or vice versa, is a common routine with the Queen's Men: it happens to the three ladies in *Three Lords and Three Ladies of London*, and Cordella, by her choice, in *King Leir*, in addition to Jane Shore.) The staging exactly repeats the pattern of the earlier Jane Shore scene, and the emblematic formality of this device recalls the tradition of interlude playing which the Queen's Men carried forward. The bits of narrative, however, show that the frightened woman is the visualization of a frightened realm. This is the literalism of the theatre at its best: provocative, obvious, demonstrative, and anti-authoritarian. Brecht could have written it.

The ultimate narrative overdetermination is to have the theatre tell a 'tale'. *The Old Wives Tale* attains its beauty by blending narrative into dramatization, instead of setting up a frame and then staging a play. The old wife's tale, as the two pages listen to it at the beginning, is a fumbling effort until the magic moment when the theatre makes its move: actors take on the narrative and act it out. The old wife and the two pages are part of this scene even if they merely remain as though they were telling and listening, but they also can take up roles here and there without violating convention. Madge's line at the end, 'When this was done, I took a piece of bread and cheese, and came my way', indicates that in some way, perhaps in her imagination, perhaps in her doubling a role (the Hostess?), she was involved in the acting of the tale.[7] This integration of narrative theatre and visual theatre, each an old-fashioned speciality of the Queen's Men, seems up-to-date wherever it is staged. It is the only one of the Queen's Men plays to be performed as anything other than an oddity today, and to the extent it depends on the blending of narrative and drama, its success follows from the staple elements of that company's dramaturgy.[8]

Staging

The Old Wives Tale is the company's most scenic play as well – the one which most fully uses emblems and properties to identify the locations of the play. The action moves among four places: a cross, a well, Sacrapant's study, and a hill with a light hidden behind removable turf. This system of staging uses emblematic props or 'houses' to indicate the locations, and because the scenic indicators remain in view throughout the action, this has sometimes been called 'simultaneous staging'. The emblematic nature of the scenic properties must be kept in mind. These are not so much acting spaces as indicators of location (although the study in *The Old Wives Tale* is ample enough for Delia to be revealed behind curtains at line 881). By keeping the locations visible and within easy reach of one another, simultaneous staging implies a containable and organized world. It was perhaps for this reason that simultaneous staging was customary at court and at other institutions of authority, where the monarch might attend and be given her special seat in an auditorium which was also carefully organized. The Queen's Men were masters of the court schedule in their early years, and (help on the settings coming from the Revels office, where new canvas 'houses' could be built and old ones pulled from storage) they must have performed many plays on the simultaneous system evident in *The Old*

Wives Tale. Three Lords and Three Ladies of London, with its stall for Simplicity and its stones of Remorse, Charity, and Care for the three ladies, also contains its action in one stage space marked out with different properties. The reference to the 'post' in *Three Lords and Three Ladies* (13v), where Fraud is bound to one post while Simplicity does violence to 'the contrary post', suggests that a permanent London theatre is assumed in this text.[9]

The usual system of staging for the Queen's Men, however, was the less decorative kind of platform acting which assumes a change of location with each clearing of the stage (Chambers called this 'successive' staging to set it off from 'simultaneous' staging). This system requires little by way of special acting areas or scenic indicators, and it travels well. For the most part, the staging avoids using structural features of the playhouse. Only in the 'city walls' scene of *The Troublesome Reign of King John* is a raised gallery (of the kind shown to the rear of the Swan drawing) called upon. Trap doors and descent machinery would be good to have in plays involving magic – *Friar Bacon, Old Wives Tale,* and *Clyomon and Clamydes* – but where special effects are called for, the directions avoid specifying the method of staging. The company's flexibility in dealing with a variety of stage conditions is the indispensable element of their plays. 'The tree appears with the dragon shooting fire' (*Friar Bacon,* E4r) leaves unanswered the question of whether the tree rises from a trap, is revealed behind curtains, or is rolled out from a stage door – probably because any of those manoeuvres might have been used in one venue or another. 'Descend Providence' in *Clyomon and Clamydes* (line 1549) suggests elaborate 'descent' machinery, but in fact Providence can descend a flight of stairs if that is what is available.

The one element of their staging which requires a free-standing scenic property is the curtained space, or 'study' (as it seems to have been known generically in the Elizabethan theatre). The magician plays did have this – a curtained cell is specified for the sorcerer in *Old Wives Tale* and for Friar Bacon's cell in *Friar Bacon and Friar Bungay.* There is no reason for thinking this to have been a structural element in the playhouse. A curtained pavilion or 'canopy' (to use the Elizabethan term) was carried on royal progresses from time to time, and the players could have used a similar portable device. It would have worked wonders for the Queen's Men as they moved from town to town in the provinces, or from one stage to another in London. A 'canopy' of virtually any size placed on stage opens up possibilities for designating part of the stage for special purposes, and these were not limited to the magicians' cells. Even in the normal convention of successive staging, the Queen's Men employed touches of simultaneous setting, and the 'canopy' which served for the magicians' cells would have served other kinds of scenes as well. In *The Famous Victories of Henry V,* the scene of Prince Hal's visit to his father divides the stage into a royal chamber and an ante-room where Hal and his reprobate companions draw aside (line 507). Thus, although Hal is already onstage, he is given a separate entrance direction when he approaches his father – that is, when he moves from the ante-room to the royal chamber where his father awaits him. A curtained enclosure of the kind useful in *Friar Bacon and Friar Bungay* – large enough to hold a bed in each play, for example – would serve to divide the royal chamber from the rest of the stage, although simpler ways of dividing space would serve well enough.[10]

What must be realized is that the royal space remains in view for some time after the first father–son interview. Hal returns to the chamber in the 'stolen-crown' episode (the King's bed now is added to the space for the royal chamber). A few minutes later, when Hal has become King, his coronation procession through the streets of London moves directly into an area where the Archbishop delivers his Salic Law interpretation, and this must be visualized as a return to the royal space, now occupied by the new King and a throne now replacing the old King's sick-bed as a sign of the realm's new vitality. Without visualizing this return to the royal space, readers of the play must suppose that the Archbishop's interpretation of Henry's right to invade France occurs in the middle of a London street where the King rejects his former cronies. This apparent absurdity causes readers to throw up their hands and declare the text a 'bad' quarto, but if the visual emphasis of the Queen's Men plays is kept in mind and if it is recognized that the procession crosses to the throne at line 756, then the theatrical normality of the text can be grasped. Viewers of the play would immediately understand the move from the streets (a procession across the platform stage) to the throne, but readers are bound to be lost for a moment in the absence of stage directions. Processions were a major routine in the repertory of the Queen's Men, and one should be imagined here, crossing the open stage to the throne-space.

A similar touch of simultaneous staging occurs in *The True Tragedy of Richard III*. The silent procession of the Queen and her children to sanctuary requires some part of the stage to be marked with religious symbolism, so the audience can see that they are seeking the protection of the church. In this case the stage direction – 'Enters the mother Queen, and her daughter, and her sonn, to sanctuary' (line 585) – makes a gesture in the direction of the reader. In the theatre, the emblem which stands for the sanctuary space must remain in view for several scenes. When the Archbishop speaks to the Queen two scenes later, it must be clear that this encounter takes place in the sanctuary. The Archbishop lets this space be invaded by Richard's men while he is speaking to the Queen, and covers up by pretending not to know why she is there: 'Madam, have you taken Sanctuary?' The terror of the scene depends on its being staged in a space marked out for 'sanctuary'.

Later in the play, the young Princes are being kept 'safe' too – in the Tower. This could well have been the same stage space that stood for 'sanctuary' earlier, the safe space of the church being no different from the safe space of the Tower when it comes to the reign of tyranny. The children 'walk up' to their Tower bedroom at line 1289, so the 'safe' space appears to have been raised and accessible from the platform, as the murderers demonstrate a moment later (line 1306) when they invade the bedroom and kill the children.

Friar Bacon and Friar Bungay carries simultaneous staging a step further by making it part of the plot. Most scenes proceed in the successive mode, but all the scenes take place in one of three locations: Fressingfield, Oxford, and court. The Oxford scenes centre on Friar Bacon's cell or study, which uses the kind of curtained pavilion or 'canopy' which is also implied in the several royal-chamber scenes in *The Famous Victories of Henry V*. (Friar Bacon's study has its own stage post against which Miles knocks his head, suggesting that the curtains referred to are for a free-standing curtained structure rather than for Bacon's bed.) The goings-on in Bacon's cell are a parody of court power, an idea spelt out by Bacon himself in scene v, when Prince Edward pays him a visit:

> Now frolic Edward, welcome to my Cell,
> Here tempers Friar Bacon many toys:
> And holds this place his consistory court,
> Wherein the devil pleads homage to his words.
>
> (lines 634–7)

He then sets up a sort of early television set, which allows those in the cell to see what is happening in Fressingfield. Since what is happening in Fressingfield is acted out on another part of the stage, the conventions of simultaneous setting are being put into action as a product of Bacon's magic.

This is the wrong way to unite the parts of England, according to this play. The second time Bacon sets up his magic glass, two sons in Bacon's Oxford cell see their fathers killing one another in Fressingfield. So the sons in the cell kill each other too. These multiple deaths cause Bacon to abjure his magic, and lead to the proper display of unification, which occurs at the real court, when fair Margaret of Fressingfield arrives on the arm of Lord Lacy and Prince Edward marries Elinor of Castile. The staging of this final scene could well turn the curtained space of Bacon's cell into a sort of canopy-space for the throne, showing that the place of the false power has turned into the place of the true. We are, of course, imagining some of these details, but the basic device of using simultaneous staging as a plot element is unmistakable.

In other words, simultaneous staging carried over occasionally into the normal successive mode employed by the Queen's Men. A broader point about this kind of stagecraft should be kept in mind. In both the successive and the simultaneous modes, the dramaturgy of the Queen's Men focuses on key visual events and images. The literalism of the theatre works this way, whether it be the pantomime battle scene, the processions which seem to exist for their own sake, or the organization of major scenes around a scenic emblem. *The Troublesome Reign of King John* uses the successive mode, but much of its meaning comes from an interplay among three emblematically focused scenes: the second coronation of John, the oath-taking of the barons at St Edmundsbury, and the concluding scene at Swinstead Abbey. (Shakespeare's *King John* omits all three scenes, as though to insist upon a different kind of dramaturgy.) Each of the three scenes is focused by a stage property: the throne for the second coronation, the altar at St Edmundsbury for the baronial swearing scene, and the banquet-table set up in the orchard for what will be John's death scene. These are not just useful properties. They carry a visual significance which is the hallmark of the style and dramatic ideology of the company.

The altar at St Edmundsbury is obviously a symbol of Catholic perfidy, and to dramatize the laying on of hands and swearing allegiance to the Pope is a stark piece of theatre. About a dozen barons are named in the stage directions and dialogue – the hired men are being called upon to fill the stage. These barons of the realm, muffled in pilgrims' outfits and pledging their obedience to a Catholic power which has nothing but death in mind for them eventually, are well on their way to proving fools.[11]

But in one way they are right. It is part of this play's sophistication to insist that John *is* a tyrant, or rather passes through a stage of tyranny before he comes to recognize his limits, and his tyranny is shown to be a reflection of the Pope's. To suppose that this play presents John simply as a Protestant martyr in a piece of anti-Catholic propaganda is to miss its most interesting point. The altar upon which the barons lay hands in allegiance to the Pope is a replacement for the throne which was the focal property for John's second coronation (Part One, scene xiii), another scene in which these barons participated, another scene which was filled out with these extras, and these two big scenes, the second coronation and the St Edmundsbury scene, relate to one another not so much by contrast as by comparison. John is in danger of falling victim to popery himself. The coronation resembles a papal installation, with the bishops placing the diadem on the head of the earthly potentate – at which point the Bastard sees the display of five moons, as though they were reflected off the 'Diadem / Placed by the Bishops on your Highness' head'. The excessiveness of the second coronation is like the excessiveness of popery, a point which is driven home by John's tyrannical behaviour at the end of the scene.

The contrast to these scenes of high pomp comes in the final scene, where the central property is no longer the throne or the altar, but a simple table set in the orchard. John allows no rank, no display – 'no pomp in penury' – in his final awareness of his reign. This is a scene of Catholic perfidy too, like the one at St Edmundsbury, but the king's inner realization is Protestant now, and the barons who denied him earlier will close ranks around him as he dies. The point is verbally driven home by the laying-on of hands. At St Edmundsbury, the barons' laying-on of hands (*Pembroke*: 'Every man lay his hand by mine, in witness of his heart's accord') was a gesture of opposition to John. Here, in the orchard scene, the barons lay their hands together to bear away the corpse of John (*Bastard*: 'Lords all, lay hands to bear your Sovereign / With obsequies of honor to his grave'). So the orchard setting opposes the altar setting, even though both are nominally Catholic. The orchard is the place of Catholic perfidy, but also the place where the barons of the realm unite against the French threat and declare 'If England's Peers and people join in one, / Nor Pope, nor France, nor Spain can do them wrong' (lines 1195–6). This is 'literalism of the theatre' working in its normal mode. The fluidity of successive staging gains points of visual emphasis through central (and transportable) properties like the altar, the throne, the table in the orchard, and the arrival of Protestant clarity in the mind of a king who passed through his own moments of Catholic pride is reflected by the contrast between the scenes focused by the first two properties and the scene focused by the third.

Versification

The writers for the Queen's Men were poets. John Bentley, their specialist in tragic acting, was said to have been moulded by the pens of Kyd, Achlow, and Watson. Greene and Peele wrote for them. Tarlton and Wilson were both poets, and it would be a mistake to imply that in their literalism of the theatre the Queen's Men were not concerned with the issues of versification that attended the growth of the commercial theatre. Indeed, their writers used every style known to the drama of the period, and sometimes used them all within one play. Just when other companies were learning what could be done with blank verse as the dominant mode of dramatic verse, the Queen's Men were busy with the fourteener, with rhyme royal, with rhymed iambic couplets, with prose, *and* with blank verse, as though all manner of writing had equal place on the stage. Wilson's conception of the 'medley' included a conviction, it would appear from his work, that a stylistic gallimaufry was part of the endeavour, and he seems to have inspired other writers for the company to follow his lead. Greene is the exception here: *Friar Bacon and Friar Bungay* does play Skeltonics and prose against blank verse in the 'medley' style, but more than the other plays of the Queen's Men it strives to imitate the style of *Tamburlaine* and establish a dominant blank verse. The 'medley' serves literalist theatre because it does not establish a dominant language, but rather creates a feeling for the impromptu – as though there will be a style for anything that comes up. This is the basic style of the Tudor interludes carried into the 1580s and 1590s. Other companies and writers used it too, and Shakespeare's early comedies are especially clever examples. But the drive toward a dominant blank-verse style can be seen developing in the other companies in the early 1590s (especially in all of Marlowe and in Shakespeare's history plays), while in the Queen's Men, the medley style remained pretty well intact.

The versification of the medley can be found at the beginning of *Three Lords and Three Ladies*. A boy representing 'London' comes forward to speak the prologue, three stanzas of rhyme royal. The three lords of London then enter with their three young pages, the lords speaking in blank verse and their pages remaining for the most part silent, although they will break out in tetrameter rhymes when their masters leave. The blank verse of the three lords is heavily end-stopped, and rhymed pentameter couplets are possible at any moment. The rhymes of the pages are gamey and spirited, as though some fun can be had once authority removes itself. Their tetrameters push against the norm and can tumble freely into longer lines, even attaining a fourteener or two. These boys are unpredictable, but good at rhymes. When the clown Simplicity enters to speak with them, he sometimes tries to join their rhyming games, but his true *métier* is prose, which allows him to ramble and chatter. 'Chapmen?', he says, when the boys insist they are not in trade, 'you are no men, neither Chapmen nor chopmen, nor chipmen nor shipmen, but if ye be chappers, choppers, or chippers, ye are but chapboys, and chapboys ye are double', which leads to a joke about the mouth. When the three ladies arrive, they speak in stanzas – slightly unstable and intricate combinations of quatrains and couplets. Here is Lucre's opening speech, which is more regular than most (the three ladies are Love, Conscience, and Lucre):

> For death we call, yet death is still in sight,
> Lucre doth scald in drops of melting gold,
> Accusing Rust, calls on eternal might [*sic?*],
> Where flames consume, and yet we freeze with cold:
> Sorrow adds Sulphur unto Fury's heat,
> And chops them ice, whose chattering teeth do beat,
> But sulphur, snow, flame, frost nor hideous crying
> Can cause them die, that ever are in dying.
> Nor make the pain diminish or increase,
> Sorrow is slack, and yet will never cease.

(D2r)

This interplay of styles marks nearly all of the plays from the Queen's Men. *The Old Wives Tale* is a more sophisticated play than *Three Lords and Three Ladies of London*, but it is a medley too, a medley in which changes of style help to create the play's subject. When Madge's narration at the beginning gives way to the entrance of the two brothers, the sense of a transformation in mode comes in part from the homely prose of the old wife's tale giving way to the blank verse of a magical dramatization. But then the blank verse gives way too, for this is a play about styles which flow into one another. No style is allowed to dominate in *The Old Wives Tale* – that is part of its marvellous quality (Huanebango is a fool because he does try to dominate with his hexameters). — *Harvey?* The two brothers no sooner play their blank verse off against Madge's prose than Erestus plays his rhymed couplets off against their blank verse, and these tetrameter couplets yield to a strange mix of blank verse and pentameter couplets in Erestus's soliloquy. When Lampriscus enters, the mode returns to prose, and before long there is a harvest-song. Anything can happen in the medley, and that is the point of *The Old Wives Tale*: anything can happen, so long as the magician is not allowed to be the mastermind of the plot (Sacrapant is the other would-be dominator).

The variation in style typical of the medley requires great versatility from the actors, but there is one thing missing almost entirely from the plays of the Queen's Men, and that is poetry capable of expressing the pressures of realistic psychological experience. That is what was taking hold in the verse of the other companies, where Edward Alleyn and Richard Burbage were setting the standards younger actors would try to achieve. Alleyn, Burbage, and their fellows were trying out new possibilities of dramatic speech at the same time as Marlowe, Kyd, and Shakespeare were trying out new possibilities of rhetoric and metaphor in dramatic writing, and these twin pressures – one cannot be said to have given rise to the other – were brought to bear on a pentameter verse which was so open-ended as to be called 'blank'. The Queen's Men used the pentameter, but they never learned the advantages to be had in the quality of the 'blank', which comes at the end of the line and refuses to close it down. George Wright has remarked that blank verse frees the actor's speech from rhyme and emphasizes metre instead.[12] The result is an opening-up of metrical variations playing against the iambic norm, and the result of *that* is speech that sounds responsive and immediate without losing its sense of underlying form. Alleyn and Burbage, Shakespeare and Marlowe, learned how to make a blank-verse line flow through into a verse paragraph, but the Queen's Men, adept at their medleys and able to theatricalize anything, thought the pentameter line should be regular and come to a pause. Their unrhymed iambic pentameter is nearly always end-stopped and metrically regular, and its goal is not variability but predictability. End-stopped iambic pentameter reaching little outbursts of rhyme – that is the

verse by which Bentley, Knell, and the other serious actors for the Queen's
Men made their mark in the company's serious vein.

Here is the beginning of *King Leir*. The King and his advisers have just come
from the funeral of the Queen (thus beginning with reference to the character
Shakespeare never mentions, the mother):

> Thus to our grief the obsequies performed
> Of our (too late) deceased and dearest Queen,
> Whose soul I hope, possessed of heavenly joys,
> Doth ride in triumph 'mongst the Cherubins;
> Let us request your grave advice, my Lords,
> For the disposing of our princely daughters,
> For whom our care is specially employed,
> As nature bindeth to advance their states,
> In royal marriage with some princely mates.

(lines 3–11)

This looks like blank verse, but the regularity of metre and the end-stopping
which is established a few lines into the speech set a pace that aims for a rounded
conclusion, and this is reached at the *states/mates* rhyme of lines 10 and 11. Trim
and repetitious, this verse is prepared not for the unexpected metaphor or
deviations in metre, but for gnomic and sententious familiarity. Daughters
without a mother's care are 'a ship without a stern, / Or silly sheep without a
Pastor's care' (lines 15–16), and the ageing father has one foot in the grave (line
24). Rhyme is the controlling feature. The first three speeches of the play end
with rhymed couplets, then the pace of rhyme picks up. The Nobleman's
speech at line 43 has three couplets, Leir's response has four, and the last half of
the scene is more than 50 per cent rhymed.

The result of this patterning through rhyme is dialogue poised and formal,
virtually an exchange of stanzas. The characters in the verse plays of the Queen's
Men do not talk to one another so much as set themselves forth in predetermined arrangements, and this technique works best in the comic medleys,
where the differences of predetermined arrangements have a variety and interest of their own. *The Old Wives Tale* is probably the best of the Queen's Men
plays for this reason. *King Leir*, with little stylistic technique besides the rhyming pace described above, seems stilted and self-conscious by contrast. Leir's
high point occurs when the would-be murderer so trembles and quakes at the
persuasions of the old men he is supposed to kill that he must drop his knives
and retreat:

> The parlosest old men, that ere I heard.
> Well, to be flat, I'll not meddle with you:
> Here I found you, and here I'll leave you:

If any ask you why the case so stands?
Say that your tongues were better than your hands.

(1751–5)

The stroke of brilliance in *King Leir* lies in playing the murderer as a comic character in the first place, one who is allowed to break the metrical norms before getting to the regular couplet at the end. He is at heart one of the Queen's Men clowns, sounding more like Simplicity from *Three Lords and Ladies of London* than the Oswald Shakespeare would later make of him. But when *Leir* grows moral, which is most of the time, the tendency toward iambic regularity and rhyme pushes the speakers into their virtual stanzas, and the action grows heavy with prefabrication.

The *Troublesome Reign of King John* is a better play than *Leir*, and one reason is that the big moments are written in real stanzas, which are formed by repetition and recapitulation.[13] The first of these is the Bastard's trance in the opening scene, when he realizes he is the son of Richard the Lionhearted:

> Methinks I hear a hollow Echo sound,
> That Philip is the Son unto a King:
> The whistling leaves upon the trembling trees
> Whistle in consort I am Richard's Son:
> The bubbling murmur of the waters fall,
> Records *Philippus regius filious*:
> Birds in their flight make music with their wings,
> Filling the air with glory of my birth:
> Birds, bubbles, leaves, and mountains, Echo, all
> Ring in mine ears, that I am Richard's Son.

(Part 1, lines 246–55)

This stanza avoids rhyme and attains its form by building a list in parallel pentameters and then recapitulating the list in the concluding lines. It is a stanza built by syntax and line-length, but not by rhyme, and it arises most effectively (as it does here) in the midst of ordinary pentameter lines, as though it is a sudden intensification. No other character hears the Bastard's speech, although the entire court is listening. This moment of realization occurs in the character's mind, and (where the modern theatre would spotlight him and shadow the others) the internalization must come across through the verse and the performance. It is a rare venture into interiority for the Queen's Men, and true to their penchant for rhyme it happens in stanza form. A moment later, the playwright will fall back on his usual device of iambic couplets ('Let land and living go, 'tis honor's fire / That makes me swear King Richard was my Sire'), but the 'list and recapitulation' stanza is a better rhetorical spotlight for the trance because it is so openly artificial.

The device is used again near the end of the play, when King John knows he is dying and thinks he has failed in everything. He is on the way to inner Protestant understanding, but first must recognize a few things about his dismal past. The 'list and recapitulation' here comes into service again:

> How have I lived, but by another's loss?
> What have I loved, but wrack of other's weale?
> When have I vowed, and not infringed mine oath?
> Where have I done a deed deserving well?
> How, what, when, and where have I bestowed a day
> That tended not to some notorious ill?

> (Part 2, lines 1057–62)

He will snap out of this despair in a moment, upon realizing that his descendants will produce Henry VIII, he who will trample upon the strumpet of Rome (Henry VIII will produce, in turn, the patroness of the company that is acting this play), but for a moment the Queen's Men are using blank verse formalized into stanzaic structure.[14]

Yet rhyme is the normal course of rhetorical oppportunity for the Queen's Men, and this is fully apparent in their use of the fourteener. Fourteeners were serious business in Tudor literature. They were a weighty line for the first generation of Elizabethan writers and translators. By the time of the Queen's Men, Golding's *Ovid* and the Heywood collection of Seneca's plays were leading examples of the appropriateness of the fourteener for serious literature. In the theatre, the fourteener was a standard medium of the interludes, old-fashioned and serviceable – and demanding resourcefulness on the part of the actors. Anyone who wants to know what the greatness of interlude acting consisted of in the earlier Tudor period should try speaking fourteeners aloud and getting an audience to listen. The line requires brilliant control from an actor, particularly because it calls attention to its own performance, and the actor has to keep pace. The sense of exuberance we have noted in the medley style and theatrical literalism of the Queen's Men can be seen quite exactly in their continued use of this form of verse, on into the later 1580s and earlier 1590s, when blank verse was obviously becoming the ruling style.

Blank verse is open to a world of experience beyond itself. The fourteener is its own world. Its reality is the enactment of a long line which exists to be answered by an echoing line, equally long, dancing its way to a rhyme. It is a speaker's ballet, and its exhilaration comes from its continually successful closure, against long odds. The Queen's Men used it most often for comic effects (as we have noted in *Three Lords and Three Ladies of London*). In the ransacking of the monastery in *The Troublesome Reign of King John*, the Friars start out speaking the silliest of Skeltonics ('Benedicamus Domini, was ever such an injury / Sweet St Withold of thy lenity, defend us from extremity'), but Philip the Bastard outrhymes them with his fourteeners and more or less beats them into his mode ('Now, bald and barefoot Bungay birds, when up the gallows climbing, / Say Philip he had words enough to put you down with rhyming!' – lines 1184 ff.). But the fourteener can be chilling and slick too. The arrest of Rivers in *True Tragedy of Richard III* (scene vii) is in fourteeners shared between the terrified Rivers and the mocking Gloucester and Buckingham.

> *Rich.* Griev'st thou that I the Gloster Duke
>   Should as Protector sway?
>   And were you he has left behind,
>   To make us both away?
>   Wilt thou be ringleader to wrong,
>   And must you guide the realm?
>   Nay, overboard all such mates I hurl
>   While I do guide the Helm.
>   I'll weed you out by one and one,
>   I'll burn you up like chaff,
>   I'll rend your stock up by the roots,
>   That yet in triumphs laugh.
> *Riv.* Alas good Dukes, for ought I know,
>   I never did offend,
>   Except unto my Prince
>   Unloyal I have been.
>   Then show just cause why you exclaim
>   So rashly in this sort,
>   So Falsely thus me to condemn,
>   Upon some false report
>
>   (lines 602–11)

As soon as Rivers is taken away, the strange formality of the fourteeners changes to Gloucester's ordinary prose. The medley technique is being used to show Gloucester's control: he can outdo Rivers in the close personal encounter of the fourteener, then switch to administrative prose to announce the closing of all highways in the realm.

Clyomon and Clamydes is entirely in long-line rhymes, a trait which has led modern readers to assume that the play must come from the period of the Tudor interlude. We have mentioned the frailty of assumption that lies behind this view of theatre history (see p. 89 above), and have argued that however old the original play may have been, the version published in 1599 belonged to the Queen's Men, just as the title-page says. The Queen's Men were purveyors of the long-line rhyme as a staple in their medley style, and their dramaturgy is founded on the Tudor interlude. *Clyomon and Clamydes* fits into their repertory because it *is* so old-fashioned. The opportunity to take this play seriously, as a play written for real actors in a real time of the theatre, should not be over-looked merely because it shows no influence from Marlowe and Shakespeare.

The rhyming hexameters and heptameters of *Clyomon and Clamydes* belong to the design of the play, which is based on the narrative overdetermination we have noted in the Queen's Men. Everyone is a narrator in *Clyomon and Clamydes*. When Rumour enters at line 1196, his function is to fill in key elements of the romance which have been left undramatized.[15] But the Queen's Men also narrate what has been dramatized, and do so at the climax of the plot. Leir's narration to Cordella in their reconciliation scene rehashes the plot at the crucial moment, and a similar recapitulation forms the recognition scene in *Clyomon and Clamydes*. Neronis has removed her disguise and stands forth for her lover to see who she is, but her lover refuses to look, so deep is his desolation over losing his lady. Always in this play resolution is on the verge of happening but is taking its time (which is the verse form of the fourteener). While the lover stares at his feet, Neronis recounts parts of the plot – and the truth dawns on the knight through her narrative. He then takes a closer look at her – yes, it *is* Neronis. This is an epitome of Queen's Men dramaturgy – truth being made plain in the telling and in the staging, and being made plain two or three times over.

The fourteener obtains its interest from the expectation of rhyme occurring over a pronounced metrical distance: one waits for the second shoe to drop, and nearly always it drops seven beats after the first. The plot of *Clyomon and Clamydes* is the larger version of this idea. The narrative overdetermination requires everyone to know that a resolution to whatever conflict comes up is within hailing distance. Wait a bit, and it will arrive, with no more uncertainty than the rhyme arrives in the verse form. (There is *some* uncertainty, by the way, for little bursts of 'sixteener' change the pace here and there, and one of Subtle Shift's comic elements is that he cannot get the fourteener right much of the time. There is even a moment of lyric beauty in Neronis's song in scene xi, as G. R. Hibbard observed.[16]) Although the play ranges over the lands known to Alexander the Great, when one knight crosses the stage, some point of honour to pursue, the knight for whom he searches will be found within a minute or two. The stage becomes a place where coincidence becomes normal and the worthy find what they are looking for, although sometimes they do not know they have found it for a while. The fourteener has a general tonal effect here: all the noble characters sound, not a little like one another, but exactly like one another, as though the language they speak comes from a predetermined design in which they are equal participants. Subtle Shift and the rustic Corin are not equal participants, but the fourteener is what they cannot quite manage, so the pattern is heard in their deviations anyhow. The characters exist to

fill out obvious patterns, which are the systematic metrical form they intend to speak and the systematic series of coincidences by which they find one another.

In xvi, Clyomon sets up his emblem of a golden shield over the corpse of an enemy he has slain. 'Ah Neronis where thou art, or where thou does abide / Thy Clyomon to seek thee out, shall rest no time or tide', he declares, but the convention of plot operates to make this unnecessary, for Neronis is in the vicinity and will come upon the emblem in a moment. To be in the vicinity is to be in a play of the Queen's Men. When Neronis enters, she misreads the emblem and thinks it betokens the death of Clyomon himself. Mistakes like this are what the fourteener renders temporary. Neronis cannot be in serious danger of misunderstanding the world so long as her bewilderment is expressed thus: 'Ah heavens, this Herse doth signify my Knight is slain, / Ah death no longer do delay, but rid the lives of twain' (lines 1534–5). She means that she is about to kill herself, but Providence descends and makes her read the emblem correctly. It tells her that Clyomon is alive and must be searched for the world over. (But he is somewhere in the vicinity, and enters the moment she leaves.)

Disguise is the perfect costuming for this kind of plot – for the true identity behind the false appearance will occur as certainly as the other forms of closure in language and event. Neronis disguises herself as a page in order to search for Clyomon. She hopes that a knight will come along to take her into his service, making the searching easier. In two lines a knight enters (line 1623) and takes her into his service. It is, of course, Clyomon, but he is disguised too. Neither recognizes the other, this page and master, disguise being the device that 'suspends' the recognition scene in a plot which has already brought its hero and heroine into contact.

The dramaturgy of *Clyomon and Clamydes* is systematic and coherent. It carries some of the stylistic interests of the Queen's Men to a logic which is virtually unplayable in the modern theatre: their tendency toward end-stopping and rhyme in their verse extends here to the fourteeners; these same fourteeners form one of the rhetorical skills of the interlude tradition which the Queen's Men carried into the 1580s and 1590s; and the narrative overdetermination of their plots, which fits their history plays as part of their motive for truth and plainness in the retailing of English themes for English audiences, now settles into a romantic plot which no one is supposed to believe any more than they believe that people talk in fourteeners.

We wish to end with two examples of the medley style creating strong effects in the Elizabethan theatre. We choose them because, along with the fourteeners of *Clyomon and Clamydes*, they indicate the versatility of the Queen's Men, who mastered these challenges that we do not spend much time even attempting. When the young Prince Arthur talks Hubert out of blinding him in *The Troublesome Reign of King John* (scene xii), rhymed iambic couplets convey the

most intricate and important moment. The scene follows directly upon the
fourteeners and tumbling rhymes of the comic nunnery scene. The rambunctiousness of the long-line rhymes now shades down to an iambic rhythm, which
listens to the blank verse that was gaining sway in the theatre but insists, as the
Queen's Men often insist, on turning blank verse into pentameter rhyme as an
encounter increases in intensity. By the time Arthur cleverly engages Hubert in
debate, they are exchanging couplets in a pattern of stichomythia which form-
ally predicts the resolution of the argument. At first each speaker completes his
own couplets:

> *Arthur* Yet God commands, whose power reacheth further,
> That no command should stand in force to murther.
> *Hubert* But that same Essence hath ordained a law,
> A death for guilt, to keep the world in awe.

> (Part One, lines 1393–6)

The harmony of the debaters becomes clear as their exchange doubles in pace,
so the rhymes are shared even as their disagreement continues.

> *Arthur* I plead not guilty, treasonless and free.
> *Hubert* But that appeal, my Lord, concerns not me.
> *Arthur* Why, thou art he that mayst omit the peril?
> *Hubert* Aye, if my Sovereign would remit his quarrel.

> (lines 1397–1400)

There is no doubt by the time Hubert is completing Arthur's rhymes that he
will eventually swing around to Arthur's point of view. That is one way rhyme
works well – to give the formal version of a personal encounter. The medley
effect is to bring the iambic rhyme out as though it emerges from other modes
– from the fourteeners of the comic scene, from some prose that introduces the
Arthur–Hubert scene, and from the blank verse with which they begin their
encounter.

The ending of *The True Tragedy of Richard III* presents a tyrant going mad,
and it uses end-stopped blank verse as the form which madness cannot sustain.
Prose takes over instead as Richard's mind gives way – prose which does not
entirely lose contact with iambic pentameter but which breaks through the
regularity which the writers for the Queen's Men assigned to blank verse. Here
is the beginning of his speech, in end-stopped blank verse:

> The hell of life that hangs upon the Crown,
> The daily cares, the nightly dreams,
> The wretched crews, the treason of the foe,
> And horror of my bloody practice past,
> Strikes such a terror to my wounded conscience,

> That sleep I, wake I, or whatsoever I do,
> Meethinks their ghosts come gaping for revenge,
> Whom I have slain in reaching for a Crown.

(lines 1874–81)

The playwright is about to get into trouble, for he will increase the formality of the speech to a universal list of things that demand revenge:

> The Sun by day shines hotly for revenge.
> The Moon by night eclipseth for revenge.
> The stars are turned to Comets for revenge.
> The Planets change their courses for revenge.
> The birds sing not, but sorrow for revenge.
> The silly lambs sit bleating for revenge.

We have interrupted the quotation just in time. It is going too far, and something ridiculous can be heard around the edge of that line about the lambs. A 'screeking Raven' will follow, 'croaking for revenge', and Shakespeare will turn this to absurdity (in *Hamlet*) by having the Raven 'bellow' for revenge, bellowing being what 'whole heads of beasts' do for revenge in the *next* line of Richard's big speech. One of the leading players of the day actually had to speak these lines for the Queen's Men. He must not have said 'heads' of beasts, though. He surely said 'herds' of beasts, and the scribe, making up the prompt-book from dictation, garbled this into 'heads'. But the list has become turgid, heads or herds notwithstanding. What brings the playwright out of this morass is the opportunity provided by the medley style, the opportunity to switch modes:

> But you villains, rebels, traitors as you are,
> How came the foe in, pressing so near?
> Where, where, slept the garrison that should a' beat them back?
> Where was our friends to intercept the foe?
> All gone, quite fled, his loyalty quite laid a bed?
> Then vengeance, mischief, horror, with mischance,
> Wild-fire, with whirlwinds, light upon your heads,
> That thus betrayed your Prince by your untruth.
> *King.*   Frantic man, what meanst thou by this mood? Now he
> is come more need to beat him back.

Richard is hallucinating at this point. It is another of the rare psychological moments for the Queen's Men, and it is achieved in a breakdown of their metrical system. Richard's madness forces a way through the end-stopping to become a sort of prose which can be bent back into iambic pentameter if the speaker insists, but which can equally well flow beyond the boundaries of metre and end-stopping. It is up to the actor. The scribe obviously did not know whether he was hearing prose or blank verse at this point, and by the time he decided on prose (the final two sentences quoted, after the mistake of a new speech prefix), the verse has reasserted itself and could well be end-stopped again. In the meantime, the scribe has wedged some prose possibilities into blank verse. It is a summary moment for the Queen's Men. Their medley style lets some ambiguity into the rhetoric of madness, the actor gets to make his own choices, and the scribe – who would never have guessed that his work would end up in print, for he was copying for the sake of a prompt-book, and these were actors he worked for, not literary sorts of men – is left guessing about what is going on. An actor can work with the ambiguity of prose and verse, but the scribe is bewildered. The richness of the moment belongs to the theatre and can only look strange on paper.

X for whom? For the writer !!

7

Marlowe and Shakespeare

The anti-Marlowe campaign

We have referred in our preface to the cultural divide which separates us from the time of the Queen's Men. We have said that theatre history tilts in favour of the Chamberlain's Men and the Admiral's Men, and that a balanced view of the past might better come from tilting the other way, toward the forgotten agents, the losers, the discarded, those whom Marlowe, Shakespeare, Alleyn, and Burbage knew so well as to be able to outdistance.

Perhaps the best way of reaching over the divide is to be very specific. At that defining moment in 1590 when playgoers standing before a London bookstall would have been pleased to see that both *Three Lords and Three Ladies of London* and *Tamburlaine* were available, they would have had a choice to make which is no longer available. We cannot buy *Three Lords and Three Ladies*, but *Tamburlaine* is still on the shelf. What was a choice in 1590 is now an outcome, as though a cultural contest has been waged and Marlowe has prevailed.

How early did the choice available in 1590 become the cultural contest in which Marlowe prevailed? Is it possible that some of our theatregoers bought both plays, or could not decide and put the choice off for a while? Some of them may have chosen *Three Lords and Three Ladies*, thinking they would not be seen with a book by that infidel Marlowe. Could *Three Lords and Three Ladies of London* have sold as many copies as *Tamburlaine* when they were new books? Was there a moment when more people thought the Queen's Men and their writer 'R. W.' had to be read if one wanted to keep up, or a moment when Marlowe seemed the flash-in-the-pan some of his rivals soon wished him to be?

Probably not. A choice between important texts there was, but *Tamburlaine* must have sold more copies from the beginning. Richard Jones brought out a second edition in 1592, but *Three Lords and Three Ladies* was never reprinted. More to the point, no play from the Queen's Men had a second edition during the 1590s. And when some of their plays were reprinted after the turn of the century – *Troublesome Reign of King John* in 1611 and *Famous Victories of Henry V* in 1617 are the earliest examples – they were being attributed to Shakespeare and the King's Men, who had staged their own versions of these history plays. The 1611 *Troublesome Reign* named the Queen's Men but added 'W. Sh.' as the author (perhaps partly in truth; see below), and the 1617 *Famous Victories* dropped the Queen's Men and substituted the King's Men. The only way to sell a second edition of a Queen's Men play, it appears, was to claim it had some connection with their rivals.

The cultural contest in which Marlowe prevailed was already under way when those two playbooks came onto the market. When our bookbuyer thumbed past the title-page of *Tamburlaine* and came upon the Prologue and its sneers at the 'jigging veins of rhyming mother wits, and such conceits as clownage keeps in pay', he was looking at a contest in progress. That Prologue is spoiling for trouble. Rhyme and clownage were the stock-in-trade of the Queen's Men and of *Three Lords and Three Ladies of London*. We are not certain that Marlowe had the Queen's Men in mind with those slurs, but it is a fair guess. Other actors clowned and rhymed, but the Queen's Men clowned and rhymed at court, in London, across the country, at least once in Dublin and at least once in Scotland. Certainly the 'high astounding terms' that Marlowe proceeded to supply instead of rhyme and clownage helped to create the blank-verse revolution that we have observed the Queen's Men failing to join.

The cultural contest was under way in 1590, and as far as we know Marlowe launched it. The publisher Richard Jones knew what he was helping to bring about. He addresses his book 'to the Gentlemen Readers: and others that take pleasure in reading Histories'. He has removed 'some fond and frivolous Jestures' that were 'gaped at' by the groundlings in the theatre. The same publisher brought out *Three Lords and Three Ladies* without a preamble about readers and the theatre. The long stage directions in *Three Lords and Three Ladies* are more elaborate than the corresponding kind in *Tamburlaine*. They are written with a consciousness of the reader in mind, but in a sense it is a false consciousness, for they apologize to the reader, saying look what hard work is involved in reading (and writing) stage directions, and if you were in the theatre you would see all this at a glance. The theatre is the only place for the Queen's Men. They are out of their element in print. Marlowe does not apologize to readers, he makes them read. He also makes spectators listen and see. There are two right places for Marlowe, his spectators in one, his readers in the other, and that is a large part of the reason why *Three Lords and Three Ladies of London*, with only the theatre as a right place, lost the contest.

There is no doubt that the Queen's Men retaliated in print. Their *Troublesome Reign of King John* came out the following year (from a different publisher) and was obviously intended to do battle with *Tamburlaine* on the bookstalls. The printed version adopts a two-part format like *Tamburlaine*'s, and its preface – addressed 'To the Gentlemen Readers', as though the Queen's

X It seems more likely from the wording
that King John came first – M.
reaching to it, "

Marlowe and Shakespeare

Men still had a chance – announces that anyone who has been trafficking with
the infidel Tamburlaine would do better to heed the story of a Christian and
an Englishman like John:

> You that with friendly grace of smoothed brow
> Have entertained the Scythian Tamburlaine,
> And given applause unto an Infidel:
> Vouchsafe to welcome (with like curtesy)
> A warlike Christian and your Countryman.

The writers of *The Troublesome Reign* also had their eye on *Dr Faustus*. King
John repeatedly passes through moments of Faustus-like despair, and these
contain references to the final soliloquy of Marlowe's play. 'Curst be the Crown,
chief author of my care, / Nay curst my will that made the Crown my care: /
Curst be my birthday, curst ten times the womb / That yielded me alive into
the world' (lines 1708–11) seems well acquainted with Faustus's 'Curst be the
parents that engendered me! / No, Faustus, curse thyself. Curse Lucifer . . .' (A
text, V.ii.113–14),[1] especially as John has just cried out 'What planet governed
my nativity?' (1705), which touches on Faustus's 'you stars that reigned at my
nativity' (V.ii.81). Later John bewails his inability to stop time or move it
ahead ('The Dial tells me, it is twelve at noon. / Were twelve at midnight past,
then might I vaunt' (Part 2, lines 120–1; see also lines 123–6). The point of
these echoes of Marlovian rhetoric is that John possesses what Marlowe's hero
lacked, the potential to overcome despair and attain Christian faith. By the
end, the 'curst' life is no longer his but Rome's, while John is able to see himself
as King David:

> Since John did yield unto the Priest of Rome,
> Nor he nor his have prospered on the earth:
> Curst are his blessings, and his curse is bliss.
> But in the spirit I cry unto my God,
> As did the Kingly Prophet David cry,
> (Whose hands, as mine, with murder were attaint)
> I am not he shall build the Lord a house,
> Or root these Locusts from the face of earth:
> But if my dying heart deceive me not,
> From out these loins shall spring a Kingly branch
> Whose arms shall reach unto the gates of Rome,
> And with his feet tread down the Strumpet's pride,
> That sits upon the chair of Babylon.

> (Part 2, lines 1075–87)

The agenda of the Queen's Men is pretty well unfolded at this point. John rises
above Faustus in hope of salvation by placing himself on the Tree of Jesse and

x all that it makes certain is that the preface was written later – it says nothing of when the play was written

predicting a major outbranching called Henry VIII. The anti-Marlowe motive is neatly dovetailed into the celebration of Elizabeth's lineage, these being the Queen's Men to the last.

The references to Marlowe make it apparent that *Dr Faustus* was on the stage well before *The Troublesome Reign of King John* was printed in 1591. The question of an early or a late date for *Faustus* seems answerable on the early side. Could the relationship flow the other way? Could the echoes between the two plays be explained as Marlowe's using *The Troublesome Reign* as he wrote a late *Dr Faustus*? Imitating the Queen's Men would not seem at all characteristic of Marlowe's artistic temperament; and *The Troublesome Reign*'s deliberate reference to *Tamburlaine* in the preface makes it virtually certain that its Faustian rhetoric comes as a reaction to Marlowe, as do the anti-Marlowe elements in other plays of the Queen's Men. *Friar Bacon and Friar Bungay* has been thought to be a reply to *Dr Faustus*, with a necromancer learning what damage he can do and undergoing a change of heart. The anti-necromancy theme runs extensively through the extant comedies of the Queen's Men: both *The Old Wives Tale* and *Clyomon and Clamydes* turn on the vanquishing of magicians.[2]

The most complex of the anti-Marlowe plays by the Queen's Men is *Selimus*. Here is the proper way to study Persian history, the Prologue announces, not through a celebration of rebellious power but through an account of the devastation that kind of power produces. The intricacy of the case, however, is that the Marlovian enemy is not just Tamburlaine but the blank-verse line itself. The Queen's Men knew exactly where the contest was likely to be lost and tried to set forth one of their own rhetorical devices – rhymed iambic pentameter, shaped as a stanza – as the sign of resistance. What has to be resisted is the tyrant who speaks in blank verse, the infidel given to Marlowe's mighty line.

That is to say, the play presents a rhetorical spectrum that runs from long set speeches in stanzaic form through to blank verse and then to the violence which blank verse is supposed to produce, which is the wordless brutality of strangulation. *Selimus* demonstrates the degeneration of a world of rhetoric into a world of violence, and Marlowe's *Tamburlaine* is not hard to detect behind the degeneration. Tamburlaine's outlook is monstrously represented by the egocentric and atheistical Selimus. The world of rhetoric which Selimus destroys is represented by – followers of *Tamburlaine* are meant to take notice – one Bajazeth, Selimus's father. At first, both father and son share in the rhetorical world of the formal stanza. Scene i consists mainly of a 115-line meditation by Bajazeth on the perils of kingship, especially when one's 'aspiring' son is not to be trusted; scene ii is a soliloquy of 150 lines by that aspiring son. Both of these speeches are fundamentally stanzaic, with slight blank-verse variations. Bajazeth's is an eight-line stanza, ababababcc, with one example of a shorter form, ababcc. Selimus's is rhyme royal, ababbcc. This distinction will vary from time to time. In scene iii Bajazeth will adopt rhyme royal, while later (scene x) he returns to the six-line ababcc. Some blank verse threads in and out of his speeches, but mainly he is a stanza-speaker – so much so that the play has sometimes been called a 'closet' play and unsuited for the theatre. It is an anti-Marlowe play instead. The rhetorical direction moves toward blank verse and violence. Both father and son (along with other characters from time to time) speak in elaborate and highly formal stanzas at the beginning of the play, and when those stanzas give way to blank verse, a process which occurs between scenes iii and x, it is Selimus who makes the unrhymed speech his own style and it is his father who tries to recover the stanzas.

By scene xviii, when Bajazeth has been forced to give Selimus the crown, the rebellious son has become an obvious imitation of Tamburlaine in both attitude and verse:

> Now sit I like the arm-strong son of Jove,
> When after he had all his monsters quell'd,
> He was receiv'd in heaven mongst the gods,
> And had fair Hebe for his lovely bride.
> As many labours Selimus hath had,
> And now at length attained to the crown,
> This is my Hebe, and this is my heaven.

(lines 1671–7)

This is a humdrum imitation of Tamburlaine's 'sweet fruition of an earthly crown' speech, but in noticing that the *Selimus* poets cannot write Marlovian blank verse with much conviction, we also notice that to do so would deny one of their intentions. If it is necessary for these poets to write mediocre blank verse, the virtue is that the mediocre blank verse is a stage in the moral degeneration that this aspiring conqueror brings about. Before long he is having his enemies strangled (those who remain after he poisons his father), and the rhetorical point of this repeated violence is that the command to strangle is just as dull a blank-verse line as any of his others: 'Why stais't thou Sinam? Strangle him, I say' (line 2310); 'Sinam strangle her, / And now to fair Amasia let us march' (lines 2320–1); 'Strangle her Hali, let her scold no more. / Now let us march to meet with Acomat' (lines 2416–17); 'Then Sinam strangle him: now he is dead' (line 2509). To read these lines according to the style of the Queen's Men, one must listen to the flat blank verse and simultaneously watch the sensationalism of the stranglings. In the literalism of the theatre, the brutality would not be masked – not in a play which repeats the scene four times. This is not to mention the scene where an old man has his eyes gouged out and both hands cut off.

Selimus announces itself as the first part of a two-part play (the second is not extant), another attempt to rival *Tamburlaine*. We are not certain when it was written, but by the time it was published in 1594, Marlowe was dead, his plays for Edward Alleyn's companies were vastly popular, and the Queen's Men were about to be written out of the permanent 'Elizabethan drama' in London, largely by a writer who listened to Marlovian verse and thought something valuable could be done with it.

Shakespeare a Queen's Man?

Eyes are gouged out and hands are cut off in other Elizabethan plays as well. They were for the most part written by Shakespeare (*King Lear*, *Titus Andronicus*), who is sometimes thought to have begun his career with the Queen's Men. This possibility is easily set forth in the absence of evidence, for no one knows where Shakespeare was, or with whom, between 1584 (when his twins were conceived in Stratford) and 1592 (when Robert Greene wrote his well-known complaint about him in London). There is no record of Shakespeare's ever being a member of the Queen's Men, but there is no record before 1594 of his being a member of any other acting company either. Greene called him an upstart crow, apparently for trying to become a writer instead of keeping to his place as a mere player and factotum. With which company he had made himself thus visible to the eye of Greene remains unknown, but Greene did write plays for the Queen's Men.

At any rate, from the eighteenth century to the present (Malone having first raised the idea), scholars have wondered if Shakespeare might have joined one of the professional companies which visited Stratford during the 1580s. The Queen's Men were the most prestigious of these companies. Queen's Men played in Stratford in 1587 and several other times before 1592. But other companies played Stratford too. That Shakespeare joined the Queen's Men and not one of the others was prominently proposed by A. W. Pollard in his introduction to one of the books which settled the 'bad' quarto theory into accepted belief, Peter Alexander's *Shakespeare's Henry VI and Richard III*.[3] Greene wrote some plays for the Queen's Men, Pollard reasoned, and so did George Peele, whom Greene was warning to beware of the upstart crow: perhaps the attack on Shakespeare was thus a manoeuvre related to this most famous company. (Pollard also noticed what is the closest thing to evidence in the case – a surprising number of Shakespeare's plays are closely based on the plots of plays performed by the Queen's Men. We shall return to this matter.)

A touch of documentary support was added in 1961 by Mark Eccles, who discovered that a leading member of the Queen's Men, William Knell, had been killed in a fight shortly before the company is recorded in Stratford in 1587. Did Shakespeare take Knell's place and go to London with the Queen's Men? The speculation has been hard to resist,[4] but while it is true that Knell died and that Shakespeare got to London, there is no evidence that Shakespeare got to London *because* Knell died. The probability of an unknown from a country town replacing a leading serious actor of the day is not strong, and the Stratford visit may have been made by a different branch of the company anyhow.

Eric Sams has recently provided a new twist to the story by supposing that Shakespeare was *already* with the Queen's Men when they reached Stratford in 1587, and that the high reward paid to the company, together with the fact that a bench was broken during one of their performances, tells us that 'the town had turned out in force to see its native son's success'.[5] This is cheerful and of no account, but Sams also takes up the more important matter of the correspondences between Shakespeare's known plays and those of the Queen's Men. Sams thinks that Shakespeare wrote *The Troublesome Reign of King John, The True Tragedy of Richard III, King Leir*, and *The Famous Victories of Henry V* for the Queen's Men (plus, perhaps for other companies, *The First Part of the Contention, The True Tragedy of Richard Duke of York, The Taming of A Shrew*, the ur-*Hamlet, Edmund Ironside, Edward III*, and upward of twenty unknown plays). The all-or-nothing rambunctiousness of these assertions may cause readers to disregard them, but they do include more than a hint of a connection between Shakespeare and the Queen's Men, and the matter should be taken seriously.

The plots of no fewer than six of Shakespeare's known plays are closely related to the plots of plays performed by the Queen's Men.[6] *King John* resembles *The Troublesome Reign* virtually scene for scene. *King Lear* and *Richard III* cover the same stories as *King Leir* and *The True Tragedy of Richard III*. The sequence of *1 Henry IV, 2 Henry IV*, and *Henry V* is in part an elaborate version of the material covered in *The Famous Victories of Henry V*. The plays of the Queen's Men are the largest theatrical source of Shakespeare's plots – if they came first and are not themselves reactions to the Shakespeare texts. For the 'bad' quarto theory has been applied to some of the Queen's Men plays, and 'bad' quartos come after their corresponding plays. Perhaps Shakespeare wrote his *Henry IV* and *Henry V* plays first, and the 'bad' quarto *Famous Victories* comes later. Perhaps Shakespeare's *King John* precedes a 'bad' quarto *Troublesome Reign*. Our chapter on 'Casting' has demonstrated our view that there is no reason to call the texts from the Queen's Men 'bad' quartos. But no one can be certain about the relative dates of the plays, and the relationship between Shakespeare's plays and those of the Queen's Men is important enough to warrant open-mindedness.

The relationship seems especially intense in that nearly half of the plays we attribute to the Queen's Men have their Shakespearean counterparts: four out of nine. Shakespeare seems to have known lines from all of these four plays, and he seems to have remembered their incidents in both his earlier and later work. Meredith Skura's shrewd psychoanalytic study of *Shakespeare the Actor* detects *King Leir* not just in Shakespere's *Lear* but in moments of *Richard II*, *Richard III*, *King John*, *Cymbeline*, and *Coriolanus*.[7] His connection with the published texts of the Queen's Men seems close and deep.

Moreover, there are signs that some in the publishing industry thought *The Troublesome Reign of King John* was Shakespeare's play. The publishers of the Shakespeare Folio of 1623 were careful to enter the titles of sixteen plays which were 'not formerly entered to other men' – that is, which had not previously appeared in print. *King John* was not among them (nor was *Taming of the Shrew*). The publishers apparently felt that the published *Troublesome Reign of King John* from the Queen's Men – and the *Taming of A Shrew*, first published in 1594 from Pembroke's Men – were versions of the plays about to appear in their Folio. Moreover, the second edition of *The Troublesome Reign*, 1611, put Shakespeare's initials on the title-page, and the third edition, 1622, gave his name as author. Those who do not believe Shakespeare wrote any part of *The Troublesome Reign* can explain these items away by mistrusting the publishers: the second and third editions may have been falsely trying to profit from Shakespeare's name, and the Folio editors may have been falling back on these title-page attributions as reasons for not having to register the Shakespeare text (but this cannot be the explanation for *Shrew*, where the quartos do not name Shakespeare). The publishers in question – Valentine Simmes, Augustine Mathewes, Isaac Jaggard, Edward Blount – had dealt with Shakespeare's texts before, however, and they were closer to the facts of the case than we are. They may have known something about the authorship of *The Troublesome Reign* that we do not know. In some sense, Shakespeare may have been involved in that authorship.

What sense might that be? (We will leave the *Shrew* problem to students of Pembroke's Men and will deal only with *John*.) The plots of *Troublesome Reign* and *King John* are closely similar from the beginning through Act 3 (in modern editions). Thereafter, the main lines of action continue to be parallel, but important differences of plot do occur, particularly in that *King John* narrates some scenes which *The Troublesome Reign* stages. A number of close verbal parallels occur – the exact number depending on what is considered close by the tabulator. There is no doubt that the author of the later play either had the text of the earlier play at hand or at least partially in memory. But which was the earlier play? *The Troublesome Reign*, published three years before any of Shakespeare's (other) plays were printed, would seem earlier to ordinary ways of thinking, but some scholars have viewed it as a redaction of Shakespeare's play, a 'bad' quarto of a rather special type, and have argued that Shakespeare was writing in London earlier than the publication dates of his known plays would suggest. The various interpretations that have been posed over the years can be grouped into three main lines: (1) that Shakespeare wrote both texts, *King John* being a thorough rewriting of his *Troublesome Reign* (Sams's argument); (2) that *King John* is Shakespeare's rewriting of someone else's *Troublesome Reign* (the most common view among Shakespeareans); (3) that *Troublesome Reign* is someone else's rewriting of Shakespeare's early *King John* (the 'bad quarto' argument).[8]

We have shown that the plays of the Queen's Men proceed from a dramaturgy which is coherent and recognizable in its own terms – the 'medley' style, the 'literalism of the theatre' – and differs in recognizable ways from the dramaturgy which Shakespeare, Marlowe, and others established in the 1590s. That is why we think it unlikely that *The Troublesome Reign* is a 'bad' quarto version of Shakespeare's play (argument 3 above) or that Shakespeare himself wrote *The Troublesome Reign* and later rewrote it as *King John* (argument 1 above). Both arguments assume that the two plays resemble one another in style, but they do not. They resemble one another in plot. The style of Shakespeare's play depends on a writer who has a knack for writing dramatic blank verse, while the style of *The Troublesome Reign* depends on actors who command the resources of a visual theatre. These are not mutually exclusive characteristics, but they do have a different emphasis and the difference in emphasis can be seen and heard in the theatre.

For example, to deal with the mysterious appearance of five moons at the time of King John's second coronation, the Queen's Men rigged up a display of the five moons themselves. That is theatrical literalism – letting the spectators see for themselves. Shakespeare's *King John* delivers this event not visually but narratively, describing the shuddering of a troubled society in images which could never be precisely seen on a stage:

> And he that speaks doth gripe the hearer's wrist,
> Whilst he that hears makes fearful action
> With wrinkled brows, with nods, with rolling eyes.
> I saw a smith stand with his hammer, thus,
> The whilst his iron did on the anvil cool,
> With open mouth swallowing a tailor's news . . .
>
> (IV.ii.190–5)[9]

The five moons stun the beholders in Shakespeare, but in the staging of this moment there are no real beholders, not of the five moons. If you wish to behold the five moons, you must see the Queen's Men's version. In Shakespeare, the stunned society comes across as words, and the only beholders in the theatre are spectators being turned into listeners. The actor makes the scene happen through words, especially through the series of active verbs and the special moment of mimicry he gains on that word 'thus'.

X   (There is a certain know-how about writing blank verse of this kind, and it comes from a sense of metrical variation which virtually does not occur in the plays of the Queen's Men. This metrical variation is most obvious when a line runs through its normal pause at the end in order to pick up a trochee at the beginning of the next line –

> Here's a stay
> That shakes the rotten carcass of old Death
> Out of his rags!
>
> (*King John*, II.i.455–7)

but the passage about the five moons is mainly end-stopped and the internal pauses come predictably after the second beat. In this case, the know-how occurs with the trochaic variations which fall just after the internal pauses in the final three lines quoted, advancing the third stress and placing it on the front of the active verbs: 'stand' and 'swallowing'. The blank verse in the plays of the Queen's Men falls short on active verbs in the first place, and only rarely does it reveal such an adventure as a trochaic variation after the second-beat internal pause in a line.

The Troublesome Reign belongs to a dramatic style which can be recognized more fully in the other plays of the Queen's Men than it can be recognized in Shakespeare's *King John*. Argument 2 above, that Shakespeare's *King John* is a rewriting of someone else's *Troublesome Reign*, is in our view the correct one. Yet it is necessary to tarry a moment at this point, and ask what 'someone else' might mean when it comes to authorship in the Elizabethan theatre. There is little reason to think of sole authorship as the model for the plays of the Queen's Men, whose 'medley' style would have especially opened itself to collaboration. The 'someone else' whose work Shakespeare later rewrote was probably more than one writer. Robert Wilson is known to have worked as a collaborator later in his career. We have noted earlier that only one of the nine Queen's Men plays was published with an author's name given in full (*Friar Bacon*, for Robert Greene: initials are given for *Three Lords and Three Ladies of London* and *Old Wives Tale*). Collaboration was a normal way of getting new plays into the repertories of the Elizabethan companies on a steady basis, and there is no doubt that Shakespeare, for example, collaborated on certain plays even after he was established as a leading writer.

Shakespeare could well have begun his career as a collaborator with other writers, and his close knowledge of their plays makes the Queen's Men the likely company in which such collaboration could have occurred. The evidence we have is circumstantial and indirect, but it does indicate an unusually substantial and detailed knowledge of the Queen's Men plays on the part of Shakespeare, and it also refuses to give clear and sustained signs of Shakespeare's style in the plays of the Queen's Men. The conjecture that best answers these conditions is that Shakespeare belonged to the Queen's Men early in his career, perhaps in some other capacity than as a writer. Greene may have been right in saying he was a player and factotum. Greene also said that this player and factotum had the audacity to attempt blank verse of his own. This may have been right too. It is not beyond question that the young Shakespeare did some writing for the Queen's Men as a collaborator – not as a principal writer, but as a 'patcher of other men's plays', let us say, who contributed here and there to the joint effort by which many Elizabethan plays got written. He would not have designed the plays or determined their style. He would have adapted his talent to a design and style set by others and set some time earlier, for this company was built on the showmanship of the Tudor interlude and its talent was both famous and old-fashioned. A fledgling writer would not dictate to principal writers but would do what he could and would learn something from the effort – would learn, perhaps, that he did not want to write that way. The publishers of *The Troublesome Reign* in its later editions, when Shakespeare was famous on his own terms, may have been telling a truth of sorts when they attributed the play to him – he may have had a hand in it.

Does it make sense to suppose that the later Shakespeare would rewrite plays from a company to which he had once belonged? The similarities lie in the plotting, not in the style and dramaturgy. The playwright in question borrowed nearly all of his plots from one well-known current source or another. Shakespeare was a lifter of other people's plots. He could have lifted plots from another acting company – there is nothing to be surprised about in this possibility.[10]

The important point in regard to Shakespeare, whether or not he belonged to the Queen's Men during his 'lost years', is that by producing his own versions of four of their plays, he was helping to write the most prestigious company of the 1580s into eventual obscurity at the same time as he was helping to make the Chamberlain's Men, where he can be placed from 1594 on, the premier organization of the 1590s. The Chamberlain's Men made their career in large part on the basis of the connected series of English history plays which Shakespeare wrote for them by the turn of the century. They were not famous for tragedy – not yet – and their success in comedy could be matched by good comedies from the Admiral's Men or the Queen's Men. No other company was taking English history so far into popularity as the Chamberlain's Men, however, with their plays on the reigns of Richard II, Henry IV, Henry V, Henry VI, and Richard III, not to mention the one on King John. Burbage

Oxford was already writing blank verse by the late '80s

and the other leading actors must have known a major change was occurring in their profession as they learned to develop and sustain an acting style across the enormous historical range of these plays. Shakespeare did not lift the comedies of the Queen's Men, he lifted their history plays. And it was his history plays which along with Marlowe's tragedies made the 1590s a revolutionary decade in English theatre.

Conclusion

We think the basis of that revolution was primarily rhetorical, and that is why we have stressed the development of blank verse as a ground of separation between the companies which would survive to be read today and the company which would be forgotten after a generation. The dialogue of the Queen's Men tends to measure the world into segments which can be arranged around the image of the queen or the themes of the queen's political interest. It varies between prose and blank verse, rhyme royal and blank verse, fourteeners and blank verse. It is 'medley' writing, a gloss on the company's open, broad theatricality, and perhaps a bit dull for the Tarlton-tradition of clownishness. The prose is rambunctious and fit for Tarlton, but the verse always looks for the pause at the end of the line, the regular caesura in the middle, steady measures for naming the status of things. (So does Tarlton's published verse, by the way – he did not write the way he clowned.)

Their inability to participate in the blank-verse revolution was in some measure a result of their political and cultural agenda. Dramatic style and politics encircle one another in the theatre, and which is the influential circle in an acting company's real work is not easy to say: making a profit is a circle too, for these companies. One has to read the circles simultaneously, yet try to discriminate between them. The Queen's Men were formed to spread Protestant and royalist propaganda through a divided realm and to close a breach within radical Protestantism. This resulted in a repertory based on English themes. The English history play came to prominence through this motive, and probably through the sheer fact of the company's size. They could do big plays, they ought to do English plays, and narrative sources for English history were being published. Such plays as *The Famous Victories of Henry V*, *The True Tragedy of Richard III*, and *King Leir* reached the stage because they could be presented as 'true' rather than 'poetic', the sort of entertainment English people could be drawn to see in crowds without abjuring the combination of God, queen, Protestant church, and nation which the government depended on. They must have caught on, these big plays of the original company, and if we are right about the signs of reduction in some of the printed texts, they were kept in

the repertory even when they had to be reduced for smaller versions of the
Queen's Men.

Among the commercial companies, it is possible to think that the Queen's
Men invented the English history play. No example from the professional
theatre can be dated earlier than *The Famous Victories of Henry V* on the basis
of factual evidence and no example was published earlier than *The Troublesome
Reign of King John*. There were academic and courtly plays on English history
well before the professional theatre took up this theme, *Gorboduc* being the
best known of these, but it is the innovation of carrying English history into
the popular theatre and making a living from it that we are considering, and in
this regard the Queen's Men appear to have been first. That they 'invented' the
genre in the professional theatre, however, is not quite right. They 'came upon'
the English history play – inventing the genre was never part of the endeavour,
because they were looking for something else. They were looking for a 'large-
cast' kind of drama that kept not so much to the genres of literary history as to
the style of performance at which they were masters. They were staging the
'true' chronicle history of this, and the 'true' tragedy of that, 'truth' being different from 'poetry', plainer and more honest than poetry, a truth the devout
Protestant could attend to without deserving the vituperation of a Stubbes or
a Northbrook. Coming upon the English history play in the course of this
endeavour is one of the more predictable outcomes in literary history, but the
intention was to be 'true' and to be men of the queen's patronage, before it was
to invent a genre.

This is to think about the Queen's Men from the Walsingham–Leicester
point of view we followed in chapter 2, whereas to stress the importance of
blank verse is to think from the writers' point of view we have followed above.
But there is a congruence between the two. The history play which the Queen's
Men came upon and which the Chamberlain's Men developed had a potential
which only one of those companies recognized, a potential that ran beyond the
'medley' style of writing. To imagine the crown politics of England as accessible to individualist aspiration, to recognize the national agony entailed by
such will-to-power – these would be the ways to develop the potential of the
history play. They are the spirit of *Tamburlaine* combined with the spirit of *Dr
Faustus* and translated into historical terms.[11] Too much emphasis on Marlowe
as the presiding genius of Elizabethan drama lies in that snapshot view, of
course. It leaves Kyd out of the picture, and the writer of the anonymous play
on Richard II which is sometimes called *Thomas of Woodstock*. The academic
drama brought blank verse and English history together well before the popular
drama. But it does not get things wrong to put Marlowe at the centre of the
commercial drama in the late 1580s and early 1590s, and the blank verse he
wrote in those years not only rang true to the psychology of individualism in

his conception of tragedy, but also made possible the extension into historical drama that Shakespeare undertook. The Queen's Men came upon the history play but they did not have the style and dramaturgy that turned the history play to long-term account.

From the perspective of the Queen's Men, with their mission to heal rifts and advance moderate ways of thinking, Marlowe was unmistakably the genius of disturbing ventures. He was advancing the new conception of popular drama, and the Queen's Men were in no position to imitate him. Instead, they called him atheist and tried to answer him with orthodoxy. If Shakespeare was a Queen's Man in his early career, he was strangely positioned – participating in plays which called Marlowe the enemy and knowing in his own talent that he must write in the enemy's way. This Shakespeare of our imaginings would then have changed his affiliations at about the time of Marlowe's death, going on to write an impressive and influential series of English history plays based in part on the plots of the Queen's Men themselves, and having no small share in bringing the career of the company he started with to an eventual end.[12]

The career of the Queen's Men ended for other reasons as well. The political motives which operated in their formation had changed in character in the 1590s. The execution of Mary Stuart and the defeat of the Armada had lessened the need for anti-Catholic propaganda, and the Marprelate controversy had borrowed the company's popular style, turning it into the rhetoric of reformist satire. The Queen's Men strained against Martin and made little headway. They were straining against a gross version of their own methods. By this time Tarlton was dead, as were Bentley, Mills, and Knell. The privy council had new concerns in the 1590s and new members to deal with them. Walsingham had died in 1590, Leicester two years before that.

We are summarizing the non-literary factors so as to surround Marlowe, Shakespeare, and the writing of blank verse with the social and political context of our earlier chapters. We will close with the issuing of plays in print, where the literary, the social, and the political combine. The growth of drama in London from the 1590s on into the next century (and in many ways down to the present day) comes from a combination of the printing and theatre industries, along with other developments like the concentration of capital and the growth of literacy in a vastly expanded population. The Queen's Men were masters of the quite different activity of moving shows from one venue to another and drawing crowds of people who were not, for the most part, readers of plays. In the 1580s they had also appealed to the literate and the sophisticated – in their dominance of the court schedule, for example – and their success ran from Whitehall to the farthest reaches of the kingdom. But no one was reading the plays of the popular theatre in the 1580s. In the years between 1589 and 1591, many things changed for the Queen's Men, who found themselves fighting

Martin in the give-and-take of the improvisational theatre just when Edward Alleyn and his fellows were learning to master *Tamburlaine* and *The Spanish Tragedy*. The age of Leicester and Walsingham was over. In the 1590s popular plays began to be published, and the underlying dramaturgy of the Queen's Men, meant to be seen rather than read, lost its hold in the centre of sophistication and capital. Most of the plays they did publish, if we are right, were prepared or revised for smaller groups of Queen's Men – either for a smaller version of the original company or for a branch of the overall company. There is an aura of the practical theatre about their published plays, and this is a sign of the company's true character. Even if we could read dozens of their plays, and read them in the full original versions (as perhaps we do with *Three Lords and Three Ladies of London* and *The Troublesome Reign of King John*), the Queen's Men would still seem a company better suited to theatres than to publication. In the provinces they continued strong, as we can see from records being retrieved by REED from provincial archives, but in London, where a different cultural record was being printed and circulated in the play texts of the Admiral's Men and then of the Chamberlain's Men, the new theatre was being made by others, and the Queen's Men were becoming a matter for history.

APPENDIX A

Recorded performances of the Queen's Men

Chapter 3 attempted to trace the performance history of the Queen's Men from a fresh perspective based upon a close survey of original manuscript sources. This survey would not have been possible without the collaboration of the Records of Early English Drama project and its many associated editors, who shared their work in progress with characteristic generosity and allowed a cumulative itinerary to be drawn up in advance of publication of their volumes in the REED series. Their individual county and city projects are recognized below, together with the document sources which we have had access to through their transcriptions and manuscript photoreproductions at the REED office in Toronto. In some instances, where REED research has not yet begun in a county, we have surveyed manuscripts ourselves in key locations and these are segregated in the list of sources below. Where originals have not survived to this century (for example, some of the Rochester civic accounts), we have used the antiquarian notes taken by Halliwell-Phillipps during his search of those records in the nineteenth century.

The itinerary can only be as detailed as our sources allow, and we would emphasize that survival of Elizabethan manuscripts can only be described as erratic. Our evidence is therefore incomplete at several levels. There are locations, especially private households, where no manuscripts from the period survive; there are others with accounts which promise much but furnish little because their entries are summary rather than detailed or, like those of Southampton (1594–1603), stop for a period of time which unhappily coincides with the career of the Queen's Men. Once into a detailed set of accounts, however, there are further stumbling blocks, the chief of which is the complex variety of accounting practices from town to town. Previously published itineraries for the Queen's Men have tended to gloss over these complexities but we have chosen to lay them bare in this appendix so that our readers can see for themselves how we have reconstructed the itinerary and recognize the uncertainties inherent in such a reconstruction.

The dates given in the date column are therefore as precise as possible, and represent the date or approximate period of payment within the accounting year of the relevant MS. Where no date is indicated, the customary accounting year of Michaelmas to Michaelmas should be assumed. In some instances, such as the Chamberlains' Accounts of Lydd where the accounting year ran from 22 July to 22 July, we have not been able to give a narrower time frame for the troupe's visit in many years. In such instances and in others where only a broad period within a year can be given, we have enclosed the account period within square brackets to indicate that any time within that date range would have been possible, although we have followed what could be called geographical logic in proposing where Lydd or others like it may have fitted into a given year's tour. Coventry is another frequently visited location with an accounting year that varies from the norm. Its payments may sometimes be fitted into more than one year's itinerary; in such cases we have indicated the uncertainty with a question mark and enclosed what we think is the less likely of the two possibilities within square brackets (e.g., the payment in the 9 December 1591 to 29 November 1592 account is listed under both our 1591–2 and 1592–3 itineraries, but we think that the earlier listing is more likely, as there are others for 1591–2 from nearby locations on the Midlands circuit).

We should also note that the date ranges given may reflect further information (in addition to published and unpublished REED transcriptions) derived from our search of annual accounts in the manuscript reproductions available to us at the REED office. While we have been conservative in assessing these sources, we have provided such further information about the approximate dating of some payments when there is sufficient evidence in context to indicate that the accounts were entered in chronological order. Where it is impossible to determine when during a year the troupe visited a generally dated location or region, we have listed such entries at the end of the year (e.g., Shrewsbury, 1582–3). We have been encouraged by the discovery that such impossibilities are few and that locations with more precise dates fitted together into regional circuits with surprising comfort as the itinerary was drafted. As explained in chapter 3, there are some years when conflicting dates indicate regional tours by divided branches of the Queen's Men.

The other column categories list in summary form the geographical location on the itinerary, the auspices under which the performance was given (city, town, university or household), the amount of payment when that can be determined, and further details such as performance venue or payment for non-performance. A + sign following a payment indicates that there was additional income for the performance (e.g., Leicester, 1582–3).

SOURCES

REED volumes

York, ed. Alexandra F. Johnston and Margaret Rogerson, 2 vols. (Toronto, 1979)
Chester, ed. Lawrence M. Clopper (Toronto, 1979)
Coventry, ed. R. W. Ingram (Toronto, 1981)
Newcastle upon Tyne, ed. J. J. Anderson (Toronto, 1982)
Norwich 1540–1642, ed. David Galloway (Toronto, 1984)
Cumberland/Westmorland/Gloucestershire, ed. Audrey Douglas and Peter Greenfield (Toronto, 1986)
Devon, ed. John M. Wasson (Toronto, 1986)
Cambridge, ed. Alan H. Nelson, 2 vols. (Toronto, 1988)
Herefordshire/Worcestershire, ed. David N. Klausner (Toronto, 1990)
Lancashire, ed. David George (Toronto, 1991)
Shropshire, ed. J. Alan B. Somerset, 2 vols. (Toronto, 1994)
Somerset including Bath, ed. James Stokes with Robert J. Alexander, 2 vols. (Toronto, 1996)
Bristol, ed. Mark C. Pilkinton (Toronto, 1997)

REED Collections in Progress

Abingdon Chamberlains' Accounts, Berkshire Record Office: A/FAc 1, extracts forthcoming in Berkshire, ed. Alexandra F. Johnston
Bess of Hardwick's Household Accounts, Chatsworth House: MSS. 7(H), 8, extracts forthcoming in Derbyshire, ed. Barbara D. Palmer and John M. Wasson
Beverley Town Accounts, Beverley Town Hall, extracts forthcoming in Beverley, ed. Diana Wyatt
Canterbury Chamberlains' Accounts, Canterbury Cathedral Archives: CA/FA18, 19, 20, extracts forthcoming in Kent: Diocese of Canterbury, ed. James M. Gibson
Congleton Order Book and Borough Account Book 1, Congleton Town Hall, extracts forthcoming in Cheshire, ed. David Mills and Elizabeth Baldwin
Francis Clifford's Household Accounts, Chatsworth House: Bolton Abbey MS. 216, extracts forthcoming in Clifford Family, ed. John M. Wasson
Dover Chamberlains' Accounts, Centre for Kentish Studies, Maidstone, extracts forthcoming in Kent: Diocese of Canterbury, ed. James M. Gibson
Dublin Treasurer's Book, Dublin City Archives: MR/35, extracts forthcoming in Ireland, ed. Alan J. Fletcher
Faversham Chamberlains' Accounts, Centre for Kentish Studies, Maidstone: FA/FAc 13, 14, 197, 17, 18, 19, 20/1, 21, 22/1, 23/1, 25, 26, 27, 30, extracts forthcoming in Kent: Diocese of Canterbury, ed. James M. Gibson
Folkestone Chamberlains' Accounts, J. O. Halliwell-Phillipps's Literary Scrapbooks, Folger Shakespeare Library: W.b. 173, extracts forthcoming in Kent: Diocese of Canterbury, ed. James M. Gibson

Fordwich Chamberlains' Accounts, Canterbury Cathedral Archives: Fordwich Bundle 8, No. 50A, extracts forthcoming in Kent: Diocese of Canterbury, ed. James M. Gibson

Hythe Assembly Book and Chamberlains' Accounts, Hythe Borough Archives: MS. 1208, extracts forthcoming in Kent: Diocese of Canterbury, ed. James M. Gibson

Leicester Chamberlains' Accounts, Leicestershire Record Office: BRIII/2/50, 52, 53, 54, 56, 58, 60, 61, 62, 63, 64, 65, 66, 68, 71, extracts forthcoming in Leicestershire, ed. Alice B. Hamilton

Lord North's Household Accounts, BL: Stowe 774, vols. 1 and 2, extracts forthcoming in Cambridgeshire, ed. Anne Brannen

Lydd Chamberlains' Accounts, Lydd Town Archives: Ly/FAc7, Ly/FPc2, Ly/FPc4, extracts forthcoming in Kent: Diocese of Canterbury, ed. James M. Gibson

Lyme Regis Mayors' Accounts, Dorset Record Office: DC/LR/G2/2, extracts forthcoming in Dorset, ed. Rosalind C. Hays and C. E. McGee

Macclesfield, Accounts of Sir Edward Fitton, Chester City Record Office: CR/63/2/341/18, extracts forthcoming in Cheshire, ed. David Mills and Elizabeth Baldwin

Maidstone Chamberlains' Accounts, Centre for Kentish Studies, Maidstone: MD/FCAI/1586, 1588, 1589, 1591, 1592, 1594, 1595, 1596; Mayor's Account, Centre for Kentish Studies, Maidstone: MD/FCAI/1593, extracts forthcoming in Kent: Diocese of Canterbury, ed. James M. Gibson

Middleton Household Accounts, Nottingham University Library: MiA62, extracts forthcoming in Nottinghamshire, ed. John C. Coldewey

Newark Alderman's Account Memorandum and Chamberlain's Warrant, Newark Museum: Bundle D6.75/H27, no. 320, D6.75/H32, extracts forthcoming in Nottinghamshire, ed. John C. Coldewey

New Romney Chamberlains' Accounts, Centre for Kentish Studies, Maidstone: NR/FAc2, 814; Halliwell-Phillipps's Literary Scrapbooks, Folger Shakespeare Library: W.b. 147, extracts forthcoming in Kent: Diocese of Canterbury, ed. James M. Gibson

Nottingham Chamberlains' Accounts, Nottinghamshire Record Office: CA 1622/23, 1625, 1626, 1629, 1630, 1631; Nottingham Court Papers, Nottinghamshire Record Office: CA 4624, extracts forthcoming in Nottinghamshire, ed. John C. Coldewey

Oxford Chamberlains' Accounts, Oxfordshire Archives: P.5.1–2, extracts forthcoming in Oxford, ed. Alexandra F. Johnston and Diana Wyatt

Oxford University: Vice-Chancellor's Accounts, Oxford University Archives: W.P. β 21.(4); Christ Church Disbursement Book, Christ Church Archives: xii.b.32; extracts forthcoming in Oxford University, ed. John M. Elliott Jr.

Poole Mayors' Accounts, Poole Borough Archives: 119 (76), 191 (A32), extracts forthcoming in Dorset, ed. Rosalind C. Hays and C. E. McGee

Reading Cofferers' Accounts, Berkshire Record Office: R/FA 2/76, 2/77, 2/81, extracts forthcoming in Berkshire, ed. Alexandra F. Johnston

Rye Chamberlains' Accounts, East Sussex Record Office: Rye 60/9, 60/10, extracts forthcoming in Sussex, ed. Cameron Louis

Sherborne, St Mary the Virgin Churchwardens' Accounts, Dorset Record Office: PE/SH/CW69, 70, extracts forthcoming in Dorset, ed. Rosalind C. Hays and C. E. McGee

Southampton Book of Fines, Southampton Record Office: SC5/3/1, extracts forthcoming in Hampshire, edited by Peter Greenfield with Jane Cowling.

Stratford upon Avon Council Book A, Chamberlains' Accounts, Shakespeare Birthplace Trust Records Office: BRU 2/1; BRU 4/12, extracts forthcoming in Warwickshire, ed. J. Alan B. Somerset

Wallingford Bailiffs' Accounts, Berkshire Record Office: W/FAb 1, extracts forthcoming in Berkshire, ed. Alexandra F. Johnston

Weymouth Mayors' Accounts, Weymouth Borough Archives: Sherren MSS. 177, 184, extracts forthcoming in Dorset, ed. Rosalind C. Hays and C. E. McGee

Winchester Chamberlains' Accounts, Hampshire Record Office: W/E1/107–8, 110–13; Proceedings Book, Hampshire Record Office: W/B2/2; Coffer Accounts, Hampshire Record Office: W/E6/1, extracts forthcoming in Hampshire, ed. Peter Greenfield with Jane Cowling

Other published sources

Chambers, E. K. (ed.), 'Players at Ipswich', *Collections*, II, Part 3, Malone Society (Oxford, 1931), pp. 258–84

Cook, David and F. P. Wilson (eds.), *Collections*, VI, Malone Society (Oxford, 1962 for 1961)

Coldewey, J. C. (ed.), 'Playing companies at Aldeburgh 1566–1635', *Collections*, IX, Malone Society (Oxford, 1977), pp. 16–23

Galloway, David and John M. Wasson (eds.), *Collections*, XI, Malone Society (Oxford, 1980/1)

George, David and Monica Ory, 'Six payments to players and entertainers in seventeenth-century Warwick', *REEDN* 8:1 (1983), 8–12

Greenfield, Peter, 'Entertainments of Henry, Lord Berkeley, 1593–4 and 1600–5', *REEDN* 8:1 (1983), 12–24

Maxwell Lyte, H. and W. H. Stevenson, *The Manuscripts of his Grace the Duke of Rutland, K. G., preserved at Belvoir Castle*, Historical Manuscripts Commission, 4 vols. (London, 1888–1905), Vol. IV, pp. 260–558

Additional original and antiquarian sources

Chelmsford Churchwardens' Accounts, Essex Record Office: D/B3/3/162

Robert Dudley's Household Accounts, Christ Church Archives: Evelyn MS. 258b

Maldon Chamberlains' Accounts, Essex Record Office: D/B3/3

Marlborough Chamberlains' Accounts, Wiltshire Record Office: G22/1/205/2

Rochester Chamberlains' Accounts, Rochester upon Medway Studies Centre: RCA/N1/9 and James Orchard Halliwell-Phillipps's Literary Scrapbooks, Folger Shakespeare Library: W.b. 173 (entries for 1592, 1594 and 1594–5)

Saffron Walden Chamberlains' Accounts, Saffron Walden Town Hall

Year	Location	Auspices	Account date	Payment
1582–3	Ipswich	Town		40s
	Aldeburgh	Town	[2 June–24 June 1583]	20s
	Kirtling	North House	3–4 June	20s
	Norwich	City	c. 15 June–1 July	40s
	Norwich	Cathedral		(part of 45s total)
	Abingdon	Town	after 24 June	20s + 16d (wine)
	Gloucester	City	after 26 May	30s
	Bath	City	c. June/July 1583	20s 7½d
	Bristol	City	24 July	£2 (Guildhall)
	Canterbury	City		40s (Court Hall)
	Faversham	Town	26 August	20s
	Dover	Town	[5 April–8 Sept.]	40s
	Lydd?	Town	[22 July 1583– 22 July 1584]	20s
	Leicester	City	after 25 July	38s 4d+
	Nottingham	Town	2 Sept.	20s
	Rye	Town	14 Sept.	20s
	Shrewsbury	Town		40s 6d
1583–4	Marlborough	Town	[15 Nov. 1583– 15 Nov. 1584]	7s
	London	City	[28 Nov.–Shrovetide] (licence to play)	
	Whitehall	Court	26, 29 Dec., 3 March	£20 (3 plays)
	Saffron Walden	Town	[Dec. 1583– Dec. 1584]	6s 2d
	Cambridge	Town	9 July	20s
	Cambridge	Univ.		50s (not to play)
	Kirtling	North House	13–14 July	10s
	Norwich	Cathedral		(part of 30s total)
	York	City	August	£3 6s 8d (Common Hall)
	York	Minster	[11 Nov. 1583– 11 Nov. 1584]	40s
	Southampton	Town		£2
	Rye	Town	19 Sept.	20s
	Lydd	Town	[22 July 1584– 21 March 1585]	20s
	Hythe	Town	[2 Feb. 1584– 2 Feb. 1585]	10s + 20s (possibly 2 visits)
	Folkestone	Town	[8 Sept. 1583– 8 Sept. 1584]	10s
	Dover	Town	Sept./Oct. 1584	40s + 3s (breakfast)[1]

Year	Location	Auspices	Account date	Payment
1584–5	Leicester	City	30 Sept.	15s 8d+
	Wollaton Hall	Middleton House	10 Oct.	12d (to boy with players)
	Greenwich	Court	26 Dec.	(part of £40 total below)
	London	Leicester House	28 Dec.	£10
	Greenwich	Court	3, 6 Jan., 23 Feb.	£40 (4 plays)
	London	Leicester House	21 April	£5
	Greenwich?	Court	17 May	40s (Tarlton)
	Cambridge	Town	[24 Feb.–July]	26s 8d
	Norwich	Cathedral		(part of 30s total)
1585–6	London	Leicester House	20 Nov.	£5
	Greenwich	Court	26 Dec., 1 Jan., 13 Feb.	£30 (3 plays)
	Bridgwater	Town	[October–October]	30s
	Exeter	City	[April–24 June]	53s 4d
	Bristol	City	[17–23 July]	20s (played not)
	Bath	City	c. June/July 1586[2]	19s 4d + 26s 8d gathered
	Abingdon	Town	after 24 June	20s
	Oxford	City		10s
	Coventry	City	[30 Nov.–15 Nov.]	40s
	Leicester	City	[after 9 June– before 8 Sept.]	24s+
	Nottingham	Town	13 August	40s
	Lynn	Town		£3 10s (part of summary total with Chamberlain's)
	Norwich	City	after perambulation day (later May)	40s
	Aldeburgh	Town		20s
	Faversham	Town	22 August	20s
	Lydd	Town	21 Sept.	20s
	Hythe?	Town	[2 Feb. 1586– 2 Feb. 1587]	20s
	Canterbury	City	27 Sept.	30s (Court Hall)
	Maidstone	Town	[7 Sept.–19 Oct.]	23s 4d (+wine?)
1586–7	Rye	Town	29 Sept.	20s
	Dover	Town	[24 Sept.–8 Oct.]	40s + 10s 8d (drinking to welcome & breakfast)
	Ipswich	Town	25 Oct.	26s 8d
	Kirtling	North House	28–9 Oct.	13s

Year	Location	Auspices	Account date	Payment
1586–7 cont.	Greenwich	Court	26 Dec., 1, 6 Jan. 28 Feb.	£40 (4 plays)
	Thame	Town	13 June	(Knell killed at White Hound by Towne)
	Abingdon	Town		10 <s?> (+ unknown sum for Guildhall windows mended)
	Saffron Walden	Town		6s 8d
	Cambridge	Trinity Coll.	24 June	30s
	Norwich	Cathedral	[after Christmas– Sept.?]	(part of 36s 8d)
	Ipswich	Town	3 July	26s 8d[3]
	Gloucester	City		30s
	Bath	City	13 July	15s+
	Aldeburgh	Town	19 July	40s
	Bristol	City	[23–9 July]	£2 (Guildhall)
	Southampton	Town	25 July	40s
	Lynn	Town	4 August	40s
	Rye	Town	12 August	20s
	Lydd?	Town	[22 July 1587– 22 July 1588]	20s
	New Romney	Town	13 August	20s
	Dover	Town	c. August	40s + 5s 2d (at departure)
	Hythe?	Town	[2 Feb. 1587– 2 Feb. 1588]	20s
	Canterbury	City		20s
	Nottingham	Town	20 August	13s 4d (with musicians)
	Beverley	Town	4 Sept.	(59s 2d, totalled with others)
	York	City	9 Sept.	£3 6s 8d (Common Hall)
	Leicester	City	[after 16 July– 28 Sept.]	24s+
	Coventry	City	Sept. (twice)	40s + 20s
	Stratford	Town	[17 Dec.–17 Dec.]	20s (+ 16d paid for mending broken form)
	Worcester	City	(later in account)	10s
1587–8	Faversham	Town	autumn?[4]	12s 2d
	Maidstone	Town	[15 Oct.–25 Dec.]	20s
	Saffron Walden	Town		3s 4d

Year	Location	Auspices	Account date	Payment
1587–8 cont.	Aldeburgh	Town	16 Dec.	20s
	Greenwich	Court	26 Dec., 6 Jan., 18 Feb.	£20 (3 plays)
	Canterbury	City	27 March	20s
	Dover	Town	c. 6 April	10s
	Hythe?	Town	[2 Feb. 1588– 2 Feb. 1589: early]	10s
	New Romney	Town	[25 March–8 April]	20s
	Lydd	Town	after 22 March?[5]	10s
	Rye	Town	10 April	20s
	Lyme Regis	Town	3 June	8s
	Exeter	City		20s
	Plymouth	Town	early–mid June	10s
	Gloucester	City	12 July	33s 6d
	Bath	City	19 July	23s
	Bristol	City	20 July	£2 (Guildhall)
	Bath	City	14 August	17s (players) +10s (tumblers)
	Bristol	City	16 August	26s 8d (Guildhall: players & tumblers)
	Worcester	City		(part of £108 2s 11d total)
1588–9	New Park	Derby House	c. 10–11 Oct.	
	Nottingham	Town	before 17 Nov.	20s (Symons & co.)
	Leicester	City	6 Nov.	10s + ('certen of her Maiestes playars')[6]
	Coventry?	City	[14 Nov. 1587– 4 Dec. 1588]	40s
	Oxford	City		10s
	Lynn	Town		26s 8d (with 2 messengers)
	Norwich	City	10 Dec.	£4 (part of 2 rewards)
	Ipswich	Town	17 Dec.	20s
	Whitehall	Court	26 Dec., 9 Feb.	£20 (2 plays)
	Dover	Town	c. Christmas	20s
	Faversham	Town	30 Jan.	20s[7]
	Canterbury	City	c. 2 Feb.	20s
	Maidstone	Town	[17 Feb.–4 March]	13s 4d
	Folkestone	Town	[8 Sept. 1588– 8 Sept. 1589]	5s

Year	Location	Auspices	Account date	Payment
1588–9 cont.	Hythe	Town	[2 Feb. 1589– 2 Feb. 1590: early]	20s
	New Romney	Town	14 Feb.	10s
	Lydd	Town	15 Feb.	20s
	Rye	Town	17 Feb.	20s
	Winchester	City	10 March	20s
	Lyme Regis	Town	[mid 1588–9]	6s 6d (tumblers)
	Lyme Regis	Town	(later payment)	10s
	Gloucester	City	17 April	20s
	Coventry?	City	[4 Dec. 1588– 26 Nov. 1589]	20s + 20s
	Nottingham	Town	after January	20s (2 Duttons et al.)
	Leicester	City	20 May	10s 8d+ ('others moe of her mayestyes Playars')[8]
	Ipswich	Town	22 May	30s
	Aldeburgh	Town	30 May	40s
	Norwich	City	3 June	(part of £4 total)
	Lathom	Derby House	6–7 July	
	Maidstone	Town	2 August	20s
	Canterbury	City	after 24 June	30s (Court Hall)
	Dover	Town	c. 23 August	40s
	Folkestone	Town		20s
	New Romney	Town	before 30 August	16s
	Lydd?	Town	[22 July 1589– 22 July 1590]	20s
	Rye	Town	25 August	20s
	Reading	Town	2 Sept.	20s
	Winchester	City	Sept.	20s
	Knowsley	Derby House	6–7 Sept.[9]	
	Carlisle	Town	[c. 10–20 Sept.]	
	Dublin	City		£3 + 1s
1589–90	Bristol	City	[5–11 Oct.]	£2 (Guildhall)
	Exeter	City	(early)	26s 8d
	Edinburgh	City	October	
	Bath	City	Nov.	15s
	Chester	Cathedral	[c. 19–25 Nov.]	20s
	[Coventry?	City	4 Dec. 1588– 26 Nov. 1589	20s + 20s]
	Richmond	Court	26 Dec.	(part of £20 below) (Duttons & Lanham)
	Faversham	Town	unspecified date + 4 Jan.	20s+ 20s (with Essex's)

Year	Location	Auspices	Account date	Payment
1589–90 *cont.*	Folkestone	Town	[8 Sept. 1589– 8 Sept. 1590]	10s
	Greenwich	Court	1 March	£20 (2 plays)
	Norwich	City	22 April	40s (Turk on ropes at New Hall)
	Knowsley	Derby House	25–6 June	(Mr Dutton *et al.*)
	Shrewsbury	Town		20s
	Shrewsbury	Town	24 July	(Cornmarket: with tumblers)
	Bridgnorth	Town	after 24 June	10s (dancing on rope)
	Ludlow	Town	July	10s + 12*d* (wine & sugar)
	Oxford	City		10s
	Oxford	Christ Church		10s
	Oxford	Univ.	[16 July 1589– 10 July 1590]	20s
	Canterbury	City	10 August	20s
	Bristol	City	[2–8 August]	30s (at Free School; players, tumbling with Turk on rope)
	New Romney	Town	20 August	20s
	Lydd?	Town	[22 July 1590– 22 July 1591]	20s
	Rye	Town	25 August	20s
	Gloucester	City	[23 August–17 Sept.]	30s (College churchyard)
	Marlborough	Town	[15 Nov. 1589– 13 Nov. 1590]	10s
	Winchester	City		20s
	Nottingham	Town	[3 August–29 Sept.]	20s
	Coventry?	City	[26 Nov. 1589– 1 Dec. 1590]	40s (with Turk)
1590–1	Chester	Cathedral	[29 Sept.–25 Nov.]	20s 10*d*
	Shrewsbury	Town		40s
	Leicester	City	30 Oct.	40s+ ('att the hall door')[10]
	Richmond	Court	26 Dec. (Duttons), 1 Jan. (Lanham)	
	Richmond	Court	3, 6 Jan. (Duttons)	
	Greenwich	Court	14 Feb. (Duttons)	£50 (5 plays)
	Maidstone	Town	2 Jan.	20s
	Canterbury	City	11 Jan.	20s
	Dover	Town	*c.* 23 Jan.	10s

Year	Location	Auspices	Account date	Payment
1590–1 cont.	Folkestone	Town	[8 Sept. 1590– 8 Sept. 1591]	10s + 5s [2 times]
	Winchester	City	Feb.	20s
	Southampton	Town	14 Feb.	20s (with Sussex's)
	Bristol	City	[28 Feb.–6 March]	26s 8d (with Sussex's at Guildhall)
	Gloucester	City		30s
	Gloucester	City		30s (with Sussex's)
	Coventry	City	24 March	15s (with Sussex's)
	Ipswich	Town	15 May	20s
	Ipswich	Town	28 May	30s ('Another company')[11]
	Maidstone	Town	28 May	10s
	Maidstone	Town		10s[12]
	Canterbury	City		(part of 30s total)
	Faversham	Town	2 June	10s
	Fordwich	Town	[7 Dec. 1590– 7 Dec. 1591]	13s 4d (Chapel Children)
	Aldeburgh	Town	c. 7 June	(servant to player buried: Humphrey Swain, youth)
	New Romney	Town	9 June	10s
	Lydd	Town	[22 July 1590– 22 July 1591]	13s 4d (Chapel Children)
	Lydd	Town	[22 July 1590– 22 July 1591]	13s 4d
	Winchester	City	June	20s
	Lynn	Town	20 June (+ another time)	£4
	Norwich	City	23 June	40s
	Cambridge	Univ.		20s (not to play)
	Saffron Walden	Town		3s 4d (+ 8d for quart of wine to 1 man)
	Southampton	Town	29 June	20s (Mr Dutton)[13]
	Poole	Town	9 July	20s + 11s gathered (with Chapel Children)
	Weymouth	Town		10s

Year	Location	Auspices	Account date	Payment
1590–1 cont.	Bath	City	[June–19 Sept.]	15s 6d+
	Bristol	City	[27 July–29 Sept.]	30s (Guildhall)
	Oxford	City	[24 Nov. 1590– 17 Nov. 1591]	13s 4d
	Newcastle	City	early August[14]	£5
	Newark	Town		20s
	Winkburn	Manners House	18 August	40s
	Leicester	City	after 26 June	26s 8d (Chapel Children)
	Coventry	City	24 August	30s
	Stratford	Town	[25 Dec. 1590– 24 Dec. 1591]	20s
	Aldeburgh	Town	c. 29 Sept.	40s
1591–2	Chester	Cathedral	[29 Sept.–25 Nov.]	40s
	Worcester	City		£4 (with trumpeters)
	Coventry	City	20 Oct.	20s
	Whitehall	Court	26 Dec.	£10 (1 play)
	Maidstone	Town	[1 Nov. 1591– 1 Nov. 1592]	30s
	Rochester	City	[1592]	20s
	Faversham	Town		40s (played 2 times)
	Canterbury	City	30 March	20s
	Fordwich	Town	[6 Dec. 1591– 4 Dec. 1592]	20s + 16d (horsemeat & beer)
	Fordwich	Town	(another time?)	6s 8d
	Folkestone	Town	[8 Sept. 1591– 8 Sept. 1592]	7s
	New Romney	Town	[25 March 1592– 24 March 1593]	10s
	Lydd	Town	[22 July 1591– 22 July 1592]	20s
	Aldeburgh	Town		20s[15]
	Ipswich	Town	1 May	33s 4d
	Norwich	City	27 May[16]	40s (played not)
	Saffron Walden	Town		6s 8d
	Cambridge	Trinity Coll.		2s 6d (1 player)
	Cambridge	Univ.	10 June	20s (not to play)
	Gloucester	City	[22 May–4 August]	30s (+ 9s 5d breakfast)
	Bristol	City	[2–15 July]	£2
	Bath	City	[June 1591– 10 June 1592]	40s
	Leicester	City	after 10 June	40s +

Year	Location	Auspices	Account date	Payment
1591–2 cont.	Nottingham	Town	[27 March–1 August]	20s
	York	City	24 July	£3 6s 8d
	York	Minster	24 July	20s
	Southampton	Town	3 August	40s
	Winchester	City		20s
	Bath	City	c. 22 August[17]	14s 9d
	Stratford	Town	[25 Dec. 1591– 25 Dec. 1592]	20s
	Coventry?	City	[9 Dec. 1591– 29 Nov. 1592]	40s[18]
	Cambridge	Town		10s
	Cambridge	Univ.	[24 August–29 Sept.] (Sturbridge Fair)	(warrant vs Dutton *et al.*)
1592–3	Aldeburgh	Town	11 October	20s
	Ipswich	Town		26s 8d
	Maidstone	Town	[2 Nov. 1592– 2 Nov. 1593]	20s
	Faversham	Town		20s
	Canterbury	City	17 Nov.	10s + 3s dinner (with music)
	Fordwich	Town	[6 Dec. 1592– 4 Dec. 1593]	6s 8d
	New Romney	Town	[25 March 1592– 25 March 1593]	10s
	[Coventry?	City	9 Dec. 1591– 29 Nov. 1592	40s]
	Reading	Town	c. Feb.	20s[19]
	Oxford	City	25 Feb.	10s
	Lyme Regis	Town	[9 Dec.–26 May]	12s 6d + 7s 6d gathered (Duttons)
	Plymouth	Town	(after Coronation Day, 15 Jan.)	9s
	Exeter	City		36s 8d
	Barnstaple	Town		10s
	Bridgwater	Town	3 April	15s
	Coventry?	City	[29 Nov. 1592– 27 Nov. 1593]	40s
	Stratford?	Town	[25 Dec. 1592– 25 Dec. 1593]	20s
	Caludon	Berkeley House	3 June	£3
	Leicester	City	20 June	24s+
	Chatsworth	Cavendish House	28 June	20s
	Kendal	Town	summer	20s
	Newcastle	City	later August[20]	£3
	York	City	Sept.	53s 4d

Year	Location	Auspices	Account date	Payment
1593–4	Ipswich	Town	before 10 March	26s 8d
	Norwich	City	18 Oct.	40s
	Maidstone	Town	[2 Nov. 1593– 2 Nov. 1594]	20s
	Faversham	Town		30s (played twice)
	Canterbury	City	[5–25 Dec.]	20s
	Southampton	Town	26 Nov.	£1 6s 8d
	Hampton Ct	Court	6 Jan.	£10
	Rochester	City	[1594]	£1
	Southwark	Rose Theatre	1–8 April[21]	(with Sussex's)
	Caludon	Berkeley House	1 July	12s
	Coventry	City	4 July	40s
	Gloucester	City	[13 Feb.–Sept.]	40s
	Bath	City	[11 Sept. 1593–Sept./ Oct. 1594]	22s 6d
	Bristol	City	[4–10 August]	30s
	Southampton	Town	after 10 August	£2
	York	Minster	2 Sept.	20s
	Leicester	City		10s+
1594–5	Gloucester	City	[before 1 Jan.]	30s
	Bath	City	[11 Sept. 1594– 10 Oct. 1595: early]	18s 4d
	Bridgwater	Town	[19 Oct.–15 Nov.]	£1
	Rochester	City	22 Feb.	20s
	Maidstone	Town	[2 Nov. 1594– 2 Nov. 1595]	20s
	Canterbury	City	[25 Dec.–March]	30s
	Dover	Town	[8 Sept. 1594– 8 Sept. 1595][22]	20s
	Folkestone	Town	[8 Sept. 1594– 8 Sept. 1595]	5s
	Lydd	Town	[22 July 1594– 22 July 1595]	3s 4d + 13s 4d (another time?)
	Rye	Town	21 March	20s
	New Romney	Town	[25 March 1595– 25 March 1596][23]	10s
	Winchester	City	3 April	20s
	Lyme Regis	Town	15 April	15s 4d
	Exeter	City	23 April	20s
	Bridgwater	Town	29 April	£1
	Oxford	City		20s
	Oxford	Univ.	[12 July 1594– 5 Aug. 1595]	20s
	Wallingford	Town		2s 6d
	Ipswich	Town	*c.* early June	26s 8d

Year	Location	Auspices	Account date	Payment
1594–5 *cont.*	Norwich	City	25 June	30s
	Lynn	Town	21 July	20s
	Leicester	City	after 16 July	40s
	Londes-borough	Clifford House	4 August	3s 4d
	York	City	8 August	£3 6s 8d
	Coventry	City	29 August	20s
1595–6	Ipswich	Town	(first entry)	26s 8d
	Lynn	Town		20s
	Saffron Walden	Town		10s
	Leicester	City	[26 Nov.–2 May]	11s +
	Coventry	City	[2 Dec. 1595–2 Dec. 1596]	10s
	Oxford	Univ.	[5 Aug. 1595–17 July 1596]	0s (not to play)
	Worcester	City		(part of £44 2½d total)
	[Coventry?	City	2 Dec. 1595–2 Dec. 1596	40s]
	Rochester	City	3 April	10s
	Rye	Town	24 April	20s
	Lydd?	Town	[22 July 1595–22 July 1596]	20s
	New Romney	Town	28 April	10s
	Folkestone	Town	[8 Sept. 1595–8 Sept. 1596]	6s
	Faversham	Town	30 April	20s
	Maidstone	Town	[2 Nov. 1595–2 Nov. 1596]	20s
	Exeter	City		13s 4d
	Bridgwater	Town	[13 May–2 July]	£1
	York	City	July	40s (Common Hall)
	York	Minster	[11 Nov. 1595–11 Nov. 1596]	20s
	Gloucester	City	(later in acct)	30s + 3s 2d (wine & sugar)
	Bristol	City	[8–21 August]	£2 (Guildhall)
	Hardwick	Hardwick House	[5–11 Sept.]	20s ('certaine of the Queens plaiers')[24]
1596–7	Coventry?	City	[2 Dec. 1595–2 Dec. 1596]	40s
	Worcester	City		(part of £44 4s 1d total)

Year	Location	Auspices	Account date	Payment
1596–7 cont.	Bridgnorth	Town	[2 Jan. 1596– 2 Jan. 1597]	20s
	Shrewsbury	Town		20s
	Ludlow	Town	[Oct.]	20s
	Leominster	Town	12 Oct.	20s
	Canterbury	City	before 20 March[25]	
	Faversham	Town	before 27 March	20s
	Rye	Town	12 March	16d (wine)
	Lydd?	Town	[22 July 1596– 22 July 1597]	20s
	Folkestone	Town	[8 Sept. 1596– 8 Sept. 1597]	6s
	Dover	Town	c. 22 March	12s
	Ipswich	Town	19 April	20s
	Dunwich	Town	[5 May–16 July]	6s
	Saffron Walden	Town	c. 24 June	3s 4d
	Cambridge	Town		20s
	Cambridge	Univ.	before 26 June	20s
	Oxford	City	before 2 July	10s
	Bath	City	[15 Oct. 1596– 15 Oct. 1597]	31s 10d (twice)
	Bristol	City	[24–30 July]	£2
	Weymouth	Town		10s (+ 2s 6d wine)
	Sherborne	Town	[18 Feb. 1597– 5 Feb. 1598]	2s (church house rental)
	Winchester	City		20s
	Oxford	City	after 2 July	10s
	Nottingham	Town	8 July	(1 of players: John Towne)
	Leicester	City	after 26 Jan.	30s+
	Coventry?	City	[1 Dec. 1596– 7 Dec. 1597]	20s
1597–8	Congleton	Town	[29 Sept.–25 Dec.]	20s
	Bristol	City	[6 Nov.–25 Dec.]	£2 (Guildhall)
	Bridgwater	Town	9 Dec.	20s (Robert Moon slain)
	Bath	City	[15 Oct. 1597– 13 Oct. 1598]	10s
	Marlborough	Town	[13 Dec. 1597– 15 Dec. 1598]	20s
	Leicester	City	9 Jan.	14s 6d+
	Worcester	City		(part of £57 1s 5d total)
	Dover	Town	22 April	13s 4d
	Faversham	Town		£1

Year	Location	Auspices	Account date	Payment
1597–8 cont.	Maldon?	Town	[6 Jan. 1598– 6 Jan. 1599]	10s
	Saffron Walden	Town		6s 8d
	Ipswich	Town	10 June	£1 6s 8d
	Norwich	City	27 June	20s
	York	City	9 August	40s (William Smith, John Garland, & John Cowper not to play; plague in York & north, March)
1598–9	Dartmouth	Town	6 Nov.	10s
	Plymouth	Town	before May	6s 8d
	Sherborne	Town	[5 Feb. 1598– 21 Jan. 1599]	2s (church house rental)
	Winchester	City	3 March	20s
	Lydd?	Town	after 25 March	20s
	Folkestone	Town	[8 Sept. 1598– 8 Sept. 1599]	6s
	Dover	Town	c. 21 April	10s
	Faversham	Town	after 14 Feb.	20s
	Chelmsford	Town		10s
	[Maldon	Town	6 Jan. 1598– 6 Jan. 1599	10s]
	Ipswich	Town		£1 6s 8d
	Dunwich	Town		6s 8d
	Reading	Town		20s
	Oxford	City		10s
	Oxford	Univ.	[18 July 1598– 18 July 1599]	(part of 25s total)
	Shrewsbury	Town		20s
	York	City	c. 12 Sept.	40s (Common Hall)
1599–1600	Leicester	City	[1–19 Jan.]	30s+
	Winchester	City		20s
	Wallingford	Town	before 24 June	2s 6d
	Ipswich	Town	20 June	20s
	Norwich	City	2 August	(permission for 4 days but not on Sabbath)
	Newark	Town		10s
	Hardwick	Hardwick House	[week of 26 Sept. 1600]	10s

Appendix A

Year	Location	Auspices	Account date	Payment
1600–1	Congleton	Town	[29 Sept.–25 Dec.]	10s
	Macclesfield	Town		10s
	Shrewsbury	Town		10s
	Ludlow	Town	6 Dec.	10s
	Leominster	Town		20s
	Coventry	City	[20 Nov. 1600– 2 Dec. 1601]	30s
	Caludon	Berkeley House	3 Jan.	20s
	Warwick	Town	[1 Nov. 1600– 1 Nov. 1601]	10s
	Bath	City	[14 Oct. 1600– 17 Oct. 1601]	20s
	Lydd	Town	10 July	20s
	New Romney	Town	25 July	10s
	Folkestone	Town	[8 Sept. 1600– 8 Sept. 1601]	5s
	Faversham	Town	*c.* 1 August	20s
	Ipswich	Town		10s
	Saffron Walden	Town		6s 8d
1601–2	Ipswich	Town	30 May	20s
	Norwich	City	4 June	40s
	York	City	27 July	£3 (Common Hall)
	Belvoir	Manners House	before 20 Sept.	10s
	Winchester	City	12 August	10s (supper)
	Bath	City	[2 Feb.– 15 Oct. 1602]	8s + 3s 2d (food & horsemeat only)
	Barnstaple	Town		15s
	Poole	Town		6s
1602–3	Leicester	City	30 Sept.	40s
	Coventry	City	[20 Dec. 1602– 17 Nov. 1603]	10s
	Congleton	Town	[25 Dec.–24 March]	13s 4d

APPENDIX B

Casting analysis

The largest moment of each play is here listed according to the definitions given in chapter 5 (pp. 99–102 above). For the texts of 1594 and later, a doubling scheme for minimum cast is then given. References are to Malone Society Reprints (MSR), Tudor Facsimile Texts (TFT), or Geoffrey Bullough, *Narrative and Dramatic Sources of Shakespeare* (Bullough).

Two plays from before 1594

Three Lords and Three Ladies of London (TFT). Final procession. Simplicity, Nemo, Pomp, Pleasure, Policy, Diligence, Fraud, Dissimulation, Love, Conscience, Lucre, Singing Wench, Wit, Wealth, Will.

Troublesome Reign of King John (Bullough). Part I, scene iv. King John, Pembroke, Salisbury, Chattilion, Bastard, King Philip, Lewes, Limoges, 1 Citizen, English Herald, French Herald, 2 Citizen, 3 Citizen, Queen Elinor, Constance, Arthur, Blanche. (Part II, scene iv would run higher if the call for 'all the Lords of France and England' were taken as literally as possible, with all the noblemen from the rest of the play brought onstage. The call for 'many Priests' in this scene also seems lavish. J. W. Sider (ed.), *The Troublesome Raigne of John, King of England* (New York, 1979), p. xii, casts the entire play for 12 men and 4 boys.

The doubling possibilities are not shown for these two plays, because they do not seem to be arranged for minimum casting. For each of the remaining seven plays, we list one of the possible minimum-casting schemes.

Five plays first entered or published in 1594

Selimus (MSR). End of xxv–beginning of xxvi: Mustaffa, Selimus, Sinam Bassa, Cali Bassa, Hali Bassa, Solima, 2 Janizars, Acomat, the Vizir, Regan, Tonombey, 2 Soldiers. The entire play can be cast from this group:

1. Selimus. Soldier (Acomat xv)?
2. Bajazeth. Tonombeius.
3. Prologue. 2 Messenger (i). Acomat. Bullithrumble.
4. Mustaffa. Soldier (xxvii).
5. 1 Mess. (i). Soldier (ii–vi). Vizir. Janizar (xviii). Page. Amurath.
6. Janizar. Aga.
7. Cherseoli. Hali Bassa. Belierbey.
8. Sinam. Janizar (viii). 2 Messenger (x). Soldier (xi–xiv).
9. Otrante. Cali Bassa. Soldier (xii–xiv).
10. Janizar.
11. Soldier (ii–vi). Regan. Abraham. Corcut. Aladin.
12. Mahomet. Solima. Queen of Amasia.
13. Soldier (ix, xxvi–xxix). Zonara. Janizar (xxi–xxiii).
14. Occhiale. Soldier (ix, xi–xxix). 1 Messenger (x).
    (Twice a soldier must change sides in under 10 lines: no. 8, in xiii–xiv; no. 14, in xxvi–xxvii. The plot of *Tamar Cam* has some rapid changes of allegiance within the scene – a change of headgear is all that is necessary. No. 10 as a Janizar can serve as 'soldier' in xvi and 'messenger' in xvii without change of costume.)

Friar Bacon and Friar Bungay (MSR). End of xiv–beginning xv: Miles, Devil, Prince Edward, Lacy, Warren, Ermsby, Bacon, Henry III, Emperor, Castile, Margaret, Elinor, 2 Lords. Casting the entire play for this group:

1. Bacon.
2. Prince Edward. 'Other' (iii).
3. Miles. Lambert.
4. Lacy. Serlsby's Son (20-line change).
5. Ralph Simnell. Devil. Hercules. Serlsby.
6. Clement. Henry III.
7. Warren. Richard. Bungay (10-line change).
8. Vandermast. Constable. Keeper. Attendant (xv).
9. Burdon. Castile. Post.
10. Mason. Emperor.
11. Ermsby. Thomas. Lambert's Son.
12. Margaret.
13. Hostess. Elinor.
14. Joan. 'Friend' (xiii). Attendant (xv).
    (The 10-line changes for Warren–Bungay are the quickest for speaking characters in the 1594 plays, but a friar can be set forth quickly in a long hooded robe worn over another costume. We assume that Bungay is part of the general exit at line 1280.)

True Tragedy of Richard III (MSR). End of xiii–beginning xiv: Buckingham, Banister, Herald, 6 Buckingham's men, Richard, Catesby, Page, 2 'others'. Casting the entire play for this group:

1. Richard III.
2. Dorset. Morton. Buckingham. Attendant (Richard). Richmond.
3. Edward IV. Rivers. Messenger (ix). Attendant (Richard). Terrell. Attendant (Buck.). Stanley.
4. Poetry. Page. 2 Messenger (xx).
5. Hastings. Innkeeper. Attendant (Edw.). Cardinal Forest. Attendant (Buck.). Stanley.
6. Lodowick. Grey. Noble (ix). Slawter. Herald. Messenger (xiv, xvi). Soldier.
7. Citizen. Vaughan. Attendant (Richard). Banister. Lovell. Messenger (xv).
8. Ghost. Catesby. Attendant (Edw.). Brokenbury. 1 Messenger (xx).
9. Perceval. Hapce. Noble (ix). Douten. Attendant (Buck.). Landoys. Soldier.
10. Attendant (Richard). 2 Citizen. Attendant (Buck.). Blunt. Soldier.
11. Truth. Queen Mother. Attendant (Richard). Soldier.
12. Shore's Wife. Prince Edward. Attendant (Buck.). George Stanley.
13. Hursly. Duke of York. Attendant (Richard). Report.
14. Elizabeth. Attendant (Richard). Attendant (Buck.).

King Leir. xxx, from line 2549 (MSR): Leir, Perillus, Gallian King, Mumford, 2 Soldiers, Chief of Town, Cordella, King of Cornwall, King of Cambria, 2 soldiers, Ragan, Gonorill. (The juxtaposition of xxix and xxx is assumed to have a gap covered by 'excursions' – i.e. it is not an 'immediate juxtaposition'.) Casting the entire play for this group:

1. Leir.
2. Skalliger. 3 Noble (iv). Messenger (xii–xix). 1 Noble (xxii). 1 Captain (xxvii–xix). Chief of Town.
3. Noble (i). Cornwall. 1 Mariner (xxiii). Naked Man (xxix).
4. Perillus. 2 Captain (xxix).
5. Gallian King.
6. Mumford.
7. 1 Noble (iv). Attendant (vi). Noble (x–xii). Naked man (xxix). English soldier (xxx).
8. 2 Noble (iv). Noble (xiv). 1 Mariner (xxiii). Gallian soldier (xxvi–xxx).
9. Cambria. 1 Watch (xxvii–xix).
10. Servant (v, xviii). Noble (x–xii). Ambassador (xviii–xxii). Gallian soldier (xxvi–xxx).
11. Servant (v). Attendant (vi). Noble (xiv). 2 Watch (xxvii–xxix). English soldier (xxx).
12. Cordella.
13. Ragan. Naked woman (xxix).
14. Gonorill. Naked woman (xxix).

Famous Victories of Henry V (Bullough). End of xix–beginning of xx. Henry V, Derick, John Cobbler, Exeter, Oxford, King of France, Dauphin, Burgundy, Secretary,

2 Attendants, Katherine, 2 Ladies. (Katherine's entrance direction is missing in xx, and we assume she is accompanied by the two ladies who attended her previous appearance.) Casting the entire play for this group:

1. Henry V.
2. Derick. French Herald.
3. John Cobbler. French Captain.
4. Exeter. Constable of France.
5. Oxford.
6. Ned. Sheriff (iii). King of France. English Soldier (xiv–xvi).
7. Oldcastle. Lord Chief Justice. Dauphin. Drummer.
8. Tom. Archbishop of Burges. French Soldier (xiii–xvii). Burgundy.
9. 2 Receiver. Henry IV. York. Secretary.
10. 1 Receiver. Thief. Porter. English Soldier (xiv). Attendant.
11. Laurence. Lord Mayor. Gaoler (15-line change). Archbishop of Canterbury. Messenger (xi). French Captain. French Soldier (xiii–xvii). Attendant.
12. Katherine.
13. Robin. Clerk. French Soldier (xiii–xiv). Lady.
14. Vintner's boy. Wife. English Soldier (xiv–xvi). Lady.

Two plays first entered or published after 1594

Old Wives Tale. Final scene. Frolic, Fantastic, 1 Brother, 2 Brother, 'Sacrapant' (i.e. Old Man restored), Eumenides, Jack, Old Wife, Venelia, Delya.

1. Frolic.
2. Fantastic.
3. 1 Brother. Huanebango. Wiggen.
4. 2 Brother. Lampriscus. Corebus.
5. Sacrapant. Harvestman. Churchwarden (5-line change.). Fiddler.
6. Antick. Eumenides. Fury (11-line change). Harvestman (12-line change). Friar.
7. Clunch. Erestus. Fury (16-line change). Jack. Sexton. Fiddler.
8. Madge.
9. Venelia. Woman (v). Zantippa. Hostess.
10. Delya. Woman (v). Celanta.
   (The rapid changes are part of the drama. See discussion in chapter 5, pp. 110–12 above.)

Clyomon and Clamydes. Scene xxii, with immediate juxtaposition of female roles at xxii and xxiii requiring a third boy. Clamydes, Clyomon, Subtle Shift, Alexander, Mustantius, 1 Lord, 2 Lord, Neronis, Queen of Strange Marches, Juliana. This casting follows that of Arleane Ralph in her critical edition (Ph.D. thesis, University of Toronto, 1996). Casting the entire play for this group:

1. Clyomon.
2. Clamydes.
3. Prologue. Subtle Shift.
4. 3 Lord (iii). Alexander. Bosun (viii). 3 Knight (x). Rumour. Corin. King of Denmark.
5. King. Bryan. Thras. Providence. Mustantius.
6. Lord (iii). Soldier (iv). Servant (vii). Lord (viii, xxii). Knight (x, xiii). Lord (xii, xvi). Lord (xxiii).
7. Lord (iii). Servant (vii). Lord (viii, xxii). Knight (x). Lord (xii, xvi). Lord (xxiii).
8. Soldier (iv). Neronis.
9. Juliana. Lady (viii). Queen of Strange Marches.
10. Herald. Lady (viii). Queen of Denmark.

APPENDIX C

Biographical notes on the Queen's Men

The actors who are known or can be reasonably surmised to have belonged to the Queen's Men at one time or another in the company's career are here listed in alphabetical order. The biographical notes are restricted to: (1) information which pertains to the Queen's Men; (2) previous company connections of the actors, when these are known; (3) references to the style, fame, and age of the players. For fuller biographical information (which is plentiful for some of these actors), and for citations of the documents which lie behind our outlines of fact, we refer the reader to the sources from which our notes are drawn: Edwin Nungezer, *A Dictionary of Actors* (New Haven, 1929); William Ingram, *A London Life in the Brazen Age: Francis Langley, 1548–1602* (Cambridge, MA, 1978), and *The Business of Playing: The Beginnings of the Adult Professional Theater in Elizabethan London* (Ithaca, NY, 1992); Mary Edmond, 'Pembroke's Men', *Review of English Studies* ns 25 (1974), 129–36; Scott McMillin, 'Simon Jewell and the Queen's Men', *Review of English Studies* ns 27 (1976), 174–7; and Mark Eccles, 'Elizabethan actors', *Notes and Queries* ns 38 (1991), 38–49; 454–61; continued in ns 39 (1992), 293–303; continued in ns 40 (1993), 165–76.

Adams, John. Member of original Queen's Men (1583) and still with them in 1588. Earlier with Sussex's Men (1576). Remembered as a comic, with Tarlton, by the stage-keeper in Jonson's *Bartholomew Fair* (Induction): 'I kept the Stage in Master Tarletons time, I thanke my starres. Ho! and that man had liv'd to have play'd in Bartholomew Fayre, you should ha' seene him ha' come in, and ha' beene coozened i' the Cloath-quarter, so finely! And Adams, the Rogue, ha' leap'd and caper'd upon him, and ha' dealt his vermine about, as though they had cost him nothing.'

Alleyn, Richard. With John Towne (q.v.) witnessed Philip Henslowe's loan to Francis Henslowe for a share in the Queen's Men in 1594. Not otherwise known to have been in the company. An actor of this name was with the Admiral's Men from 1597 until his death in 1601.

Attewell (or Ottewell), George. Possibly a Queen's Man in 1595, when he witnessed a loan from Philip Henslowe to Francis Henslowe for a half-share in an acting company. The company is unnamed, but Francis Henslowe was a sharer in the

Queen's Men a year earlier. Attewell had been with the Strange's/Admiral's company in the winter of 1590–1 and is probably the actor connected with 'Attewell's Jig' (1595).

Bentley, John. Member of original Queen's Men (1583). Briefly imprisoned with John Singer because of an affray in Norwich in June 1583. Dead in 1585, age 32. Known for tragic and heroic parts; an undated letter to Edward Alleyn refers to a wager that Alleyn could equal Bentley and Knell in their parts. Lauded (with Tarlton, Knell, and Alleyn) by Nashe in *Pierce Penilesse* (1592). Said in Dekker's *A Knight's Conjuring* (1607) to have been moulded out of the pens of the poets and perhaps to have been one of them himself. Remembered in Thomas Heywood's *Apology* (1612) as a great actor of the previous age.

Cooke, Lionel. Member of original Queen's Men (1583) and still with them in 1588. May be the 'Mr. Cooke' mentioned (with other names connected with the Queen's Men) in Simon Jewell's will, 1592.

Cowper, John. Recorded with William Smith and John Garland as Queen's players in York, August 1598.

Davis, Hugh. With John Towne (q.v.) witnessed Philip Henslowe's loan to Francis Henslowe for a share in the Queen's Men in 1594. Not otherwise known to have been in the company, or even a player.

Dutton, John. Member of original Queen's Men (1583) and still with them in 1588, 1590, 1591. Earlier connections with Warwick's Men and Oxford's Men. Gave age as about 60 in 1608. May have been connected with Duke of Lennox's Men, *c.* 1608. Died in 1614.

Dutton, Laurence. Brother of John Dutton. Not in original company. First known as a Queen's Man in a Nottingham record of 1589. Earlier connections with Warwick's Men and Oxford's Men. Some vivid personal touches are recorded in Eccles, *Notes and Queries*, ns 38 (1991), 48–9.

Garland, John. Member of original Queen's Men (1583) and still with them in 1588, 1598. In 1595, granted an annuity by the queen of 2 shillings per day for the rest of his life. Mentioned as 'owld garlland' by Philip Henslowe in 1604. Associated with Duke of Lennox's Men (along with Francis Henslowe, Abraham Savery) after the queen's death in 1603.

Heminges, John. Sometimes thought to have been a Queen's Man because he married the widow of William Knell on 10 March 1588. With Strange's Men by 6 May 1593, and with the Chamberlain's Men from 1594.

Henslowe, Francis. Borrowed £15 from Philip Henslowe, his uncle, 'to laye downe for his share to the Quenes players' in May 1594. (Henslowe's *Diary* gives the year as 1593, but Greg's correction to 1594 seems right.) The loan was witnessed by John Towne (q.v.) among others. Further loan of £9 from Philip Henslowe for a half-share 'with the company which he dothe play with all' in June 1595, witnessed by 'Wm Smyght player' (see Smith, William), 'gorge attewell player' (see Attewell, George), and 'Robard nycowlles player' (see Nichols, Robert). With Duke of Lennox's Men, together with John Garland (q.v.), Abraham Savery and one 'symcockes' in 1605. Died 1606 (born 1566).

Jewell, Simon. Known as an actor through his will, probated in August 1592, which refers to actors otherwise linked to the Queen's Men. See Cooke, Lionel; Johnson, William; Nichols, Robert; Smith, William.

Johnson, William. Member of original Queen's Men (1583) and still with them in 1588. Earlier with Leicester's Men. Apparently the 'Mr. Johnson' mentioned in Simon Jewell's will (1592) who was owed for his share in Jewell's company, as though he had recently withdrawn as sharer.

Knell, William. Not in original Queen's Men (1583), but with the company by June 1587, when he was killed in a fight with John Towne (q.v.). Several times compared with John Bentley (q.v.) as a heroic or tragic actor; may have joined the company as Bentley's replacement in 1585. Said to have played the Prince in *Famous Victories of Henry V*. Remembered in Thomas Heywood's *Apology* (1612) as a great actor of the previous age.

Lanham, John. Member of original Queen's Men (1583) and still with them in 1588, 1591. Previously with Leicester's Men. Remembered in Thomas Heywood's *Apology* (1612) as a great actor of the previous age.

Mills, Tobias. Member of original Queen's Men (1583). Dead in July 1585. Remembered in Thomas Heywood's *Apology* (1612) as a great actor of the previous age.

Moon, Robert. A player, slain in Bridgwater in December 1597, at about the time the Queen's Men were performing there. The possibility that Moon was a Queen's Man is discussed by Herbert Berry in his article with James Stokes, 'Actors and town hall in the sixteenth century', *Medieval and Renaissance Drama in England*, VI (1993), 73–80.

Nichols, Robert. A player who witnessed a loan to Francis Henslowe (q.v.) for a half-share in an acting company, perhaps the Queen's Men, in 1595. Other witnesses were George Attewell (q.v.) and William Smith (q.v.). Both Nichols and Smith were colleagues of Simon Jewell, according to Jewell's will, 1592.

Shank, John. Claimed late in a long life of acting to have once served Queen Elizabeth, but nothing else connects him with the Queen's Men.

Singer, John. Member of original Queen's Men (1583) and still with them in 1588. Previous company unknown. Involved in the Norwich affray of June 1583, and briefly gaoled. Joined Admiral's Men by autumn of 1594, and is not recorded with the Queen's Men again (although he was an ordinary Groom of the Chamber at the time of Elizabeth's funeral in 1603). Known for comic acting and improvisation. Remembered in Thomas Heywood's *Apology* (1612) as a great actor of the previous age.

Smith (or Smyght), William. A player who witnessed a loan to Francis Henslowe (q.v.) for a half-share in an acting company, perhaps the Queen's Men, in 1595. Other witnesses were George Attewell (q.v.) and Robert Nicholls (q.v.). Recorded as a Queen's Man, along with John Garland and John Cowper, in York, 1598. Smith and Nichols were colleagues of Simon Jewell, according to Jewell's will, 1592.

Symons, John. A tumbler connected with various acting companies from time to time, including the Queen's Men in 1588–9.

Tarlton, Richard. Member of original Queen's Men (1583) and still with them in 1588. Previously with Sussex's Men. Died in September 1588. The most famous actor of his day, known for comic routines and improvisations. Also a poet, dramatist, and fencer. Much biographical information, anecdote, and recollection given in Nungezer and Eccles.

Towne, John. Member of original Queen's Men (1583) and still with them in 1588, 1597. Killed his fellow actor William Knell with his sword in June 1587.

Wilson, Robert. Member of original Queen's Men (1583). Not in list of company from 1588, but this may be incomplete. Previously with Leicester's Men. Often linked with Tarlton for exemporal wit. Also a playwright. One of the extant plays from the Queen's Men, *Three Lords and Three Ladies of London*, appears to be his. In later 1590s, was writing for companies at Henslowe's Rose. Dead in 1600. Remembered in Thomas Heywood's *Apology* (1612) as a great actor of the previous age.

NOTES

Preface

1 Andrew Gurr, *The Shakespearian Playing Companies* (Oxford, 1996).
2 Bernard Beckerman, *Shakespeare at the Globe* (New York, 1962); Roslyn Knutson, *The Repertory of Shakespeare's Company, 1594–1613* (Fayetteville, Arkansas, 1991); J. Leeds Barroll, *Politics, Plague, and Shakespeare's Theater* (Ithaca, NY, 1991).

1 The London theatre of 1583

1 E. K. Chambers, *William Shakespeare: A Study of Facts and Problems*, 2 vols. (Oxford, 1930), I, 28; V. C. Gildersleeve, *Government Regulation of the Elizabethan Drama* (New York, 1908), p. 166.
2 'Three reluctant patrons and early Shakespeare', *Shakespeare Quarterly* 44 (1993), 159–74, and in private correspondence. Issues of patronage and politics are also covered in Leeds Barroll, *The Revels History of Drama in England*, vol. III, ed. Barroll *et al.* (London, 1975), pp. 3–27.
3 For 'the struggle between City and Court', see E. K. Chambers, *The Elizabethan Stage*, 4 vols. (Oxford, 1923), I, chap. IX (hereafter cited as *ES*). For the patronage system and the importance of offering gifts of love to the queen, see Wallace MacCaffrey, 'Place and patronage', in *Elizabethan Government and Society*, ed. S. T. Bindoff *et al.* (London, 1961); *Patronage in the Renaissance*, ed. Guy Fitch Lytle and Stephen Orgel (Princeton, NJ, 1981); and Leonard Tennenhouse, *Power on Display* (London, 1986), pp. 30–6.
4 For the children's companies, see W. Reavley Gair, *The Children of Paul's* (Cambridge, 1982); and Michael Shapiro, *Children of the Revels: The Boys' Companies of Shakespeare's Time and Their Plays* (New York, 1977).
5 For play publication we have followed *Annals of English Drama: 975–1700*, ed. A. Harbage, S. Schoenbaum, and S. Wagonheim, 3rd edn (London, 1989). Other information is based on Chambers, *ES*, vol. II for companies and theatres, and vol. III for playwrights. For the Red Lion, see Janet Loengard, 'An Elizabethan lawsuit: John Brayne, his carpenter, and the building of the Red Lion Theatre', *Shakespeare Quarterly* 34 (1983), 298–310. For the theatre at Newington Butts, see William Ingram, 'The playhouse at Newington Butts: a new proposal', *Shakespeare Quarterly* 21 (1970), 385–97.

6 R. Mark Benbow, 'Dutton and Goffe versus Broughton: a disputed contract for plays in the 1570s', *Records of Early English Drama Newsletter* (1981: 2), 3–9.

7 See Muriel C. Bradbrook, *The Rise of the Common Player* (Cambridge, MA, 1962), pp. 162–77.

8 Essex's Men played at court in February 1578; Berkeley's were in a London brawl in July 1581. There is no London record for Worcester's Men before 1583, but of course the evidence for the commercial playhouses of this time is scant. See *ES*, vol. II, under each company.

9 Recent studies of the travelling theatre and of London's position in the developing industry include Sally-Beth MacLean, 'Tour routes: "provincial wanderings" or traditional circuits?', and William Ingram, 'The costs of touring', both in *Medieval and Renaissance Drama in England*, VI (New York, 1993), pp. 1–14 and 57–62. See also Ingram, *The Business of Playing: The Beginnings of the Adult Professional Theater in Elizabethan England* (Ithaca, NY, 1992), pp. 14 and 89.

10 The 'duopoly' created for the Admiral's Men and the Chamberlain's Men in 1594 is a major theme of Gurr, *The Shakespearian Playing Companies*.

11 See Barbara Freedman, 'Elizabethan protest, plague, and plays: rereading the documents of control', *English Literary Renaissance* 26 (1996), 17–45.

12 *The English Drama: 1485–1585* (Oxford, 1969), p. 172.

13 Leeds Barroll's account in *The Revels History of Drama in English*, III, 1–27, can be consulted for a more complex interpretation, as can Gildersleeve's *Government Regulation*, p. 167.

14 For the development of weekday performances and the controversy over Sunday plays, see Wickham, *Early English Stages*, II, pt. 1 (New York, 1963), pp. 75–121.

15 The documents are reprinted in Chambers, *ES*, IV, under 'Documents of control'.

16 Gair, *Children of Paul's*, pp. 96–9; Chambers, *ES*, II, 15–40.

17 An estimate mid-way between the small bands of interluders before the 1570s and the large companies established in London playhouses by about 1590. See David Bevington, *From Mankind to Marlowe* (Cambridge, MA, 1962), pp. 86–113.

18 See M. B. Pulman, *The Elizabethan Privy Council in the Fifteen Seventies* (Berkeley, CA, 1971), pp. 128–34; and David Cressy, 'Binding the nation: the bonds of association, 1584 and 1696', in *Tudor Rule and Revolution*, ed. D. J. Guth and J. W. McKenna (Cambridge, 1982), pp. 217–34.

19 Chambers, *ES*, I, 269–307; Wickham, *Early English Stages*, II, pt. 1, 54–98. For an interpretation of the 1597 order different from Wickham's, see William Ingram, *A London Life in the Brazen Age* (Cambridge, MA, 1978), pp. 167–96. For a recent, thorough study of the 1572 items, see Peter Roberts, 'Elizabethan players and minstrels and the legislation of 1572 against retainers and vagabonds', in *Religion, Culture, and Society in Early Modern Britain: Essays in Honour of Patrick Collinson*, ed. Anthony Fletcher and Peter Roberts (Cambridge, 1994).

20 The chart is derived from the 'Court Calendar' in Chambers, *ES*, IV. Leeds Barroll in *The Revels History of Drama in English*, III, 1–27, gives useful emphasis to court patronage.

21 W. R. Streitberger, 'On Edmund Tyllney's biography', *Review of English Studies* ns 29 (1978), 11–35.

22 For the economic motive, see Gildersleeve, *Government Regulation*, p. 167; and Streitberger, 'Tyllney's biography', p. 23.

2   Protestant politics: Leicester and Walsingham

1 The patent, dated 10 May 1574, is now at the Public Record Office. A transcript appears in *Collections*, 1, Part 3, Malone Society (Oxford, 1909), pp. 262–3.

2 The Dudley Household Account Book was discovered by Sally-Beth MacLean among the Evelyn Family Collection on deposit in the Archives of Christ Church, Oxford (Evelyn MS. 258b); for further details, see MacLean, 'Leicester and the Evelyns: new evidence for the continental tour of Leicester's Men', *Review of English Studies* ns 39 (1988), 487–93. More recently, Leicester's biographer, Simon Adams, has published an edition of this with other Dudley account books in *Household Accounts and Disbursement Books of Robert Dudley, Earl of Leicester, 1558–1561, 1584–1586*, Camden Society 5th ser., vol. 6 (Cambridge, 1995). The provincial itinerary for Leicester's Men has been compiled by MacLean, from REED collections in print and in progress, for a separate study of that troupe.

3 The following records survive for the 1580–2 provincial performances by Leicester's Men. South-east: for 1580, Canterbury (Chamberlains' Accounts, Canterbury Cathedral Archives: CA/FA 18, f. 118), Faversham (Wardmote and Account Book, Faversham Borough Records: FA/AC 1, f. 239), and Fordwich (Chamberlains' Accounts, Canterbury Cathedral Archives: Fordwich Bundle 8, No. 45, f. iv); for 1581, New Romney (Chamberlains' Accounts, Centre for Kentish Studies, Maidstone: NR/FAC 7, f. 289) and Fordwich (Chamberlains' Accounts, Canterbury Cathedral Archives: Fordwich Bundle 8, No. 45, f. 3v). East Anglia: for 1580, Kirtling (BL: Stowe 774, f. 124); Ipswich (Chamberlains' Account Book 14, as transcribed by E. K. Chambers for Malone Society *Collections* II.3 (Oxford, 1931), p. 271), and Cambridge (Letter from John Hatcher, the Vice-Chancellor, to Lord Burghley, PRO: SP12/139, f. 76); for 1581, Norwich (Chamberlains' Accounts IX, Norwich Record Office: 18.a, f. 32); for 1582, Ipswich (Register A, transcribed in *Collections* II.3, p. 272, payment listed, more familiarly, for 'Lord Robts players'). North-east via Coventry: for 1580, Durham (Cathedral Treasurers' Accounts, University of Durham, Dept. of Palaeography and Diplomatic: Book 12, f. 25), Newcastle upon Tyne (Chamberlains' Account Books, Tyne and Wear County Council Archives Department: 543/16, f. 138) and Coventry (Chamberlains' and Wardens' Account Book II, Coventry Record Office: A 7(b), p. 45). South: for 1582, Salisbury (Corporation Ledger B, Wiltshire Record Office: G23/1/2, f. 339a), Winchester (Chamberlains' Accounts, Hampshire Record Office: W/EI/103, mb [5]) and Southampton (Book of Fines, Southampton City Record Office: SC 5/3/1, f. 182v). West Midlands via Coventry: for 1581–2, Shrewsbury (Town Payment Claims, Shropshire Record Office: 3365/525, single sheet) and Coventry (Chamberlains' and Wardens' Account Book II, Coventry Record Office: A 7(b), p. 78).

4 They first appear at Sudbury on 2 June 1585; see *Collections*, XI (Oxford, 1980/1), p. 197.

5 For more details see Sally-Beth MacLean, 'The politics of patronage: dramatic records in Robert Dudley's household books', *Shakespeare Quarterly* 44 (1993), 175–82.

6 This new evidence has been transcribed from the original MS. but is now available in Simon Adams's edition, *Household Accounts*. The queen's players were paid £10 by Leicester on 28 December 1584; £5 on 21 April and again on 20 November 1585.

7 The evidence from the lost household account has been published by R. C. Bald, 'Leicester's Men in the Low Countries', *Review of English Studies* 19 (1943), 395–7. Wilson was paid 40s on 4 March 1586 before returning to England with Sir Thomas Shirley (Bald, p. 396). He is recorded in BL: Harleian MS. 1641, f. 19v for carrying letters to the Low Countries in January 1586, presumably after the Queen's Men had played at court. He may well not have been part of their Shrovetide perform- ance in mid February. For a discussion of Leicester's role as governor of the Nether- lands, see Wallace T. MacCaffrey, *Queen Elizabeth and the Making of Policy, 1572–1588* (Princeton, NJ, 1981), pp. 348–91, and Conyers Read, *Mr Secretary Walsingham and the Policy of Queen Elizabeth*, 3 vols. (Oxford, 1925), III, 115–65.

8 For an account of the restoration of lands and offices to the Dudley affinity, see Simon Adams, 'The Dudley clientele, 1553–1563', in *The Tudor Nobility*, ed. G. W. Bernard (Manchester, 1992), pp. 241–65.

9 For analysis of Dudley's role as 'the most assiduous and restless politician in the realm', see MacCaffrey, *Queen Elizabeth*, pp. 440–8.

10 The letter, dated 10 June 1559, is now bound in Lambeth Palace Library: MS. 3196. For a longer discussion of the first years of Dudley's troupe, see MacLean, 'Politics of patronage'.

11 See 'Robert Dudley and the Inner Temple Revels', *The Historical Journal* 13, 3 (1970), 365–78.

12 Norman Jones and Paul Whitfield White have collaborated on an article addressing the political and theatrical aspects of the account: see '*Gorboduc* and royal marriage politics: an Elizabethan playgoer's report of the premiere performance', *English Literary Renaissance* 26 (1996), 3–16. Other instances of Leicester's use of drama to advance his causes were first suggested by White in an article, 'Patronage, Protes- tantism, and stage propaganda in early Elizabethan England', *Yearbook of English Studies* 21 (1991), 39–52. Right up to the end of his career Leicester was using drama to lobby the queen. See Richard Dutton, *Mastering the Revels: The Regulation and Censorship of English Renaissance Drama* (Iowa City, 1991), pp. 67–9, for the sug- gestion that Robert Wilson's play, *The Cobbler's Prophecy*, was the comedy that caused the queen's annoyance with Leicester for its anti-Spanish theme in 1588.

13 Rosenberg, *Leicester: Patron of Letters* (New York, 1955), p. xviii.

14 Conyers Read, 'Walsingham and Burghley in Queen Elizabeth's privy council', *EHR* 28 (1913), 41. The relationship broke down in 1586 after Sir Philip Sidney's death but Read sums up the previous decade as follows: 'For ten years the two of them had stood together upon all important matters of public policy and had been

generally regarded as the two foremost champions of militant Protestantism in the Privy Council' (*Mr Secretary Walsingham*, III, 166).

15 Haynes, *Invisible Power: The Elizabethan Secret Service 1570–1603* (Stroud, Gloucestershire, 1992), p. 16. For the triumvirate of spymasters, see Haynes, p. 103.

16 Sidney makes reference to the mishap in his letter of 24 March 1586, edited by Albert Feuillerat in *The Complete Works of Sir Philip Sidney*, 4 vols. (Cambridge, 1926), III, 167.

17 Ian Arthurson, 'Espionage and intelligence from the Wars of the Roses to the Reformation', *Nottingham Mediaeval Studies* 35 (1991), 134–54, especially p. 144.

18 Read, 'William Cecil and Elizabethan public relations', in *Elizabethan Government and Society: Essays Presented to Sir John Neale* (London, 1961), p. 21.

19 *Ibid.*, p. 27.

20 We use 'puritan' in the cautious spirit of Patrick Collinson. See his *Elizabethan Essays* (London, 1994), pp. 59–86. Replying to G. R. Elton's undermining of the myth of a coherent puritan movement (*The Parliament of England, 1559–1581* (Cambridge, 1986)), Collinson places Walsingham with those who 'favoured policies which were inspired by a more than formal Protestantism and were calculated to preserve the Protestant ascendancy actively rather than passively' (p. 66). 'Puritan' is not a well-defined term for this complex position and it serves only as shorthand.

21 Conyers Read, *Mr Secretary Walsingham*, III, 437. Two quite different books which explore Marlowe's relations with the Walsingham family are William Urry, *Christopher Marlowe and Canterbury* (London, 1988) and Charles Nicholl, *The Reckoning* (London, 1992).

22 Muriel C. Bradbrook, *The Rise of the Common Player* (Cambridge, MA, 1962), pp. 162–77.

23 See also Andrew Gurr, 'Three reluctant patrons and early Shakespeare', *Shakespeare Quarterly* 44 (1993), 159–74. Gurr suspects that a key figure in forming the new Queen's Men was Charles Howard, working behind the scenes of the privy council. Howard would have held expectations of succeeding Sussex as Lord Chamberlain, an appointment that would have given him a position on the privy council, where he would have strengthened the Sussex side in the Leicester–Sussex dispute. Tilney was closely related to Howard interests and would have been concerned, perhaps more keenly than anyone else, over the appointment of the next Lord Chamberlain; and it is on record that Tilney owed Howard his appointment to the Mastership in the first place. See Richard Dutton, *Mastering the Revels* (Iowa City, 1991), pp. 44–5. Walsingham's role in appointing the new company would seem to have been a counter-thrust to Howard's interests, and it may be that the mysterious company that toured under the Master of the Revels's own patronage in 1583–4 was part of the Howard–Tilney manoeuvring (see *ES*, I, 318; II, 223, and, for the entries at Bath, Gloucester and Ludlow: James Stokes, with Robert J. Alexander (eds.), *Somerset including Bath*, REED, 2 vols. (Toronto, 1996), I, 13; Audrey Douglas and Peter Greenfield (eds.), *Cumberland/Westmorland/Gloucestershire*, REED (Toronto, 1986), p. 309; and J. Alan B. Somerset, *Shropshire*, REED, 2 vols.

(Toronto, 1994), I, 87). In the event, Howard did become Chamberlain, but not until six months after Sussex's death.

24 For the lord lieutenancy system, see Wallace MacCaffrey, *The Shaping of the Elizabethan Regime* (Princeton, NJ, 1968), p. 337; Lawrence Stone, *The Causes of the English Revolution* (London, 1972), p. 74; and Penry Williams, 'The crown and the counties', in Christopher Haigh (ed.), *The Reign of Elizabeth I* (London, 1984), pp. 126–8. The importance of patronage systems in breaking down regional differences is studied in Linda Peck, 'Court patronage and government policy: the Jacobean dilemma', in Guy Fitch Lytle and Stephen Orgel (eds.), *Patronage in the Renaissance* (Princeton, NJ, 1981). For the espionage system, along with Read's volumes on Walsingham see John Michael Archer, *Sovereignty and Intelligence: Spying and Court Culture in the English Renaissance* (Stanford, CA, 1993); Haynes, *Invisible Power*; and Alison Plowden, *The Elizabethan Secret Service* (New York, 1991). Nationwide administrative systems were greatly aided by advances in the technology of mapmaking in the 1580s. See P. D. A. Harvey, *The Maps of Tudor England* (Chicago, 1993), especially chapter 3. For the cult of Eliza, see Simon Adams, 'Eliza enthroned? The court and its politics', in Haigh (ed.), *The Reign of Elizabeth I*; Philip Edwards, *Threshold of a Nation* (Cambridge, 1979), pp. 38–65; and Stone, *Causes*, pp. 88–9. As for the outlays to Walsingham, Conyers Read, *Mr Secretary Walsingham*, II, 370–1, appears to have missed the larger items. The Signet Book, PRO: SO 3/1, includes a June 1585 payment of £5,000 which Read does not include, and an April 1586 payment of £6,000, followed by another of £4,000, plus smaller ones, most of which Read does not include. All of these payments are entered with the same formulas as are used in the payments Read does include: 'to be employed by him about her majesty's special service', 'according to her majesty's direction, without any accompt to be set upon him his heirs', etc.

25 W. R. Streitberger, *Edmond Tyllney, Master of the Revels and Censor of Plays: A Descriptive Index to His Diplomatic Manual on Europe* (New York, 1986), pp. 22–3.

26 The Declared Accounts are to be found in PRO: E351/542. The account book of Sir John Petre for October 1576 is now in the Essex Record Office. We owe this citation to Alan H. Nelson.

27 See n. 7 above.

28 PRO: E351/542, 6 and 21 May 1583 for Garland; BL: Harleian MS. 1644, f. 73 for Garland and Smith; Chambers gives references for the Duttons, *ES*, II, 314.

29 The messenger John Garland can be traced through Simon Adams, *Household Accounts*, p. 471 (where he is listed as servant to Leicester), into J.S. Brewer (ed.), *Calendar of Carew Papers*, II (1868), 486, 492, and III, 25–37, where his vivid letters on Irish affairs are quoted at length.

30 *ES*, I, 266n. Will Kempe is paid 10s on 4 May 1585 as 'one of the pleyers' in Leicester's 1584–6 Household Account Book.

31 The phrase is from Thomas Dekker, *A Knight's Conjuring*, 1607. For writers, espionage, and the Walsingham circles, see Archer, *Sovereignty and Intelligence*; F. S. Boas, *Christopher Marlowe: A Biographical and Critical Study* (Oxford, 1940), pp. 116–28; Katharine Duncan-Jones, *Sir Philip Sidney, Courtier Poet* (London,

1991); Arthur Freeman, *Thomas Kyd: Facts and Problems* (Oxford, 1967); William Ringler, 'Spenser and Thomas Watson', *Modern Language Notes* 69 (1954), 77–86.

32 The will is P. C. C. 63 Harrington. See Mary Edmond, 'Pembroke's Men', *Review of English Studies* ns 25 (1974), 129–36.

33 See Michael Brennan, *Literary Patronage in the Renaissance: The Pembroke Family* (London, 1988); Alan Sinfield, 'The cultural politics of the *Defence of Poetry*', in *Sir Philip Sidney and the Interpretation of Renaissance Culture*, ed. Gary F. Waller and Michael D. Moore (London, 1984); and Gary F. Waller, *Mary Sidney, Countess of Pembroke* (Salzburg, 1979).

34 *Birthpangs of Protestant England: Religious and Cultural Change in the Sixteenth and Seventeenth Centuries* (London, 1988), pp. 98 and 112.

35 *Theatre and Reformation: Protestantism, Patronage, and Playing in Tudor England* (Cambridge, 1993), pp. 42–66.

36 *Ibid.*, p. 204.

37 Collinson, *Birthpangs of Protestant England*, p. 114.

38 Chambers, *ES*, I, 3.

39 *Sovereignty and Intelligence*, chapter 2.

3   The career of the Queen's Men

1 The most frequently consulted sources for the history of individual professional companies in this period remain Chambers's *Elizabethan Stage* (cited as *ES*), II, and John Tucker Murray, *English Dramatic Companies 1558–1642*, 2 vols. (London, 1910). Andrew Gurr has recently published an updated account of the London playing companies for the period 1560 to 1642 in *The Shakespearian Playing Companies*. For the Queen's Men, see *ES*, II, 104–15; Murray, *English Dramatic Companies*, I, 3–25; and Gurr, *Shakespearian Playing Companies*, pp. 196–217. See also G. M. Pinciss's account of the 'rise and fall' of the company in 'The Queen's Men, 1583–1592', *Theatre Survey* II (1970), 50–65.

2 The new evidence has been accumulated during the past twenty years of collaborative research in original documentary sources by an international team of scholars co-ordinated by the Records of Early English Drama (REED) project based at the University of Toronto in Canada. Details relating to the itinerary of the Queen's Men in the provinces from 1583 to 1603 are presented, with full acknowledgements, in Appendix A (pp. 170–88 above).

3 The most reliable evidence is published in the county and city volumes of the REED series (17 vols. to date; University of Toronto Press, 1979–). Both Chambers and Murray derived their Renaissance company itineraries largely from printed sources, many inconsistently dated and erratically transcribed.

4 Two articles by Sally-Beth MacLean reflect recent study of medieval and Renaissance tour routes: 'Players on tour: new evidence from Records of Early English Drama', *The Elizabethan Theatre X*, ed. C. E. McGee (Port Credit, 1988), pp. 55–72, and 'Tour routes: "provincial wanderings" or traditional circuits?', in *Medieval and Renaissance Drama in England*, VI (New York, 1993), 1–14.

5 One example of a family with a long-standing tradition of sponsoring entertainers, both at home in Essex and abroad in their regions of influence, was the de
Veres, the family of the Earls of Oxford. The appearance of the 16th Earl's troupe
in Southwark in 1547 is indicative of how elusive evidence of unofficial performances in the London area can be: we owe knowledge of this single event to a letter
written by a visiting bishop, frustrated that they had lured his congregation away
from a dirge for the king at St Saviour's (PRO: SP 10/1, ff. 8–9; for transcript
see *Letters of Stephen Gardiner*, ed. James Arthur Muller (Cambridge, 1933),
pp. 253–4).

6 See Wallace T. MacCaffrey, 'Place and patronage in Elizabethan politics', in *Elizabethan Government and Society: Essays Presented to Sir John Neale*, ed. S. T. Bindoff,
J. Hurstfield, and C. H. Williams (London, 1961), pp. 95–126, and for a specific
study of a town's relationship with its patron, Catherine F. Patterson, 'Leicester
and Lord Huntingdon: urban patronage in early modern England', *Midland
History* 16 (1991), 45–62.

7 In 1579–80 they are also on record in the south-east, at Faversham (Wardmote
and Account Book, Faversham Borough Records: FA/AC 1 f. 239); further west
at Winchester in 1580–1 and 1581–2 (Hampshire Record Office: W/EI/102, mb 5d;
W/EI/103, mb 5); and in 1582–3 at Liverpool near their patron's seat (see *Lancashire*,
ed. David George, REED (Toronto, 1991), for this entry from the Liverpool Town
Book and other dramatic records from the county). The court calendar in Chambers, *ES*, IV, Appendix A, remains a useful and generally accurate summary of
performances at court, although it is usefully supplemented by Leeds Barroll in
The Revels History of Drama in England, vol. III, ed. Barroll *et al.* (London, 1975).

8 It is intriguing that this prominent company does not appear at court or on tour
after 1582. It is unfortunate that the names of company members are not on record;
without names we can only speculate that when Tilney chose twelve of the best
for the queen's troupe, he looked to Derby's for some of them.

9 See, for example, a happy conjunction of related specific dates for a southern tour
in the spring of 1595: Rye (21 March), Winchester (3 April), Lyme Regis (15 April),
Exeter (23 April) and Bridgwater (29 April). Around the same period we may
tentatively put other south-eastern stops for which there is no day and month of
payment ascribed by their accountants: Maidstone (after 2 November 1594), Canterbury (25 December 1594–March 1595), Dover (8 September 1594–8 September
1595), Folkestone (8 September 1594–8 September 1595), Lydd (22 July 1594–22
July 1595) and New Romney (25 March 1595–25 March 1596).

10 See F. M. Stenton, 'The road system of medieval England', *Economic History
Review* 7 (1936), 21.

11 Ohler, writing about Europe generally, notes that the increasing speed of travel in
the later Middle Ages and Renaissance was partly the result of 'the breeding of
faster horses, establishment of staging-posts, the building of roads and bridges,
regularly operating ferries, better provisions for men and horses on the way, and
building of faster (and more comfortable) ships'. See *The Medieval Traveller*,
tr. Caroline Hillier (Woodbridge, Suffolk, 1989), p. 99.

12 The details from the now lost manuscript journal of Nicholas Assheton were first printed in *An History of the Original Parish of Whalley and Honor of Clitheroe*, ed. T. D. Whitaker (London, 1818), p. 314. Examples of what could be accomplished at high speed come from a different part of the country: in the south-west a messenger is on record in 1595 as covering the approximately 180 miles from Plymouth in Devon to Hartford Bridge in Hampshire in 31 hours, an average of 6 miles an hour including stops, while a queen's messenger in the same year rode from Plymouth to the court outside London in less than 36 hours (cited by Gilbert Sheldon, *From Trackway to Turnpike* (London, 1928), p. 74).

13 Our thanks to Anne Brannen for sharing with us her transcriptions from Lord North's Household Accounts (BL: Stowe 774). The 1583 payment appears in vol. 2, f. 35v; two payments in 1578 to Leicester's men are recorded in vol. 1, ff. 79v–80.

14 Norwich Chamberlains' Accounts IX, Norwich Record Office: 18.a, f. 97v. For this and other transcriptions from Norwich, see *Norwich 1540–1642*, ed. David Galloway, REED (Toronto, 1984), pp. 65–76.

15 A survey of town accounting payments of this kind quickly reveals that rewards were established according to the prominence or local influence of a patron and varied less than we might expect from year to year. Unsurprisingly, the royal troupes always receive the highest payments. The variation in amount from town to town in the 1580s is probably more indicative of the relative prosperity of the towns than their attitude toward the quality of the performances or their degree of respect for the royal patron.

16 The Leicester Chamberlains' Accounts, for example, typically enter the official reward to players with the phrase 'more than was gathered'. The first entry for the Queen's Men in the 1582–3 accounts is an example: '. . . Item gevon to the Queenes maiesties Playors more then was gathered xxxviij s iiij d' (Leicestershire Record Office: BRIII/2/50, mb 2).

17 See *Cumberland/Westmorland/Gloucestershire*, pp. 306–7, for the 3 November 1580 decision in the Gloucester Corporation Common Council Minute Book.

18 See *Norwich 1540–1642*, p. 70. The exact amount of the Dean and Chapter's reward cannot be given as it is part of a summary payment of 45s awarded various acting troupes during the year.

19 *Norwich 1540–1642*, p. 71.

20 Browne had been able to make bail by 28 July; he would have been able to claim exemption from prosecution by secular courts for felony and homicide by simply demonstrating literacy (see further Thomas Andrew Green, *Verdict according to Conscience: Perspectives on the English Criminal Trial Jury, 1200–1800* (Chicago, 1985), pp. 105–52).

21 The relevant records are in Quarter Session Minute Books, Norwich Record Office: 20.a, ff. 44v–59v and the depositions taken 15 and 17 June 1583 about the affray at Norwich and presented by Mayor John Suckling in June 1585 before the King's Bench in Westminster (the King's Bench scribe was understandably confused by the two Suckling mayors involved in the case and mistook John, mayor in 1584–5, for Robert, mayor in 1582–3). The depositions were placed in the third section

of the King's Bench Roll (PRO: K.B. 29/219), where writs of mandamus some-times ordered lower courts to take further action, but in this case there is no evidence that writs were issued. We are indebted to Herbert Berry for studying these records at the Public Record Office and to both him and Abigail Ann Young, REED's legal expert, for help with the interpretation offered here.

22 See the Aldeburgh Chamberlains' Accounts (as transcribed by John Coldewey for Malone Society *Collections*, IX (Oxford, 1977 for 1971), p. 20).

23 Although the payment to the Queen's Men in the Ipswich Chamberlains' Accounts is listed first under the heading 'Rewards to players of Interludes' above another, for 6 October 1582, to Lord Morley's players, it seems probable that the reward was indeed to the new Queen's company although listed out of chrono-logical sequence in these Michaelmas 1582 to Michaelmas 1583 accounts. There is no evidence that the queen's former troupe, the interluders, were still in existence in 1582 and certainly they have not shown up in the provincial records after 1576. See *Collections* II.3, pp. 272–3.

24 See, for example, the 1579–80 payment of 6s to Shrewsbury's troupe or the 1580–1 rewards to Worcester's Men (6s 10d) and Derby's Men (5s) in the Abingdon Chamberlains' Accounts, Berkshire Record Office: A/FAc1, ff. 174, 178v. Although Oxford's troupe also received 20s in 1583, they were not favoured with wine in addition. See Abingdon Chamberlains' Accounts at the Berkshire Record Office: A/FAc2, f. [7a].

25 For this and other entries from the Gloucester Chamberlains' Accounts see Peter Greenfield's transcriptions in *Cumberland/Westmorland/Gloucestershire*, especially p. 308.

26 For this and other transcriptions from the Bristol Mayors' Audits, see Mark C. Pilkinton's transcriptions in *Bristol*, REED (Toronto, 1997), especially pp. 123–4.

27 For this and other entries from the Bath Chamberlains' Accounts see Robert J. Alexander's transcriptions in *Somerset, including Bath*, vol. 1, especially p. 13.

28 Account payments are to be found in the following: Faversham Chamberlains' Accounts at the Centre for Kentish Studies, Maidstone: FA/FAc 13, mb 7; Lydd Chamberlains' Accounts in the Lydd Town Archives: Ly/FAc7, p. 18; Rye Cham-berlains' Accounts, East Sussex Record Office: 60/9, f. 218v; Dover Chamber-lains' Accounts at the Centre for Kentish Studies, Maidstone: uncatalogued MS., f. 60; and Canterbury Chamberlains' Accounts at the Canterbury Cathedral Archives: CA/FA6, f. 265v.

29 The 1582–3 Dover Chamberlains' Account entry for Stafford's Men is on f. 58 and the 1583–4 payments to Oxford's and Berkeley's Men on ff. 92v and 95v.

30 See Nottingham Chamberlains' Accounts, Nottinghamshire Record Office: CA 1622/23, f. 19v. The Leicester accounts are very detailed in their chronology and appear to be in order in this period. The payment to the Queen's Men, while undated itself, is the last entry for the account year ending on 29 September 1583. See Leicester Chamberlains' Accounts at the Leicestershire Record Office: BRIII/2/50, mb 2 and n. 16 above.

31 See *Shropshire*, ed. J. Alan B. Somerset, REED, 2 vols. (Toronto, 1994), I, for this (p. 235) and other dramatic records for that county.

32 Marlborough Chamberlains' Accounts, Wiltshire Record Office: G22/1/205/2, f. 16.

33 *Shakespearian Playing Companies*, p. 202.

34 'A record of London inn-playhouses from *c.* 1565–1590', *Shakespeare Quarterly* 22 (1971), 22. See also Ingram, *The Business of Playing* (Ithaca, NY, 1992), p. 230. Gurr, *Shakespearian Playing Companies*, p. 202, notes anecdotes about Tarlton which have him playing at the Theatre and the Curtain, as well as at the city inns.

35 It was long-established custom for active troupes to travel for profit outside the Christmas or Shrovetide seasons when their patrons might require their services. In the case of Leicester's Men, Dudley's household accounts suggest that that company was more often seen at court during the festive seasons than at their patron's residence, but as Dudley himself was in constant attendance on the queen, this is scarcely surprising.

36 See *Collections*, I, part 2, Malone Society (Oxford, 1908), pp. 163–8.

37 Quoted in *ES*, IV, 298.

38 See Andrew Gurr, 'Three reluctant patrons and early Shakespeare', *Shakespeare Quarterly* 44 (1993), 159–74.

39 The Saffron Walden Chamberlains' Accounts are still held by the town council. The first entry to the Queen's players is on p. 115.

40 See *Cambridge*, ed. Alan H. Nelson, REED, 2 vols. (Toronto, 1988), I, for this (p. 311) and other dramatic records relating to the town and university of Cambridge.

41 It is possible that further records of the tour along this route will be discovered, as REED research for Huntingdonshire and Lincolnshire is still in its early stages. No relevant accounts for the towns along the southern end of the road in Hertfordshire have survived and the chamberlains' bills and vouchers for Newark in Nottinghamshire are fragmentary in the late sixteenth century.

42 See *York*, ed. A. F. Johnston and Margaret Rogerson, REED, 2 vols. (Toronto, 1979), I, for these (pp. 409, 413) and other dramatic records relating to the city and cathedral of York.

43 The sources are the Leicester Chamberlains' Accounts, Leicestershire Record Office: BRIII/2/52, mb 2, and the Middleton Household Account Book, Nottingham University Library: MS. MiA62, f. 14. The remarkable Elizabethan mansion designed by Robert Smythson was commissioned by Sir Francis and built between 1580 and 1588. The Queen's Men would have performed in the old hall, erected in the late fifteenth century. For further details, see Alice T. Friedman, *House and Household in Elizabethan England: Wollaton Hall and the Willoughby Family* (Chicago, 1989).

44 Payments occur in the civic records from Southampton (Southampton Record Office: Book of Fines, f. 188) and the chamberlains' accounts from Rye (East Sussex Record Office: 60.9, f. 218v), Lydd (Lydd Town Archives: Ly/FAc7, p. 26), Hythe (Borough Archives: MS. 1208, ff. 116v–17), Folkestone (J. O. Halliwell-Phillipps's Literary Scrapbook, Folger Shakespeare Library: W.b. 173, p. 68) and Dover (Centre for Kentish Studies, Maidstone: uncatalogued MS.,

f. 124v). The Dover and Hythe entries are not specifically dated, but their context suggests a late summer appearance by the troupe at both locations.

45 We follow Chambers's dating of the petition and the subsequent reply of the City, *ES*, IV, 298–9.

46 *ES*, IV, 301.

47 See *ES*, IV, 160. The Leicester House payment appears in Robert Dudley's Household Account Book, Christ Church, Oxford: Evelyn MS. 258b. See also Scott McMillin, 'Building stories: Greg, Fleay, and the plot of *2 Seven Deadly Sins*', *Medieval and Renaissance Drama in England*, IV (1989), 53–62.

48 The queen was in Surrey and Sussex during July and August 1583, and visited various locations in Surrey, Berkshire and Hampshire in August and September 1584. See Chambers's court calendar in *ES*, IV, 100.

49 Foakes and Rickert (eds.), *Henslowe's Diary* (Cambridge, 1961), p. 7. Henslowe's date was 1593, but Greg's argument that it was 1594 (in his earlier edition of the *Diary*) is generally accepted.

50 *Shakespearian Playing Companies*, pp. 55–67.

51 *A London Life in the Brazen Age* (Cambridge, MA, 1978), pp. 116–20.

52 See, for example, Mark Eccles, 'Elizabethan actors IV', *Notes and Queries* ns 40 (1993), 169. Gurr gives a useful discussion of Henslowe's word 'broke' in *Shakespearian Playing Companies*, pp. 22–3.

53 W. W. Greg, *Two Elizabethan Stage Abridgements* (Oxford, 1923). The account of the Queen's Men is on pp. 352–7.

54 Mark Eccles summarized the case in *Shakespeare in Warwickshire* (Madison, WI, 1961), pp. 82–3. The document is among the Patent Rolls, PRO: c66/130, mb 20. There are no borough records from the period to confirm the visit to Thame by the Queen's Men in this or any other year. Neither Chambers nor Murray seems to have known the details of Knell's death; Edwin Nungezer lists him in his *Dictionary of Actors*, pp. 228–9, but does not mention the date or cause of his death.

55 Patrick Collinson writes shrewdly about Martin Marprelate as the resurrection of Tarlton and his theatrical style. See 'Religious satire and the invention of puritanism', in *The Reign of Elizabeth I: Court and Culture in the Last Decade*, ed. John Guy (Cambridge, 1995), especially pp. 158–9. A good guide to the Marprelate tracts is Leland H. Carlson, *Martin Marprelate, Gentleman* (San Marino, 1981), from which our quotations are taken. The first is from *Mar Martine*, the second from *A Whip for an Ape*, both of 1589.

56 Quoted in Carlson, *Marprelate*, p. 73.

57 See Carlson, *Marprelate*, pp. 71–4, and Janet Clare, *'Art made tongue-tied by authority': Elizabethan and Jacobean Dramatic Censorship* (Manchester, 1990), pp. 24–5.

58 *Mastering the Revels*, pp. 74–6.

59 In East Anglia, their recorded take from annual tours, principally in the summer and fall, was approximately £57 during the first decade.

60 The Dorset years were 1588, 1589, 1591, and 1593. The Queen's Men stopped at Southampton and/or Winchester in 1584, 1587, 1589 (twice), 1590, 1591 (twice),

1592 and 1593, but in 1584 there is no indication that they were on route to or from the south-west.

61 Official rewards to the Queen's Men from 1583 to 1593 approximated £57.

62 Although there are eight years on record for the troupe visiting the southern counties of Wiltshire, Dorset and Hampshire, the total reward comes to approximately £22. While we can assume that more was earned along the way, it is obvious that the south coast was a longer and less lucrative route than the one through the Thames Valley to the actors' mecca at Bristol. The Thames Valley route is on record in the first decade for the tours to or from the south-west in 1583, 1586, 1587, 1593, and possibly 1589.

63 Town accounts of this period survive for Kingston upon Thames, Reading, Abingdon and Oxford.

64 See Chambers, *ES*, IV, 105–7.

65 For the importance of the royal progresses in maintaining contact with her subjects, see Christopher Haigh's chapter on Elizabeth and the people in *Elizabeth I*, pp. 146–8.

66 See 'Lord Burghley's Map of Lancashire, 1590', *Miscellanea IV*, Catholic Record Society (London, 1907), pp. 162–223.

67 Although the volumes for the counties of Cumberland, Westmorland, Lancashire and the cities of Newcastle upon Tyne and York have appeared in the REED series, research continues in Cheshire, Durham, and Yorkshire West Riding. Work on the Beverley records has been completed but the rest of the East Riding, the North Riding, and Northumberland remain to be surveyed.

68 See Coward, *The Stanleys, Lords Stanley and Earls of Derby 1385–1672: The Origins, Wealth and Power of a Landowning Family* (Manchester, 1983), pp. 145–6. Apparently, the earl and his heir, with some political prudence to their credit, did not support William Stanley's plans to invade England, but, as Coward points out (p. 146), 'The fact, though, that the earls of Derby gave no encouragement to the crown's opponents did little to lessen royal suspicions that they *might* do so . . .'

69 See extracts from the Derby Household Book for 1586–90 in *Lancashire*, pp. 180–2.

70 For the letter from Henry Scrope, governor of Carlisle, to William Ashby, the English ambassador in Scotland, see *Lancashire*, pp. 182–3 and endnote. Knowing their itinerary, we can deduce that his reference to their stay in 'the furthest parte of Langkeshier' was, in fact, to Knowsley, near Liverpool.

71 The letter from Ashby to Burghley on 22 October 1589 is quoted in an endnote, *Lancashire*, p. 356. The players apparently waited in Edinburgh for about a month before returning south via Chester.

72 York, for example, paid an average of £3 6s 8d for the civic performance while Newcastle paid £5 in 1591. See *York*, I, 409, 430, and 449, and *Newcastle upon Tyne*, ed. J. J. Anderson, REED (Toronto, 1982), p. 79.

73 The evidence for the Manners family is spotty at best, because their valuable collection of manuscripts, still housed at Belvoir Castle, is not available for con-

sultation. We must be satisfied for the time being with sample extracts published by H. Maxwell Lyte and W. H. Stevenson in *The Manuscripts of his Grace the Duke of Rutland, K. G., preserved at Belvoir Castle*, Historical Manuscripts Commission, 4 vols. (London, 1888–1905), vol. 4. We are more fortunate with the Clifford family collection which has been surveyed at Chatsworth by John M. Wasson for the REED series; although there are no accounts extant for the first decade of the Queen's Men's travels, household records are relatively complete from 1594 onwards. The Middleton records are now held by the Nottingham University Library; the principal run of household accounts is sixteenth-century and of these only the 1584 account is relevant for the Queen's Men.

74 For visits to Chester in 1589–91, see *Chester*, ed. Lawrence M. Clopper, REED (Toronto, 1979), pp. 159, 162, 166. The chance survival of a letter from Henry Scrope, presumably to the ambassador to Scotland, William Ashby, makes passing reference to their trip through the north-western border town of Carlisle in September 1589 on route to the royal court at Edinburgh but as there are no civic accounts surviving for Carlisle before 1602, we cannot trace them further at this location (see *Cumberland/Westmorland/Gloucestershire*, p. 65).

75 See *Shropshire*, I, 19, 88, 235 and 248, and *Herefordshire/Worcestershire*, ed. David N. Klausner, REED (Toronto, 1990), pp. 24, 32, and 122–3.

76 Although the Queen's Men performed in the Midlands most often in the summer, they appeared or returned during the fall in four of the ten years concerned (1584, 1588, 1590 and 1591). In one of these years they also visited the area in the spring (1591). For the less documented West Midland circuit, they are recorded for three summer tours, the latest extending into the fall (1583, 1587 and 1590), and one other fall tour (1591).

77 The north-eastern total of approximately £24 derives from a search of a handful of major centres such as York, Durham, Newcastle upon Tyne and Beverley. A complete survey of Yorkshire East and North Ridings and Northumberland remains to be done by the REED project, while the edited records of the West Riding have not yet been submitted to the Toronto office. We have been informed by the editors of that collection, Barbara Palmer and John Wasson, that one of the key stops on the road north, at Doncaster, yields no payments to the Queen's Men, although the civic accounts include numerous, previously unpublished, rewards to travelling entertainers preceding and following the 1583–1603 era. The official rewards in the Midlands presently known total almost £50.

78 Church performances were more numerous than is sometimes assumed. For a useful account, see Paul Whitfield White, 'Drama in the church: church-playing in Tudor England', *Medieval and Renaissance Drama in England*, VI (1993), 15–35.

79 'The costs of touring', cited at p. 199 above, n. 9.

80 Conflicting itinerary dates similar to those itemized above for 1583 and 1584 also occur in 1586, 1587, 1589, 1590, 1591 and 1592. Division into two branches for touring seems the most plausible explanation for these parallel appearances in different parts of the country.

81 See p. 29 above and p. 204, n. 32.

82 Quoted from Mary Edmond, who published the text of the will in 'Pembroke's Men', 129–36.

83 See the Chamberlains' Accounts, Nottinghamshire Record Office: CA 1629, p. 17. Four years later the Jewell will does not name either the Duttons or Lanham, but it does not list all six sharers either.

84 *Lancashire*, p. 182; Southampton Book of Fines, Southampton Record Office: SC5/3/1, f. 226v; and the Lyme Regis Mayors' Accounts, Dorset Record Office: DC/LR/GG2/2, p. 55.

85 See *Cambridge*, I, 340–1.

86 See *Collections*, VI, pp. 26–7.

87 See the Poole Mayor's Account, Poole Borough Archives: 119, f. [2].

88 For the history of this company and its association with Paul's Boys in the early 1580s see Shapiro, *Children of the Revels*. See also *Norwich 1540–1642*, p. 86, and *Collections* II.3, p. 274, for payments to the Children by the Norwich and Ipswich city chamberlains.

89 For specific payments to the Children of the Chapel see Fordwich Chamberlains' Accounts, Canterbury Cathedral Archives: Fordwich Bundle 8, No. 49, f. 2; Lydd Chamberlains' Accounts, Lydd Town Archives: Ly/Fac7, p. 92; and Leicester Chamberlains' Accounts, Leicestershire Record Office: BRIII/2/58, mb 2.

90 For the court payment to the Duttons for their Shrove Sunday performance, see the extract from the Chamber accounts, printed in *Collections* VI, p. 27. The Queen's Men are paid with Sussex's at the following locations in 1591: Southampton, 14 February (Book of Fines, Southampton Record Office: SC5/3/1, f. 225); Bristol, during the week of 28 February to 6 March (*Bristol*, p. 140); Gloucester (*Cumberland/Westmorland/Gloucestershire*, p. 312); and Coventry, 24 March (*Coventry*, p. 332).

    There are a couple of other instances of adjacent account payments that may indicate sharing of the performance bill. In 1589, the Dublin treasurer recorded a payment to Essex's troupe immediately following the reward to the Queen's Men (Dublin Corporation Archives: MR/35, p. 431), and at Faversham during the following January the two troupes are paid 20s together (Faversham Chamberlains' Accounts, Centre for Kentish Studies, Maidstone: FA/FAc 19, mb 5).

91 See *Henslowe's Diary*, p. 21.

92 See Nottingham Chamberlains' Accounts, Nottinghamshire Record Office: CA 1629, p. 11 and, for payments to Symons at court, see the extracts from the Chamber accounts, *Collections*, VI, pp. 21–4.

93 Quoted from 'Dr Taylor's History'; for a full transcription see *Shropshire*, I, 247.

94 See Nottingham Chamberlains' Accounts, Nottinghamshire Record Office: CA 1626, f. 13; Canterbury Chamberlains' Accounts, Canterbury Cathedral Archives: CA/FA 20, f. 32; and *Herefordshire/Worcestershire*, p. 449, for the entry from the Worcester City Accounts. Canterbury records have recently shown that players named 'Symcox' and 'Edwards' were accused in 1592 of trying to 'inveigle' Canterbury schoolboys into joining them as actors. These may have been Queen's

Men. See Peter Roberts, ' "The studious artizan": Christopher Marlowe, Canterbury, and Cambridge', in *Christopher Marlowe and English Renaissance Culture*, ed. Darryll Grantley and Peter Roberts (Aldershot, 1996).

95 For the privy council order, see Chambers, *ES*, IV, 313, and see *ibid.*, pp. 347–9, for his summary of the plague between 1592 and 1594.

96 For the full text of the letter, see *Cambridge*, I, 346–7.

97 For comparative purposes, the approximate figures for official rewards on tour are East Anglia: £20; south-east: £24; and south-west: £29.

98 The still incomplete total for the southern route is approximately £8. The Winchester payment can be found in Hampshire Record Office: w/EI/113, mb 5.

99 The profits presently known total £14 10s.

100 In the Midlands, the company's profits presently total approximately £23; the meagre £1 on record for the north-west cannot reflect reality. In the West Midlands their take included at least £8 13s 4d.

101 For problems of access relating to the Manners household accounts, see note 73 above. Our limited information for Winkburn and Belvoir comes from volume 4 of the Historical Manuscripts Commission report on the Duke of Rutland's collection, pp. 400, 452. The payments from the Berkeley household accounts for Caludon were published by Peter Greenfield in 'Entertainments of Henry, Lord Berkeley, 1593–4 and 1600–5', *REED Newsletter* 8:1 (1983), 14–18. Relevant entries in the Cavendish household accounts for Chatsworth and Hardwick Hall can be found at Chatsworth House: MS. 7 (H), ff. 63v, 161v, and MS. 8, f. 92; the Clifford accounts are also held at Chatsworth House (Bolton Abbey MS. 216, f. 58).

102 *Bristol*, p. 128. See *Norwich 1540–1642*, p. 102, for the payment of 40s in May 1592 (the MS. reads 'May 1593', an apparent error for 1592 in accounts otherwise covering the accounting year Michaelmas 1591 to Michaelmas 1592).

103 There is a noticeable decline in Bristol's official rewards to players of any sort after 1600, possibly because of puritan inclinations among those in power. For the Common Council ordinance see *Bristol*, p. 148.

104 See *Cambridge*, I, 313, 332, 338, 340–3.

105 See *ibid.*, I, 311, 313, 338, 319, 337.

106 See *ibid.*, I, 342–3.

107 See *ibid.*, I, 369.

108 Alan Somerset, ' "How chances it they travel?" Provincial touring, playing places, and the King's Men', *Shakespeare Survey* 47 (1994), p. 59. Somerset's census of provincial playing spaces drawn from records printed in Malone Society or REED volumes published or undergoing publication is found on pp. 56–7.

109 See n. 93 above and the Gloucester Corporation Chamberlains' Accounts in *Cumberland/Westmorland/Gloucestershire*, p. 311. Among surviving playing places in Norwich, David Galloway has listed the yard of the Red Lion – 'its dimensions not much changed from what they were in Shakespeare's time' (*Norwich 1540–1642*, p. xxx). This is an overly optimistic assessment of the present yard, surrounded as it is by nineteenth- and twentieth-century buildings. The Red Lion is now only a distant memory, reflected in the name of the street along which it

stood and the continuing existence of a courtyard, however changed its dimensions and irregular its shape. The site of the inn, which was renamed the Cricket-
ers' Arms in a later era, is now occupied by a bank.

110 For more on the Free School see p. 215 below, n. 123.

111 See Canterbury Chamberlains' Accounts for 1582–3, 1585–6, 1588–9, Cathedral
Archives: CA/FA 18, ff. 265v, 412v, and CA/FA 19, f. 71v; Norwich Chamberlains'
Accounts for 1589–90 transcribed in *Norwich*, p. 96; York Chamberlains' Accounts for 1584, 1587, 1596, 1599 and 1602 transcribed in *York*, 1, 409, 430, 471, 487
and 501; Abingdon Chamberlains' Accounts for 1586–7, Berkshire Record Office:
A/FAc 2, f. 75v; Bristol Mayors' Audits for 1582–3, 1586–7, 1587–8, 1589–90, 1590–
1, 1595–6 and 1597–8, transcribed in *Bristol*, pp. 124, 131, 133, 135, 140, 148 and 151;
Leicester Chamberlains' Accounts for 1590–1, Leicestershire Record Office: BRIII/
2/58, mb 1d. There were at least two halls known in Canterbury in the sixteenth
century, a Market Hall built *c.* 1520 and a Guildhall. The 'Sessions Hall' sometimes referred to may have been one of these two and it seems likely that the
Court Hall is the same location. None of the Canterbury halls remain. The Bristol Guildhall, formerly in Broad Street, does not survive, nor does the Abingdon
Hall, purchased by the town in 1560 and converted from the former chapel and
hospital of St John Baptist *c.* 1563.

112 The Guildhall, in Guildhall Lane, was built next to the church of St Martin, now
the cathedral.

113 See Somerset, ' "How chances it they travel?" ', p. 59. The estimate is Somerset's,
based on Andrew Gurr's calculation that each seated spectator required approximately 18 inches × 18 inches. For a more detailed introduction to the Guildhall,
see *The Leicester Guildhall: A Short History and Guide*, published by the Leicester
City Council.

114 Other later features include the seventeenth-century panelling on the south wall
of the dais with an opening at the upper level from the Jury Room above the
Mayor's Parlour which would have allowed views over activities in the great hall
but not during the lifetime of the Queen's Men.

115 The surrender of the Blackfriars' house probably occurred in October 1538. The
city paid £81 for the buildings in 1540 and, four years later, a further £152 for the
roof lead. For more information on these transactions and other historical and
architectural details, see Helen Sutermeister, *The Norwich Blackfriars* (Norwich,
1977), especially pp. 8–9, and Nikolaus Pevsner, *North-East Norfolk and Norwich*
(Harmondsworth, Middlesex, 1962). The former nave, then Common Hall, is
known today as St Andrew's Hall, a flint and freestone building facing St George's
Street near the River Wensum.

116 The north aisle windows are perpendicular, in keeping with the period when
most of the nave was constructed. However, the five decorated windows in the
south aisle date from the mid fourteenth century when the first Blackfriars church
on the site was completed. This building was largely destroyed by fire in 1413.
The large west window is a much later addition from the period of mid-
nineteenth-century restoration.

117 See Sutermeister, *Norwich Blackfriars*, pp. 17, 21. The original western porch experienced major change in the mid sixteenth century when kitchens and several other outbuildings were put up around it to cater for feasts (Sutermeister, *Norwich Blackfriars*, pp. 10, 18); these were demolished during the Victorian restoration.

118 See Sutermeister, *Norwich Blackfriars*, p. 10, and photographs of the modern interior, Plates 5 and 6, p. 72 above.

119 See Sutermeister, *Norwich Blackfriars*, p. 17.

120 For a description of the Guildhall which lies along the River Ouse in St Helen's Square near Coney Street, see *An Inventory of the Historical Monuments in the City of York*, vol. v: *The Central Area* (Royal Commission on Historical Monuments, 1981), pp. 76–80 and ground plan, p. 81. The Guildhall was shared by the religious guild of St Christopher and the mayor and commonalty of York from its erection in the mid fifteenth century until the dissolution. By 1546 the civic administration was in sole possession of the hall, which continued to be known as the 'Common' Hall during the period when the Queen's Men played in York.

121 Copies of the photographs, taken by Robert L. S. Catcheside, are held at the York City Archives Office (Acc 453, Box 181, Photonumbers 52 and 56).

122 The doorway in the south aisle at the west end was added *c.* 1810, according to the *Inventory of Historical Monuments*, p. 79. Although only one survives along the west wall, the screen enclosing the dais had more than one door, according to mid-sixteenth-century records of repair (*ibid.*, p. 78).

123 See *Bristol*, pp. 135–6. The Free Grammar School was refounded in 1532 and housed in the ancient St Bartholomew's Hospital on the north bank of the River Frome by the bridge. See C. P. Hill, *A History of Bristol Grammar School* (London, 1951) and Roger Price, *Excavations at St Bartholomew's Hospital Bristol* (Bristol, 1979) for further details. As noted above (p. 68), it is also possible that it was the courtyard rather than an indoor hall which was used by the Queen's Men for their rope-walking act (see Price, *Excavations*, p. 17, fig. vi for the post-medieval ground plan).

124 See All Hallows Churchwardens' Accounts for 1596/7–7/8 and 1597/8–8/9, Dorset Record Office: pe/sh/cw69, mb 2 and pe/sh/cw70, mb 1.

125 The smaller medieval parish church of All Hallows built along the west wall of the abbey was demolished after the parish of Sherborne purchased the abbey church in 1540. The church house, an unusual survival of its kind, was built *c.* 1534. See John Newman and Nikolaus Pevsner, *Dorset* (Harmondsworth, Middlesex, 1972), pp. 368, 382.

126 See Rosalind Conklin Hays, 'Dorset church houses and the drama', *Research Opportunities in Renaissance Drama* 31 (1992), 13–23. Further information with transcriptions is forthcoming in her edition, with C. E. McGee, of Dorset dramatic records, for the REED series. Hays's detailed description of the building is based upon an examination of the site in 1986 by her collaborator, C. E. McGee.

127 Although the ground-floor entrances and windows have been substantially altered over the years, the windows on the second level of the south side and the larger window (now blocked) at the west end are mostly original, with the exception of

two enlarged modern windows in the south-west section now occupied by an estate agent.

128 The roof and room length measurements have been proposed by C. E. McGee, as reported by Hays, 'Dorset church houses', p. 14.

129 For this staircase, known in the period as the 'king's stair', see Hays, 'Dorset church houses', p. 14 and n.

130 Hays, 'Dorset church houses', pp. 14–15.

131 For an analysis of the relative popularity of the western route through Shaftesbury, Sherborne and Yeovil, see Sally-Beth MacLean's article, 'At the end of the road: an overview of the south-western touring circuits', in a proposed book of essays edited by Gloria Betcher on culture and politics in the south-west.

132 See Alan H. Nelson's edited version of the Trinity College Steward's Book 2 in *Cambridge*, I, 319. Nelson is cautious about accepting the hall for performances other than those known to have been mounted by college players (for which stage construction payments survive). In correspondence with the authors he suggests other options that could have been used for college-sponsored performances by touring players: outdoors on college grounds or at undesignated playing places elsewhere in the town. There is another payment of 2*s* 6*d* to one of the Queen's Men in the 1592 Trinity College accounts, but the smaller amount may indicate that this was not for a full performance (*Cambridge*, I, 337).

133 Alan Nelson, *Early Cambridge Theatres: College, University, and Town Stages, 1464–1720* (Cambridge, 1994), p. 5. Nelson (p. 5) notes in passing that the 'sometimes romantically styled "minstrels' galleries"' played a negligible role in early theatre.

134 See Christ Church Disbursement Book, Christ Church Archives: xii.b.32, f. 12.

135 The Bereblock Commentary (Bodleian Library: Rawlinson D 1071) will be published in the REED collection for Oxford, edited by John M. Elliott, Jr. An analysis of the description and diagram of the hall conversion for theatrical production was done by Glynne Wickham in *Early English Stages 1300 to 1660*, 3 vols. (London and Henley, 1980), vol. 1: *1300 to 1576*, Appendix H, pp. 355–9. For an account of a somewhat later use of this hall for royal theatrical production, see John Orrell, 'The theatre at Christ Church, Oxford, in 1605', *Shakespeare Survey* 35 (1982), 129–40. The rectangular layout of the hall allowed for more than one type of stage set-up and the 1605 design for stage and auditorium by Inigo Jones and Simon Basil is described by Orrell, p. 128, as 'the first adequately documented neo-Roman theatre in England'.

136 As Orrell (p. 129) points out, 'Many English medieval and Tudor halls measured about 40 ft wide internally, including those for example at Hampton Court (which is extant) and Whitehall (destroyed by fire late in the seventeenth century). Christ Church hall was famous, however, for its exceptional length.' Hampton Court hall, for instance, was 97 feet long.

137 For further architectural details see *An Inventory of the Historical Monuments in the City of Oxford* by the Royal Commission on Historical Monuments: England (London, 1939), pp. 33–4.

138 A third door to the right end of the dais leads only into a cupboard. The main entrance, a double door at the east end, was renovated in the nineteenth century when the windows were restored and the two central fireplaces placed in the north and south walls. The roof was damaged by fire in 1720 and repaired so that 'it is now difficult or impossible to say what parts are original Tudor work and what are repairs of this age' (*Inventory of Historical Monuments in the City of Oxford*, p. 34).

139 The magnificent buildings of present-day Chatsworth postdate our period. Construction work on the residence visited by the Queen's Men began in 1557; of this 'nothing visible to the eye survives', according to Nikolaus Pevsner (*Leicestershire and Rutland*, rev. edn Elizabeth Williamson and Geoffrey K. Brandwood (Harmondsworth, Middlesex, 1984), p. 82). The third Clifford family residence at Londesborough does not survive. Lathom House, the principal seat of the Stanleys, was destroyed in the Civil War; New Park, on its grounds, suffered the same fate. Knowsley is now the principal family residence but little of the much-renovated building dates from before the second half of the seventeenth century.

Belvoir paid the price as a royalist garrison during the Civil War: the castle was slighted in 1646 and demolished in 1649. The present residence was completed *c.* 1830 (for further details see Pevsner, *Leicestershire and Rutland*, pp. 95–100).

Caludon is now an evocative ruin. The only hints of its former grandeur are derived from its moat and a mid-fourteenth-century wall with two of four large transomed two-light windows on the upper floor, presumably part of the original great hall. See Nikolaus Pevsner and Alexandra Wedgwood, *Warwickshire* (Harmondsworth, Middlesex, 1966), p. 281, and *A History of the County of Warwick*, ed. H. Arthur Doubleday *et al.*, Victoria County History, 8 vols. (London, 1904–69), VIII, 121–2.

For further architectural details of the new hall built by Smythson between 1580 and 1588 at Wollaton, see Nikolaus Pevsner, *Nottinghamshire* (Harmondsworth, Middlesex, 1951; 2nd edn, rev. Elizabeth Williamson, 1979), pp. 275–9. Very little survives of the late-fifteenth-century manor house visited by the Queen's Men in 1584 (see Friedman, *House and Household in Elizabethan England*, pp. 38–40). The old hall near the church had been turned into three or four farmhouses by the seventeenth century.

The remains of the Elizabethan residence of Roger, 2nd Baron North, lie a few miles south of Newmarket and the main Cambridge–Norwich road in lovely, easily traversed countryside. The red brick gatehouse tower of a large sixteenth-century house still stands, although most of the residence was pulled down in 1801 and rebuilt. However, the moat, the largest in Cambridgeshire, is still filled on two sides with water (see I. S. Bailey, *A Short Guide to All Saints Church, Kirtling* (Kirtling, 1991) and Nikolaus Pevsner, *Cambridgeshire*, 2nd edn (Harmondsworth, Middlesex, 1970), p. 420).

140 For a detailed guide to the new house, see Mark Girouard, *Hardwick Hall* (London, 1996). Girouard, p. 56, notes that although Bess moved her household into

the new hall in 1597, the carefully co-ordinated decorations of the High Great Chamber remained to be completed two years after, in 1599. The Queen's Men had visited Hardwick before, in 1596, but their performance would have been in one of the now crumbling formal rooms of the old hall. Hardwick Hall continued to be used by her Cavendish descendants after Bess's death but largely escaped the renovating enthusiasms of subsequent generations, in part because it was of secondary importance to their principal seat at Chatsworth. The house was surrendered for death duties in 1956 and is now administered by the National Trust.

141 Girouard, *Hardwick Hall*, p. 33; Girouard notes that the great chamber had taken the place of the great hall in all large Elizabethan houses. See also *The Building of Hardwick Hall*, ed. David N. Durant and Philip Riden, Derbyshire Record Society, vols. IV and IX (Chesterfield, 1980, 1984).

142 Girouard, *Hardwick Hall*, p. 56; see also Nikolaus Pevsner, *Derbyshire*, rev. edn Elizabeth Williamson (Harmondsworth, 1978), p. 234.

143 Girouard, *Hardwick Hall*, p. 70. The tapestries and firedogs are the only fittings which can be surely identified as still in their original location, although other items like the cupboard are elsewhere in the house. The furniture and wall panelling now in the High Great Chamber come from a later era.

144 The withdrawing chamber would have been used by Bess and her guests between banqueting and the setting up of the High Great Chamber for entertainment. Actors would have been likely to use either of the two entrances at the south end rather than the private space reserved for their hostess.

145 Robert Tittler's study of town halls illuminates the subject: see *Architecture and Power: The Town Hall and the English Urban Community c. 1500–1640* (Oxford, 1991).

146 For examples, see Tittler, *Architecture and Power*, pp. 146–7. The Abingdon chamberlains' accounts have a damaged entry for the mending of the Guildhall windows after a 1586–7 performance by the Queen's Men (Berkshire Record Office: A/FAc/2, f. 75v).

147 Hays, for example, itemizes both kitchen and military equipment available to users of the Sherborne church house from late-sixteenth-century inventories kept by the churchwardens ('Dorset church houses', pp. 14–15).

148 Richard Southern's outline of evidence from provincial records remains a useful introduction to the type of limited information we have about how temporary stages were set up in provincial halls. See *The Staging of Plays before Shakespeare* (New York, 1973), pp. 329–41, and Robert Tittler, *Architecture and Power*, pp. 144–5. The 'screen-end' staging assumed by earlier studies has not been confirmed by Alan Nelson's work on Cambridge college productions, which had stages placed at the upper end of their halls. See *Early Cambridge Theatres*, p. 124.

4   The Queen's Men in print

1 Dates are from *Annals of English Drama*, 3rd edn, ed. Alfred Harbage, Samuel Schoenbaum, and Sylvia Stoler Wagonheim (New York, 1988).

1A See G. M. Pinciss, 'Thomas Creede and the repertory of the Queen's Men, 1583–1592', *Modern Philology* 67 (1970), 321–30.
2 The Revels edition of *The Old Wives Tale* (Manchester, 1980), p. 7.
3 See *ES*, IV, 25.
4 See *ES*, II, 25, and Pinciss, 'Thomas Creede'.
5 See Geoffrey Bullough, *Narrative and Dramatic Sources of Shakespeare*, 8 vols. (London, 1957–75), IV, 4.
6 *ES*, III, 515. See also Pinciss, 'Thomas Creede', pp. 321–30.
7 The early dating is in Chambers, *ES*, IV, 6, and Betty J. Littleton, *Clyomon and Clamydes: A Critical Edition* (The Hague, 1968), pp. 30–3.
8 See Pinciss, 'Thomas Creede'; Arleane Ralph, who has recently completed a critical edition as a Ph.D. dissertation at the University of Toronto, favours an early date for the play, but helped us to see the possibility that the Queen's Men may have revived it.
9 Bullough, *Narrative and Dramatic Sources*, IV, 167.
10 See Peter Corbin and Douglas Sedge (eds.), *The Oldcastle Controversy* (Manchester, 1991), pp. 26–7.
11 See Alice-Lyle Scoufos, *Shakespeare's Typological Satire* (Athens, Ohio, 1979), p. 168.
12 As a Malone Society Reprint, edited by W. L. Renwick.
13 See W. L. Renwick's introduction to the Malone Society Reprint of *John of Bordeaux* (Oxford, 1936) and S. McMillin, 'The ownership of *The Jew of Malta, Friar Bacon*, and *The Ranger's Comedy*', *English Language Notes* 9 (1972), 249–52.
14 See Harold Jenkins, 'Peele's *Old Wives Tale*', *Modern Language Review* 34 (1939), 177–85.
15 For discussion of this play in connection with *Selimus*, see Peter Berek, '*Locrine* revised, *Selimus* and early responses to *Tamburlaine*', *Research Opportunities in Renaissance Drama* 23 (1980), 33–44.
16 See Patricia Binnie's Revels edition of *The Old Wives Tale*, p. 5.
17 See Scott McMillin, 'Building stories: Greg, Fleay, and the plot of *2 Seven Deadly Sins*', *Medieval and Renaissance Drama in England*, IV (New York, 1989), pp. 53–62.
18 Mark Eccles, *Shakespeare in Warwickshire* (Madison, WI, 1961), pp. 82–3.
19 See the Revels edition by Patricia Binnie, pp. 5–6.

5 Casting and the nature of the texts

1 Laurie Maguire, *Shakespearean Suspect Texts* (Cambridge, 1996) summarizes the major turns in twentieth-century scholarship and gives a text-by-text account of the quartos in question. Paul Werstine's 'Narratives about printed Shakespeare texts: "foul papers", and "bad" quartos', *Shakespeare Quarterly* 41 (1990), 63–86, along with Randall McLeod (Random Cloud, pseud.), 'The marriage of good and bad quartos', *Shakespeare Quarterly* 33 (1982), 421–31, provide a valuable account of the issue. Recent books which sharpen our understanding of new possibilities in textual scholarship include David Bradley, *From Text to Performance in the*

Elizabethan Theatre (Cambridge, 1992), Grace Ioppolo, *Revising Shakespeare* (Cambridge, MA, 1991), and Kathleen O. Irace, *Reforming the 'Bad' Quartos: Performance and Provenance of Six Shakespearean First Editions* (Newark, 1994).

2 See Leo Kirschbaum, 'A census of bad quartos', *Review of English Studies* 14 (1938), 20–43; Kirschbaum, 'An hypothesis concerning the origin of the bad quartos', *PMLA* 60 (1945), 697–715; Alfred Hart, *Stolne and Surreptitious Copies* (Melbourne, 1942), p. 18; J. A. Lavin (ed.), *Friar Bacon and Friar Bungay* (London, 1969), p. xxxiii; Peter Berek, '*Locrine* revised, *Selimus* and early responses to *Tamburlaine*', *Research Opportunities in Renaissance Drama* 23 (1980), 43; Betty J. Littleton (ed.), *Clyomon and Clamydes: A Critical Edition* (The Hague, 1968), p. 18; Patricia Binnie (ed.), *The Old Wives Tale*, Revels Plays (Manchester, 1980), p. 20.

3 See W. W. Greg, *Dramatic Documents from the Elizabethan Playhouses: Commentary* (Oxford, 1931); *The Editorial Problem in Shakespeare* (Oxford, 1942); and R. B. McKerrow, 'The Elizabethan printer and dramatic manuscripts', *The Library* series 4, 12 (1931), 253–75.

4 See Stephen Booth, 'Speculations on doubling in Shakespeare's plays', in *Shakespeare: The Theatrical Dimension*, ed. Philip C. McGuire and David A. Samuelson (New York, 1979), pp. 103–32.

5 Ringler, 'The number of actors in Shakespeare's early plays', in *The Seventeenth Century Stage*, ed. G. E. Bentley (Chicago, 1968), pp. 110–34; Bradley, *From Text to Performance in the Elizabethan Theatre*. Our method of casting agrees with the first four 'rules' set forth by Bradley, pp. 41–2: count two for all cases of unnumbered attendants; avoid immediate juxtapositions; avoid casting boys in men's roles; take care over unusually 'swollen' scenes. Bradley's fifth rule, which holds that actors would not normally double alternating roles, seems unwarranted to us for two reasons: it is contradicted by leading Elizabethan evidence in the plot of *The Battle of Alcazar* (as Bradley admits); and it introduces as a hypothesis a point which is under investigation. The companies may very well have doubled alternating roles when casting was tight, as the *Alcazar* plot indicates, and the possibility should be left open in the gathering and presentation of evidence. Bradley's casting estimates for the Queen's Men generally run higher than ours because of his rule against doubling alternating roles, but the only serious disagreement is with *The Old Wives Tale*, where he counts sixteen (p. 54) and we count ten (see p. 192 above). That is because *The Old Wives Tale* presents many opportunities for doubling alternating roles.

6 Alfred Harbage, S. Schoenbaum, and Sylvia S. Wagonheim (eds.), *Annals of English Drama*, 3rd edn (New York, 1988). Act and scene references in the following list are from the Malone Society Reprints in all but the following: *A Shrew* is from the F. S. Boas edition (London, 1908); the Shakespeare quartos are adjusted to the act and scene references of the New Arden editions of *2 Henry VI* and *Titus Andronicus*.

7 The pathbreaking work on casting is David Bevington, *From Mankind to Marlowe* (Cambridge, MA, 1962). Recent books include Bradley's *From Text to Performance*, T. J. King, *Casting Shakespeare's Plays* (Cambridge, 1992), and Scott McMillin, *The Elizabethan Theatre and the Book of Sir Thomas More* (Ithaca, NY, 1987).

8 When the text omits entrance and exit directions, as happens frequently, the presence of characters must be indicated by speech prefixes or by references in the dialogue.

9 Evidence from the plots can be seen in King, *Casting Shakespeare's Plays*.

10 See the Lavin edition, cited at n. 2 above. The earlier Brooke-Paradise edition (Boston, 1933) also omitted Saxony.

11 For Strange's Men of the early 1590s in this regard, see McMillin, *The Elizabethan Theatre and the Book of Sir Thomas More*, ch. 3. Andrew Gurr has recently developed this point more fully in *The Shakespearian Acting Companies*.

12 The large number of roles for boys in *The Old Wives Tale* has led some to think the play must have been performed by a children's company. There are six female roles, a large number, yet never do more than three of these roles appear together or in immediate juxtaposition. One may feel that a number of the male roles would properly be played by boys, but the version we have in the quarto of 1595 refuses to demonstrate that the male roles are for children. Instead, it presents several roles for 'youths': Jack is said to be '15 or 16 years' (line 701), the three lost males in the opening scene are called 'masters', and one of them, Antick, is called 'lad'. We have met this 'youth' language before, in the 1594 group of Queen's Men plays, with indications that the company of that period had a number of young male actors, who could play younger or older male roles. The text makes several adjustments to ensure, in our view, that no more than three roles for boys appear at once or in immediate juxtaposition.

13 Harold Jenkins, 'Peele's *Old Wives Tale*', *Modern Language Review* 34 (1939), 184.

14 See Bevington, *From Mankind to Marlowe*, p. 72, and Arleane Ralph's edition, a Ph.D. dissertation at the University of Toronto (1996). Ralph prefers a cast of 11, but shows that 10 can cover all roles. We are indebted to her for letting us see this work at an early stage.

15 'Peele's *Old Wives Tale*', pp. 177–85.

16 For Symons, see the summary in Patricia Binnie's edition of *Old Wives Tale*, p. 63. On Jewell as a Queen's Man, see Scott McMillin, 'Simon Jewell and the Queen's Men', *Review of English Studies* 27 (1976), 174–7.

17 If one inquires as to what role the previous actor of Erestus is playing in the final scene, one will begin to see how extensive the idea of doubled identity is as a subject of this play. He will be playing the youth Jack, who is dead but on hand as a sort of resurrected spirit. The interplay between resurrection and doubling is extensive.

18 Quoted in Peter Corbin and Douglas Sedge (eds.), *The Oldcastle Controversy* (Manchester, 1991), p. 21 n. The editors are A. R. Humphries, in the 1960 Arden edition of *1 Henry IV*, and J. H. Walter, in the 1954 Arden edition of *Henry V*. More recent editors have expressed sounder views. See David Bevington's 1987 Oxford edition of *1 Henry IV*, for example, and Andrew Gurr's 1992 Cambridge edition of *Henry V*.

19 Akihiro Hamada, *Thomas Creede: Printer to Shakespeare and his Contemporaries* (Tokyo, 1994).

20 See G. I. Duthie's edition of *King Lear* (Oxford, 1949); D. L. Patrick, *The Textual History of Richard III* (Stanford, CA, 1936); and Greg, *Two Elizabethan Stage*

Abridgements. The Heywood quotation is given more fully, along with a possibly related quote from Humphrey Moseley about actors making transcriptions of what they acted, as opposed to what the author wrote, in Paul Werstine, 'Narratives about printed Shakespeare texts', pp. 84–5.

21 Corbin and Sedge, *Oldcastle Controversy*, p. 187 n.

22 For the late preparation of the prompt-book, see Fredson Bowers, *On Editing Shakespeare and the Elizabethan Dramatists* (Philadelphia, 1955), pp. 111–12, along with McMillin, *The Elizabethan Theatre and the Book of Sir Thomas More*, pp. 39–50, where it is shown that some of the 'additional' passages appear just where doubling is tight. See also Trevor Howard-Hill, 'Crane's 1619 manuscript of *Barnavelt* and theatrical processes', *Modern Philology* 86 (1988), 146–70, which recognizes a distinction between the 'book of the play', used for parts and other rehearsal purposes, and the 'prompt-book' used to regulate performances.

23 We owe this point to Andrew Gurr and Patrick Spottiswoode, in private conversations.

24 Betty J. Littleton's edition of *Clyomon and Clamydes* (The Hague, 1968), p. 18, notes 'certain phonetic spellings', such as 'Serbarus' and 'Cur Daceer', and suggests these were 'the work of a scribe who had heard the words pronounced but who gave no attention to accuracy'. In an unpublished edition of *The Troublesome Reign of King John* (University of Michigan, 1969), J. F. Dominic thought scribal mishearings were the cause of 'Shattilion' for 'Chattilion', 'Hughbert' for 'Hubert', 'Nidigate' for 'Newdigate', etc. See the edition by John Sider (New York, 1979), p. xiii, although Sider himself does not accept these as mishearings. See also Patricia Binnie's edition of *Old Wives Tale*, cited above.

25 *Old Wives Tale* is well printed, but Frank S. Hook's edition (in *The Dramatic Works of George Peele*, vol. 3 (New Haven, 1970)) notes about a dozen examples of mislineation.

6 Dramaturgy

1 For the staging of Marlowe's play, see William A. Armstrong, *Marlowe's Tamburlaine: The Image and the Stage* (Hull, 1966); David Bevington, *Tudor Drama and Politics* (Cambridge, MA, 1968), p. 191; and David H. Zucker, *Stage and Image in the Plays of Christopher Marlowe* (Salzburg, 1972), pp. 20–79.

2 Quotations from plays of the Queen's Men have been modernized from the edition cited under each title in the Casting Analysis, pp. 189–93 above.

3 New Mermaid edition, ed. J. W. Harper (London, 1971), I.i.35–43.

4 Quoted from M. C. Bradbrook, *The Rise of the Common Player* (Cambridge, MA, 1962), p. 175. Tarlton's style is vividly described in Andrew Gurr, *Playgoing in Shakespeare's London* (Cambridge, 1987), pp. 121–8.

5 See David Bevington, *Tudor Drama and Politics* (Cambridge, MA, 1968), pp. 197–201, for the Hal of *Famous Victories* as 'the hero of thieves and commoners' and for a comparison with the Bastard's role in *Troublesome Reign*.

6 Alexander Leggatt, *English Drama: Shakespeare to the Restoration* (London, 1988), p. 16, praises the clowns' battlefield scene of *Famous Victories* in useful ways. Quoted in Peter Corbin and Douglas Sedge (eds.), *The Oldcastle Controversy* (Manchester, 1991), p. 27.

7 Our casting scheme in chapter 5 does not have Madge double, for the point is admittedly speculative.

8 See Thelma N. Greenfield, *The Induction in Elizabethan Drama* (Eugene, OR, 1969), pp. 105–8, for a sensitive discussion of *Old Wives Tale*.

9 We owe this point to Andrew Gurr.

10 Sedge and Corbin introduce a curtained space for the royal chamber in their edition, p. 167.

11 We are indebted to Philip Virgen's dissertation now being written for a Cornell University Ph.D. for emphasizing the visual elements of *The Troublesome Reign*.

12 *Shakespeare's Metrical Art* (Berkeley, CA, 1988), p. 97.

13 Technically, the stanza form is *synathroismos* overlapping with *percusio/collectio*. We are grateful to Brian Vickers for advice on the rhetorical figures involved.

14 The use of rhymed stanzas in *Selimus* will be further considered in chapter 7, where it will be treated as part of the Queen's Men attack on Marlowe.

15 This Rumour tells the truth – it is quite in keeping with the emphasis on the 'true' in the Queen's Men that even Rumour should be trustworthy, and our belief that this play comes from the late 1590s puts it close to a very different kind of Rumour, Shakespeare's, in *2 Henry IV*.

16 'From "iygging vaines of riming mother wits" to "the spacious volubilitie of a drumming decasillabon"', in *The Elizabethan Theatre XI* (Port Credit, 1990), pp. 55–74.

7 Marlowe and Shakespeare

1 *Dr Faustus and Other Plays*, ed. David Bevington and Eric Rasmussen (Oxford, 1995). All quotations from play texts have been modernized.

2 See Irving Ribner, 'Greene's attack on Marlowe: some light on *Alphonsus* and *Selimus*', *Studies in Philology* 52 (1955), 162–71; and Peter Berek, '*Locrine* revised, *Selimus* and early responses to *Tamburlaine*', *Research Opportunities in Renaissance Drama* 23 (1980), 41–4. The reception of *Tamburlaine* is surveyed in Richard Levin, 'The contemporary reception of Marlowe's *Tamburlaine*', *Medieval and Renaissance Drama in England*, 1 (New York, 1984), pp. 51–70.

3 Cambridge, 1929.

4 See, for example, Russell Fraser, *Young Shakespeare* (New York, 1988), p. 78.

5 *The Real Shakespeare: Retrieving the Early Years, 1564–1594* (New Haven, 1995), p. 58.

6 See also G. M. Pinciss, 'Shakespeare, Her Majesty's Players, and Pembroke's Men', *Shakespeare Survey* 27 (1974), 129–36; and David George, 'Shakespeare and Pembroke's Men', *Shakespeare Quarterly* 32 (1981), 305–23.

7 Chicago, 1993, pp. 285–6. Skura also cites Jacqueline Pearson, 'The influence of *King Leir* on Shakespeare's *Richard II*', *Notes and Queries* 29 (1982), 113–15. See also Martin Mueller, 'From *Leir* to *Lear*', *Philological Quarterly* 73 (1994), 195–218.

8 The 'bad' quarto argument has recently been summarized by Brian Boyd, '*King John* and *The Troublesome Raigne*: sources, structure, sequence', *Philological Quarterly* 74 (1995), 37–56. L. A. Beaurline, in his New Cambridge edition (1990) and E. A. J. Honigman, Arden edition (1954) are both on the 'bad' quarto side. The standard view is fully set forth in A. R. Braunmuller's Oxford edition (1989).

9 Quotations from Shakespeare are from the Riverside edition, ed. G. Blakemore Evans *et al.* (Boston, 1974).

10 In fairness to the 'bad' quarto argument, however, it is not characteristic of Shakespeare to follow his sources so closely as *King John* and *The Shrew* resemble the plots of *Troublesome Reign* and *A Shrew*.

11 See David Riggs, *Shakespeare's Heroical Histories: Henry VI and Its Literary Tradition* (Cambridge, MA, 1971).

12 The path to the Chamberlain's Men may also have included stints with the Pembroke's Men of 1592–3 and Sussex's Men of 1594. The Pembroke connection has long been suspected. For a summary, see Andrew Gurr, 'Three reluctant patrons and early Shakespeare', *Shakespeare Quarterly* 44 (1993), 159–74. For the Sussex connection, see Scott McMillin, 'Sussex's Men in 1594', *Theatre Survey* 32 (1991), 214–23.

Appendix A: Recorded performances of the Queen's Men

1 Dover's annual accounts appear to have been entered periodically, with the date of recording entered in the left margin. This payment to the Queen's Men is grouped with others recorded 24 October early in the accounts (Centre for Kentish Studies, Maidstone: Chamberlains' Accounts for 1584–5, f. 124v).

2 The payment to the Queen's players is the first in the annual accounts running 15 June 1586 to 14 June 1587. As these accounts appear to have been kept chronologically during this period, a June/July approximate dating seems reasonable.

3 There is another payment of 20s entered in the Ipswich accounts for 14 July to 'the Quenes players being the Childeren' which in this year at least should be considered part of a separate tour as there is no corroborative evidence from elsewhere to indicate joint performances (see *Collections* II.3, p. 274).

4 The tentative season for the visit is suggested by the fact that this is the first payment given for Faversham's Michaelmas–Michaelmas year (Chamberlains' Accounts, Centre for Kentish Studies, Maidstone: FA/FAc17, mb 6).

5 If these accounts are, in fact, chronological, it is worth noting that the Queen's Men payment follows several entries after a payment specifically dated 22 March on the previous page (Lydd Town Archives: Ly/FAc7, pp. 53–4).

6 Leicester Chamberlains' Accounts, Leicestershire Record Office: BRIII/2/56, mb 1.

7 There are two payments to the Queen's Men this year, the first by Nicholas Upton, deputy mayor, and the second, presumably later, by John Castlock, mayor from

Michaelmas 1587 to Michaelmas 1588 (see below in this year). Our thanks to Duncan Harrington and Patricia Hyde, historians of Faversham, for their help in verifying this information.

8 Leicester Chamberlains' Accounts, Leicestershire Record Office: BRIII/2/56, mb 1.

9 The Queen's Men were at Knowsley on the same day as Essex's troupe, but their performance was in the afternoon and Essex's performed in the evening (*Lancashire*, p. 182).

10 Under the receipts heading for the same date is recorded 10s collected at the hall (i.e. the Guildhall) door; see Leicester Chamberlains' Accounts, Leicestershire Record Office: BRIII/2/58, mb 1d.

11 *Collections* II.3, p. 276.

12 This second payment is found among some miscellaneous entries at the end of the year's accounts, apparently out of strict chronological order (Centre for Kentish Studies, Maidstone: MD/FCAI/1591, f. 2v). As it appears near another entry in the same group dated for the end of May, it is possible that this payment relates to the same visit by the Queen's Men to Maidstone as the first, especially as the two payments together would make up the typical amount paid by civic officials to the troupe.

13 Southampton Book of Fines, Southampton Record Office: SC5/3/1, f. 226v.

14 The Newcastle accounts are dated by the lunar month year, a system explained by J. J. Anderson in his introduction to *Newcastle upon Tyne*, pp. xxi–xxii. The payment to the Queen's Men this year is entered for '1 week September' (pp. 78–9) but should be converted to an earlier date in August according to the lunar system.

15 Despite the fact that an entry for Coronation Day in January appears further down on the same folio (as noted in *Collections*, IX), the MS. makes it apparent that the year's accounts are not in chronological order. The 11 October 1592 entry for the Queen's Men, for example, precedes this one, which presumably fell within the range of the account for Aldeburgh's Michaelmas 1591 to Michaelmas 1592 year. See Suffolk Record Office (Ipswich Branch): EE1/12/1, ff. 328–31.

16 The entry concerned is dated 27 May 1593 in the MS., a presumed error for 1592 as it falls within the annual accounts for Michaelmas 1591–Michaelmas 1592 (*Norwich 1540–1642*, p. 102).

17 This payment occurs in an accounting year that ran 11 June 1592 through 10 September 1593 (see *Somerset including Bath*, p. 15). As there is no other evidence for the Queen's Men in the south-west in the summer of 1593, the payment has been listed under the earlier of the two possible years.

18 Also in this year's account is a payment of 5s to a 'mr duttons players' (*Coventry*, p. 336) but the payment is low for a branch of the Queen's Men and the Mr Dutton referred to may be a local patron rather than one of the Dutton brothers.

19 This payment occurs near several relating to the appointment of the Earl of Essex as high steward of Reading. The burgesses elected Essex to the post on 21 January 1593 (see *Reading Records: Diary of the Corporation*, ed. J. M. Guilding, 4 vols. (London, 1892–6), vol. 1, p. 416). There is another payment of 3s 4d to 'the Quenes men' later in the accounts for the same year but it is quite possible that these were other royal servants, as 'players' are usually so specified in these records.

20 The payment is entered, by the lunar month system, as the third week of September (*Newcastle upon Tyne*, p. 92).

21 See Henslowe's *Diary*, p. 21, where income of £14 8s is recorded as income for this week of performances.

22 These Dover accounts appear to have been entered periodically with their date of recording noted in the margin. This payment occurs within a group of others entered 23 August at the end of the accounting year.

23 A reimbursement to Mr Allen, former mayor, in the 1596–7 accounts (New Romney Chamberlains' Accounts, Centre for Kentish Studies, Maidstone: NR/FAc8, f. 80v) is for a payment to the Queen's Men in the previous year, 1595–6, when he held office.

24 Chatsworth House: MS. 7(H), f. 161v.

25 A local presentment dated 20 March 1597 found by James Gibson reveals that a man named Foscew had been involved in a brawl with one of the Queen's Men on an unspecified occasion (Quarter Sessions Jury Presentment, Canterbury Cathedral Archives: JQ 396a).

BIBLIOGRAPHY

Printed and manuscript sources for the provincial visits of the Queen's Men are consolidated in the headnote to Appendix A (pp. 172–4 above) and are not repeated here.

Adams, Simon (ed.), *Household Accounts and Disbursement Books of Robert Dudley, Earl of Leicester, 1558–1561, 1584–1586*, Camden Society 5th ser., vol. 6 (Cambridge, 1995)
  'Eliza enthroned? The court and its politics', in Christopher Haigh (ed.), *The Reign of Elizabeth I*. London, 1984
  'Faction, clientage, and party: English politics, 1550–1603', *History Today* 32 (1982), 33–9
  'The Dudley clientele, 1553–1563', in *The Tudor Nobility*, ed. G. W. Bernard (Manchester, 1992), pp. 241–65
Alexander, Peter. *Shakespeare's Henry VI and Richard III*. Cambridge, 1929
  Shakespeare's Life and Art. London, 1939
An Inventory of the Historical Monuments in the City of Oxford. Royal Commission on Historical Monuments, London, 1939
An Inventory of the Historical Monuments in the City of York, vol. v: *The Central Area*. Royal Commission on Historical Monuments, 1981
Anon. *Clyomon and Clamydes: A Critical Edition*, ed. Betty J. Littleton. The Hague, 1968
  The Famous Victories of Henry V, in *Narrative and Dramatic Sources of Shakespeare*, vol. iv, ed. Geoffrey Bullough (London, 1960)
Anon ('R. W.'). *Three Ladies of London*. Tudor Facsimile Texts, 1911
  Three Lords and Three Ladies of London. Tudor Facsimile Texts, 1912
Anon. *The Tragical Reign of Selimus*. Malone Society Reprint, 1909
  The Troublesome Reign of King John, in *Narrative and Dramatic Sources of Shakespeare*, vol. iv, ed. Geoffrey Bullough (London, 1960)
  The Troublesome Raigne of John, King of England, ed. J. W. Sider. New York, 1979
  The True Chronicle Historie of King Leir, in *Narrative and Dramatic Sources of Shakespeare*, vol. vii, ed. Geoffrey Bullough (London, 1973)
  The True Tragedy of Richard III. Malone Society Reprint, 1929
Archer, John Michael. *Sovereignty and Intelligence: Spying and Court Culture in the English Renaissance*. Stanford, CA, 1993

Armstrong, William A. *Marlowe's Tamburlaine: The Image and the Stage*. Hull, 1966

Arthurson, Ian. 'Espionage and intelligence from the Wars of the Roses to the Reformation', *Nottingham Mediaeval Studies* 35 (1991), 134–54

Axton, Marie. 'Robert Dudley and the Inner Temple Revels', *The Historical Journal* 13, 3 (1970), 365–78

Bailey, I. S. *A Short Guide to All Saints Church, Kirtling*. Kirtling, 1991

Bald, R. C. 'Leicester's Men in the Low Countries', *RES* 19 (1943), 395–7

Barroll, J. Leeds. *Politics, Plague, and Shakespeare's Theater*. Ithaca, NY, 1991
   The Revels History of Drama in England, vol. III, ed. Barroll *et al*. London, 1975

Beckerman, Bernard. *Shakespeare at the Globe*. New York, 1962

Beier, A. *The Problem of the Poor in Tudor and Early Stuart England*. London, 1985

Benbow, R. Mark. 'Dutton and Goffe versus Broughton: a disputed contract for plays in the 1570s', *Records of Early English Drama Newsletter* (1981: 2), 3–9

Berek, Peter. '*Locrine* revised, *Selimus* and early responses to *Tamburlaine*', *Research Opportunities in Renaissance Drama* 23 (1980), 33–44

Berry, Herbert, and James Stokes. 'Actors and town hall in the sixteenth century', *Medieval and Renaissance Drama in England*, VI (1993), 73–80

Bevington, David. *From Mankind to Marlowe*. Cambridge, MA, 1962
   Tudor Drama and Politics. Cambridge, MA, 1968

Blackstone, Mary. 'Patrons and Elizabethan acting companies', in *Elizabethan Theatre X*, ed. C. E. McGee. Port Credit, Ontario, 1988

Boas, F. S. *Christopher Marlowe: A Biographical and Critical Study*. Oxford, 1940

Bossy, John. *Giordano Bruno and the Embassy Affair*. New Haven, 1991

Bradbrook, M. C. *The Rise of the Common Player*. Cambridge, MA, 1962

Bradley, David. *From Text to Performance in the Elizabethan Theatre*. Cambridge, 1992

Brennan, Michael. *Literary Patronage in the Renaissance: The Pembroke Family*. London, 1988

Brownstein, O. L. 'A record of London inn-playhouses from *c*. 1565–1590', *Shakespeare Quarterly* 22 (1971), 17–24

Bullough, Geoffrey. *Narrative and Dramatic Sources of Shakespeare*. 8 vols. London, 1957–75

Calderwood, William. *The Elizabethan Protestant Press: A Study of the Printing and Publishing of Protestant Religious Literature in English, Excluding Bibles and Liturgies, 1558–1603*. Univ. of London Ph.D. thesis, 1977

Carlson, Leland H. *Martin Marprelate, Gentleman*. San Marino, 1981

Chambers, E. K. *The Elizabethan Stage*. 4 vols. Oxford, 1923
   William Shakespeare: A Study of Facts and Problems. 2 vols. Oxford, 1930

Clare, Janet. *'Art made tongue-tied by authority': Elizabethan and Jacobean Dramatic Censorship*. Manchester, 1990

Clemen, Wolfgang. *English Tragedy Before Shakespeare: The Development of Dramatic Speech*, trans. T. S. Dorsch. New York, 1961

Collinson, Patrick. 'Religious satire and the invention of puritanism', in *The Reign of Elizabeth I: Court and Culture in the Last Decade*, ed. John Guy. Cambridge, 1995
   Elizabethan Essays. London, 1994

The Birthpangs of Protestant England: Religious and Cultural Change in the Sixteenth and Seventeenth Centuries. London, 1988

Corbin, Peter, and Douglas Sedge (eds.), *The Oldcastle Controversy*. Manchester, 1991

Coward, Barry. *The Stanleys, Lords Stanley and Earls of Derby 1385–1672: The Origins, Wealth and Power of a Landowning Family*. Manchester, 1983

Cressy, David. 'Binding the nation: the bonds of association, 1584 and 1696', in *Tudor Rule and Revolution*, ed. D. J. Guth and J. W. McKenna. Cambridge, 1982

Doubleday, H. Arthur, *et al.* (eds.), *A History of the County of Warwick*. Victoria County History, 8 vols. London, 1904–69

Duncan-Jones, Katharine. *Sir Philip Sidney, Courtier Poet*. London, 1991

Durant, David N. and Philip Riden (eds.), *The Building of Hardwick Hall*. Derbyshire Record Society, vols. IV and IX. Chesterfield, 1980, 1984

Duthie, G. I. *Shakespeare's King Lear: A Critical Edition*. Oxford, 1949

Dutton, Richard. 'Patronage, politics, and the Master of the Revels, 1622–1640: the case of Sir John Astley', *English Literary Renaissance* 20 (1990), 287–319

Mastering the Revels: The Regulation and Censorship of English Renaissance Drama. Iowa City, 1991

Eccles, Mark. 'Brief lives', *Studies in Philology* 79 (1982), 1–135

'Elizabethan actors', *Notes and Queries* ns 38 (1991), 38–49; 454–61; ns 39 (1992), 293–303; ns 40 (1993), 165–76

Marlowe in London. Cambridge, MA, 1934

Shakespeare in Warwickshire. Madison, WI, 1961

Edmond, Mary. 'Pembroke's Men', *Review of English Studies* ns 25 (1974), 129–36

Edwards, Philip. *Threshold of a Nation*. Cambridge, 1979

Elton, G. R. *The Parliament of England, 1559–1581*. Cambridge, 1986

Feuillerat, Albert. *The Complete Works of Sir Philip Sidney*, 4 vols. Cambridge, 1926

Foakes, R. A. and R. T. Rickert (eds.), *Henslowe's Diary*. Cambridge, 1961

Fraser, Russell. *Young Shakespeare*. New York, 1988

Freedman, Barbara. 'Elizabethan protest, plague, and plays: rereading the documents of control', *English Literary Renaissance* 26 (1996), 17–45

Freeman, Arthur. *Thomas Kyd: Facts and Problems*. Oxford, 1967

Friedman, Alice T. *House and Household in Elizabethan England: Wollaton Hall and the Willoughby Family*. Chicago, 1989

Gair, Reavley. *The Children of Paul's: The Story of a Theatre Company, 1553–1608*. Cambridge, 1982

George, David. 'Shakespeare and Pembroke's Men', *Shakespeare Quarterly* 32 (1981), 305–23

Gildersleeve, V. C. *Government Regulation of the Elizabethan Drama*. New York, 1908

Girouard, Mark. *Hardwick Hall*. London, 1996

Gooch, Jane Lytton. *The Lamentable Tragedy of Locrine: A Critical Edition*. New York, 1981

Green, Thomas Andrew. *Verdict according to Conscience: Perspectives on the English Criminal Trial Jury, 1200–1800*. Chicago, 1985

Greene, Robert. *Friar Bacon and Friar Bungay*. Malone Society Reprint, 1926

Greenfield, Thelma N. *The Induction in Elizabethan Drama*. Eugene, OR, 1969

Greg, W. W. *Dramatic Documents from the Elizabethan Playhouses: Commentary*. Oxford, 1931

    The Editorial Problem in Shakespeare. Oxford, 1942

    Two Elizabethan Stage Abridgements. Oxford, 1923

Guilding, J. M. (ed.) *Reading Records: Diary of the Corporation*. 4 vols. London, 1892–6

Gurr, Andrew (ed.), *Politics, Patronage and Literature in England, 1558–1658*. Yearbook of English Studies 21 (1991)

    'The chimera of amalgamation', *Theatre Research International* 18 (1993), 85–93

    Playgoing in Shakespeare's London. Cambridge, 1987

    The Shakespearean Stage. 3rd edn. Cambridge, 1992

    The Shakespearian Playing Companies. Oxford, 1996

    'Three reluctant patrons and early Shakespeare', *Shakespeare Quarterly* 44 (1993), 159–74

Haigh, Christopher. *Elizabeth I*. London, 1988

Hamada, Akihiro. *Thomas Creede: Printer to Shakespeare and his Contemporaries*. Tokyo, 1994

Hamilton, Donna B. *Shakespeare and the Politics of Protestant England*. Lexington, KY, 1992

Harbage, Alfred, S. Schoenbaum, and Sylvia S. Wagonheim (eds.), *Annals of English Drama*, 3rd edn. New York, 1989

Hart, Alfred. *Stolne and Surreptitious Copies*. Melbourne, 1942

Harvey, P. D. A. *The Maps of Tudor England*. Chicago, 1993

Haynes, Alan. *Invisible Power: The Elizabethan Secret Service, 1570–1603*. Stroud, 1992

    The White Bear: Robert Dudley, the Elizabethan Earl of Leicester. London, 1987

Hays, Rosalind Conklin. 'Dorset church houses and the drama', *Research Opportunities in Renaissance Drama* 31 (1992), 13–23

Higham, F. M. G. *The Principal Secretary of State*. Manchester, 1923

Hill, C. P. *A History of Bristol Grammar School*. London, 1951

Hill, J. W. F. *Tudor and Stuart Lincoln*. Cambridge, 1956

Hook, Frank S. (ed.), *Old Wives Tale*, in *the Dramatic Works of George Peele*, vol. 3. New Haven, 1970

Howard, Jean E. *The Stage and Social Struggle in Early Modern England*. London, 1994

Howard-Hill, Trevor. 'Crane's 1619 manuscript of *Barnavelt* and theatrical processes', *Modern Philology* 86 (1988), 146–70

Ingram, William. *A London Life in the Brazen Age*. Cambridge, MA, 1978

    The Business of Playing: The Beginnings of the Adult Professional Theater in Elizabethan London. Ithaca, NY, 1992

    'The costs of touring', in *Medieval and Renaissance Drama in England*, VI (1993), 57–62

    'The playhouse at Newington Butts: a new proposal', *Shakespeare Quarterly* 21 (1970), 385–97

Ioppolo, Grace. *Revising Shakespeare*. Cambridge, MA, 1991

Irace, Kathleen O. *Reforming the 'Bad' Quartos: Performance and Provenance of Six Shakespearean First Editions*. Newark, 1994

Jenkins, Harold. 'Peele's *Old Wives Tale*', *Modern Language Review* 34 (1939), 177–85

Jones, Norman, and Paul Whitfield White. '*Gorboduc* and royal marriage politics: an Elizabethan playgoer's report of the premiere performance', *English Literary Renaissance* 26 (1996), 3–16

King, John N. *English Reformation Literature: The Tudor Origins of the Protestant Tradition*. Princeton, NJ, 1982

King, T. J. *Casting Shakespeare's Plays: London Actors and Their Roles, 1590–1642*. Cambridge, 1992

Kirschbaum, Leo. 'A census of bad quartos', *Review of English Studies* 14 (1938), 20–43
'An hypothesis concerning the origin of the bad quartos', *PMLA* 60 (1945), 697–715

Knutson, Roslyn. *The Repertory of Shakespeare's Company, 1594–1613*. Fayetteville, Arkansas, 1991

Leggatt, Alexander. 'The companies and actors', in *The Revels History of Drama in English*, vol. 3, ed. Leeds Barroll *et al*. London, 1975
English Drama: Shakespeare to the Restoration. London, 1988

Loengard, Janet S. 'An Elizabethan lawsuit: John Brayne, his carpenter, and the building of the Red Lion Theatre', *Shakespeare Quarterly* 34 (1983), 298–310

Lytle, Guy Fitch, and Stephen Orgel (eds.), *Patronage in the Renaissance*. Princeton, NJ, 1981

MacCaffrey, Wallace. 'Place and patronage in Elizabethan politics', in *Elizabethan Government and Society*, ed. S. T. Bindoff *et al*. London, 1961
Queen Elizabeth and the Making of Policy, 1572–1588. Princeton, NJ, 1981
The Shaping of the Elizabethan Regime. Princeton, NJ, 1968

— MacLean, Sally Beth. 'Leicester and the Evelyns: new evidence for the continental tour of Leicester's Men', *Review of English Studies* ns 39 (1988), 487–93
'Players on tour: new evidence from Records of Early English Drama', in *The Elizabethan Theatre X*, ed. C. E. McGee (Port Credit, Ontario, 1988)
— 'The politics of patronage: dramatic records in Robert Dudley's household books', *Shakespeare Quarterly* 44 (1993), 175–82
'Tour routes: "provincial wanderings" or traditional circuits?', in *Medieval and Renaissance Drama in England*, VI (1993), 1–14

McMillin, Scott. 'Building stories: Greg, Fleay, and the plot of *2 Seven Deadly Sins*', *Medieval and Renaissance Drama in England*, IV (1989), pp. 53–62
'Simon Jewell and the Queen's Men', *Review of English Studies* ns 27 (1976), 174–7
'Sussex's Men in 1594: the evidence of *Titus Andronicus* and *The Jew of Malta*', *Theatre Survey* 32 (1991), 214–23
— 'The ownership of *The Jew of Malta, Friar Bacon*, and *The Ranger's Comedy*', *English Language Notes* 9 (1972), 249–52
'The Queen's Men and the London theatre of 1583', in *Elizabethan Theatre X*, ed. C. E. McGee. Port Credit, Ontario, 1988
The Elizabethan Theatre and the Book of Sir Thomas More. Ithaca, NY, 1987

Maguire, Laurie. *Shakespearean Suspect Texts*, Cambridge, 1996

Manley, Lawrence. 'Fictions of settlement: London 1590', *Studies in Philology* 88 (1991), 201–24

Mann, Irene. 'A lost version of *The Three Ladies of London*', *PMLA* 59 (1944), 586–9

Martin, C. T. (ed.), *Journal of Sir Francis Walsingham from December 1570 to April 1583*. Camden Society, CIV, part 3, 1871; repr. New York/London, 1968

Merrington, John. 'Town and country in the transition to capitalism', in Paul Sweezy *et al.*, *The Transition from Feudalism to Capitalism*. London, 1976

Mueller, Martin. 'From *Leir* to *Lear*', *Philological Quarterly* 73 (1994), 195–218

Muller, James Arthur (ed.), *Letters of Stephen Gardiner*. Cambridge, 1933

Murray, John Tucker. *English Dramatic Companies 1558–1642*, 2 vols. London, 1910

Nelson, Alan. *Early Cambridge Theatres: College, University, and Town Stages, 1464–1720*. Cambridge, 1994

Newman, John, and Nikolaus Pevsner. *Dorset*. Harmondsworth, Middlesex, 1972

Nicholl, Charles. *The Reckoning*. London, 1992

Nungezer, Edwin. *A Dictionary of Actors*. New Haven, Conn., 1929

Ohler, Norbert. *The Medieval Traveller*, trans. Caroline Hillier. Woodbridge, Suffolk, 1989

Orrell, John. 'The theatre at Christ Church, Oxford, in 1605', *Shakespeare Survey* 35 (1982), 129–40

   The Human Stage: English Theatre Design, 1567–1640. Cambridge, 1988

Patrick, D. L. *The Textual History of Richard III*. Stanford, CA, 1936

Patterson, Annabel. *Censorship and Interpretation: The Conditions of Writing and Reading in Early Modern England*. Madison, WI, 1984

Patterson, Catherine F. 'Leicester and Lord Huntingdon: urban patronage in early modern England', *Midland History* 16 (1991), 45–62

Peck, Linda. 'Court patronage and government policy: the Jacobean dilemma', in G. F. Lytle and S. Orgel (eds.), *Patronage in the Renaissance*. Princeton, NJ, 1981

Peele, George. *The Old Wives Tale*. Revels edition, ed. Patricia Binnie. Manchester, 1980

Pevsner, Nikolaus, and Alexandra Wedgwood. *Warwickshire*. Harmondsworth, Middlesex, 1966

Pevsner, Nikolaus. *Cambridgeshire*. 2nd edn. Harmondsworth, Middlesex, 1970

   Derbyshire. Rev. edn Elizabeth Williamson. Harmondsworth, Middlesex, 1978

   Leicestershire and Rutland. Rev. edn Elizabeth Williamson and Geoffrey K. Brandwood. Harmondsworth, Middlesex, 1984

   North-East Norfolk and Norwich. Harmondsworth, Middlesex, 1962

   Nottinghamshire. Rev. edn Elizabeth Williamson. Harmondsworth, Middlesex, 1951; 2nd edn, 1979

Pinciss, G. M. 'Thomas Creede and the repertory of the Queen's Men, 1583–1592', *Modern Philology* 67 (1970), 321–30

   'The Queen's Men, 1583–1592', *Theatre Survey* 11 (1970), 50–65

   'Shakespeare, Her Majesty's Players, and Pembroke's Men', *Shakespeare Survey* 27 (1974), 129–36

Plowden, Alison. *The Elizabethan Secret Service*. New York, 1991

Poole, Kristen. 'Saints alive! Falstaff, Martin Marprelate, and the staging of puritanism', *Shakespeare Quarterly* 46 (1995), 47–75

Price, Roger. *Excavations at St Bartholomew's Hospital Bristol*. Bristol, 1979

Pulman, M. B. *The Elizabethan Privy Council in the Fifteen Seventies*. Berkeley, 1971

Read, Conyers. 'Walsingham and Burghley in Queen Elizabeth's privy council', *EHR* 28 (1913), 34–58

 'William Cecil and Elizabethan public relations', in *Elizabethan Government and Society: Essays Presented to Sir John Neale*. London, 1961

 Mr Secretary Walsingham and the Policy of Queen Elizabeth. 3 vols. Oxford, 1925

Ribner, Irving. 'Greene's attack on Marlowe: some light on *Alphonsus* and *Selimus*', *Studies in Philology* 52 (1955), 162–71

Riggs, David. *Shakespeare's Heroical Histories: Henry VI and its Literary Tradition*. Cambridge, MA, 1971

Ringler, William A. 'The number of actors in Shakespeare's early plays', in *The Seventeenth Century Stage*, ed. G. E. Bentley. Chicago, 1968

 'Spenser and Thomas Watson', *Modern Language Notes* 69 (1954), 484–6

Roberts, Peter. '"The studious artizan": Christopher Marlowe, Canterbury, and Cambridge', in *Christopher Marlowe and English Renaissance Culture*, ed. Darryll Grantley and Peter Roberts. Aldershot, 1996

 'Elizabethan players and minstrels and the legislation of 1572 against retainers and vagabonds', in *Religion, Culture, and Society in Early Modern Britain*, ed. Anthony Fletcher and Peter Roberts. Cambridge, 1994

Rosenberg, Eleanor. *Leicester: Patron of Letters*. New York, 1955

Sams, Eric. *The Real Shakespeare: Retrieving the Early Years, 1564–1594*. New Haven, 1995

Scoufos, Alice-Lyle. *Shakespeare's Typological Satire*. Athens, Ohio, 1979

Shakespeare, William. *2 Henry IV*, ed. Giorgio Melchiori. Cambridge, 1989

 King John, Arden edition, ed. E. A. J. Honigman. London, 1954

 King John, ed. A. R. Braunmuller. Oxford, 1989

Shapiro, Michael. *Children of the Revels: The Boy Companies of Shakespeare's Time and Their Plays*. New York, 1977

Sheldon, Gilbert. *From Trackway to Turnpike*. London, 1928

Sinfield, Alan. 'The cultural politics of the *Defence of Poetry*', in *Sir Philip Sidney and the Interpretation of Renaissance Culture*, ed. Gary F. Waller and Michael D. Moore. London, 1984

Skura, Meredith Anne. *Shakespeare the Actor and the Purposes of Playing*. Chicago, 1993

Somerset, J. A. B. '"How chances it they travel?" Provincial touring, playing places, and the King's Men', *Shakespeare Survey* 47 (1994), 45–60

 'The Lords President, their activities and companies: evidence from Shropshire', *Elizabethan Theatre X*, ed. C. E. McGee. Port Credit, Ontario, 1988

Southern, Richard. *The Staging of Plays before Shakespeare*. New York, 1973

Stenton, F. M. 'The road system of medieval England', *Economic History Review* 7 (1936), 1–21

Stone, Lawrence. *The Causes of the English Revolution.* London, 1972

Streitberger, W. R. 'On Edmond Tyllney's biography', *Review of English Studies* 29 (1978), 11–35

    Edmond Tyllney, Master of the Revels and Censor of Plays: A Descriptive Index to His Diplomatic Manual on Europe. New York, 1986

Strong, R. C. and J. A. Van Dorsten. *Leicester's Triumph.* Leiden, 1964

Sutermeister, Helen. *The Norwich Blackfriars.* Norwich, 1977

Taylor, Rupert. 'A tentative chronology of Marlowe's and some other Elizabethan plays', *PMLA* 51 (1936), 643–88

Tennenhouse, Leonard. *Power on Display.* London, 1986

Tittler, Robert. *Architecture and Power: The Town Hall and the English Urban Community c. 1500–1640.* Oxford, 1991

Urry, William. *Christopher Marlowe and Canterbury.* London, 1988

Waller, Gary F. and Michael D. Moore (eds.), *Sir Philip Sidney and the Interpretation of Renaissance Culture.* London, 1984

Waller, Gary F. *Mary Sidney, Countess of Pembroke.* Salzburg, 1979

Werstine, Paul. 'Narratives about printed Shakespeare texts: "foul papers", and "bad" quartos', *Shakespeare Quarterly* 41 (1990), 63–86

Westfall, Suzanne R. *Patrons and Performance: Early Tudor Household Records.* Oxford, 1990

Whitaker, T. D. (ed.). *An History of the Original Parish of Whalley and Honor of Clitheroe.* London, 1818

White, Paul Whitfield. 'Drama in the church: church-playing in Tudor England', *Medieval and Renaissance Drama in England*, VI (1993), 15–35

    'Patronage, Protestantism, and stage propaganda in early Elizabethan England', *Yearbook of English Studies* 21 (1991), 39–52

    Theatre and Reformation: Protestantism, Patronage, and Playing in Tudor England. Cambridge, 1993

Wickham, Glynne. *Early English Stages 1300 to 1660*, 3 vols. New York, 1963–

Wiles, David. *Shakespeare's Clown: Actor and Text in the Elizabethan Playhouse.* Cambridge, 1987

Williams, Penry. 'The crown and the counties', in Christopher Haigh (ed.), *The Reign of Elizabeth I.* London, 1984

Wilson, F. P. *Shakespearian and Other Studies*, ed. Helen Gardner. Oxford, 1969

    The English Drama, 1485–1585. Oxford, 1969

Wright, George T. *Shakespeare's Metrical Art.* Berkeley, CA, 1988

Zucker, David H. *Stage and Image in the Plays of Christopher Marlowe.* Salzburg, 1972

INDEX

Abingdon: guildhall 68, 82, 177, 214, 218;
official rewards 43–4; performances 175–7;
town accounts 172
accidents: *see* Paris Garden
Achlow, Thomas 29, 143
acrobats xii, 55, 63, 130
Act for the Punishment of Vagabonds 13
acting companies xi–xii, 5, 6, 11, 102–3,
143–5; board for 38, 59, 60; combinations
44, 49, 55, 58, 62–3, 195; expansion 8;
finances 7, 12, 38, 60–1, 67; membership
12, 160; personnel xii (*see also* actors);
reorganization 49, 85; repertories 5–6, 12,
164; style xiii; tours 5, 6, 7, 37, 60, 67–8,
82, 121, 208; *see also* control; licences;
plays; *and individual companies*
acting style: *see under* Queen's Men
actors xi, xiii, 3, 54, 98–9, 148, 164; as
messengers 22–3, 28–9; as musicians 63;
condemnation of 30, 124; contracts 7;
dishonest 52, 120; hired men 11, 12, 52,
60–1, 142; in plays 22, 54; leading 1, 11, 12,
24, 34, 53, 102, 121, 128, 137, 153, 160–1,
165–6, 195–7 (*see also* Tarlton); minor 97,
100–1; servant 181; students 63–4, 212;
see also children; dictation; *under* Queen's
Men, casting and personnel; *and*
individual actors
Acts against Retainers 13
Adam, in *James IV* 142
Adam, in *Looking Glass for London* 91
Adams, John xiv, 12, 91–2, 128, 194
Admiral's Men 8, 54; combinations 195;
court performances 53, 67; dominance of
xiv, 16, 49–51, 67, 85, 155, 169; personnel
xiv, 194–6; repertory 51, 84, 86, 92–3, 121,
160, 165

admissions 3, 10
affrays: *see under* Norwich
Agincourt, battle of 107, 115
Airedale 39
Aladin, in *Selimus* 134
Aldeburgh: performances and rewards 41, 43,
175–9, 181–3; town accounts 225
Alexander, Peter 160
All Hallows' Church, Sherborne 215
allegorical devices 121, 124, 126–7
Allen, Mr 226
Alleyn, Edward xiv, xv–xvi, 5, 6, 53, 93, 102,
145, 155, 160, 169; wager with Bentley and
Knell 196
Alleyn, Richard 194
Alphonsus of Aragon 91
altar, as prop 142–3
ambassador, to Scotland 58, 211
Amurath, in *Selimus* 134
anecdotes 89–90
angels, in *Three Lords and Three Ladies* 126
Anne of Denmark 58
annuities, for actors 195
Antick, in *Old Wives Tale* 221
antiquarian sources 20, 170, 172–4
ape 54
Apology for Actors, An 195–7
Apology for Poetry, An 30
archbishops, as play characters 117, 131, 140
Archer, John Michael 35
aristocracy: *see* noblemen *and individual*
members
Armada 26, 32, 57, 89, 95, 124–5, 133, 168
art, as propaganda 30
Arthurson, Ian 23
Ashby, William 211
Assheton, Nicholas 41, 206

York 41, 58, 215; performances and rewards 47, 58, 64, 175, 177, 183–5, 187–8, 195–6, 211; St Christopher guild 215
York, Archbishop of, in *True Tragedy* 117, 131
York, Duke of *see* princes in the Tower
York Common Hall 68, 74–6, 175, 176, 185, 187, 188, 215

York Minster, performances and rewards 47
Yorkshire 39, 47, 57, 210, 211; East Riding 79
youths 8, 30, 181; in plays 107, 221; *see also* children

Zantippa, in *Old Wives Tale* 111
Zeal 33
Zenocrate, in *Tamburlaine* 122

Questions:

Is it known where The Bull and The Ball
were located? Was the Bull outside or inside
the City walls?